W9-CNC-731

The Forgotten Legacy of Stella Walsh

The Forgotten Legacy of Stella Walsh

The Greatest Female Athlete of Her Time

SHELDON ANDERSON

ROWMAN & LITTLEFIELD
Lanham • Boulder • New York • London

Published by Rowman & Littlefield
A wholly owned subsidiary of The Rowman & Littlefield Publishing Group, Inc.
4501 Forbes Boulevard, Suite 200, Lanham, Maryland 20706
www.rowman.com

Unit A, Whitacre Mews, 26-34 Stannary Street, London SE11 4AB

British Library Cataloguing in Publication Information Available

Library of Congress Cataloging-in-Publication Data

Names: Anderson, Sheldon R., 1951– author.
Title: The forgotten legacy of Stella Walsh : the greatest female athlete of
  her time / Sheldon Anderson.
Description: Lanham, Maryland : Rowman & Littlefield, 2017. | Includes
  bibliographical references and index.
Identifiers: LCCN 2016058110 (print) | LCCN 2017002523 (ebook) | ISBN
  9781442277557 (hardback : alk. paper) | ISBN 9781442277564 (electronic)
Subjects: LCSH: Walsh, Stella, 1911-1980. | Women track and field
  athletes—Poland—Biography. | Women track and field athletes—United
  States—Biography. | Olympic athletes—Poland—Biography. | Polish
  American athletes—Biography. | Intersex athletes—Poland—Biography. |
  Intersex athletes—United States—Biography.
Classification: LCC GV1061.15.W37 A64 2017 (print) | LCC GV1061.15.W37
  (ebook) | DDC 796.42092—dc23
LC record available at https://lccn.loc.gov/2016058110

Printed in the United States of America

Contents

Acknowledgments

I have many people to thank for making this book possible. The generous hospitality of Chris and Karen Elzey, and Betsy and Paige Piper-Bach, facilitated my research at the Library of Congress. Sean Martin and other archivists at the Western Reserve Historical Society in Cleveland were very helpful, as were the librarians at the LA84 Foundation Library in Los Angeles and the University of Minnesota Immigration Center. Miami University supported my research with travel funds to these libraries. Trina Galauner of the Polish Genealogical Society of Greater Cleveland provided key documents on Stella Walsh's early life. Matt Tullis of Ashland University generously shared his research, as did filmmaker Rob Lucas. Jeff and Linda Kimball offered crucial feedback on the biography. Grace Butcher shared invaluable personal insights on her relationship with Walsh. I owe a special thanks to Marilyn Elzey, who proofread the manuscript, and Gracia Lindberg, who did the cartography. Finally, I am forever grateful to my wife, Kristie; son, O. Maxwell; and daughter, Lauren, for their enduring love and support.

Prologue

On August 2, 1932, the six finalists in the women's Olympic 100 meters, two Americans, one Canadian, one German, and one Pole, warmed up on the cinder track of the Los Angeles Coliseum. The magnificent arena, an architectural marvel of neo-classicism, had been built in 1923, as a football venue for the University of Southern California, and still serves that purpose today. Before the Olympics, the Coliseum had been expanded to hold more than 100,000 spectators, the largest capacity of any stadium in the world. The crowd was relatively sparse that day, but all eyes were on the starting line as the sprinters dug out their footholds with small trowels.

This was only the second time that women's track and field had been included on the Olympic program. At the 1928 Amsterdam Games, women competed in five athletic events: the 800 meters, the 4 × 100-meter relay, the high jump, the discus, and the 100 meters. Sixteen-year-old Chicagoan Betty Robinson was the surprise winner in the 100 meters in Amsterdam, and would have defended her Olympic title at Los Angeles but had been severely injured in a plane crash a year earlier.

With Robinson out, the favorite on this day was a muscular, curly haired twenty-one-year-old from Cleveland, Ohio. Stanisława Walasiewicz did not have USA on her shirt, but rather the Polish eagle in the red and white colors of her native country. As an infant, Stanisława had come with her mother to the United States from a little village in Russian Poland and had never been naturalized as a U.S. citizen. It was an unlikely odyssey for a girl born in the Russian Empire to compete in America's greatest sports arena in the world's biggest athletic spectacle.[1]

At the starter's gun, the diminutive Canadian Hilde Strike broke first off the line, but Walasiewicz's long strides enabled her to catch Strike at the halfway mark. The local favorite, Californian Wilhelmina von Bremen, fell off the world-record pace as Strike strained to hold off the bigger Pole. Strike and Walasiewicz hit the tape in a near-dead heat. The timers clocked both runners in 11.9 seconds. The judges huddled for several minutes before declaring Walasiewicz the winner. Von Bremen finished third. At the awards ceremony, the winners climbed onto the three perches of the medals podium. Walasiewicz stood on the top tier as the fastest woman in the world, a gold medal and world record in hand. She was feted in Poland and her Polish American community in Cleveland, but many American sports fans were disappointed that she had not won gold for the United States.

Walasiewicz's victory at the Los Angeles Olympic Games was her signature achievement, but it was only the beginning of a long and incomparable career. For a quarter-century, she was the best all-around female athlete in the world; in addition to the Olympic gold medal, she set at least fifty world records and won forty-one U.S. Track and Field National Championships. Walasiewicz was the first woman to run the 100-yard dash in less than eleven seconds. She was also one of premier female basketball and softball players of her time, and in 1951, the Helms Athletic Foundation in Los Angeles named her the "greatest woman athlete" of the first half of the twentieth century.

On a cold wintry night in Cleveland, in 1980, Walasiewicz went shopping at a strip mall not far from her house in the Polish neighborhood where she had lived for most of her life. In the parking lot, two local thugs brandished a gun and demanded her money. She tried to grab the gun and was shot in the stomach. She died at the hospital that night at the age of sixty-nine. Clevelanders were stunned by the news of the murder of their local hero, but her death was barely noticed throughout the rest of the country. Newspapers in Poland, where she was born and the country for which she had won her Olympic gold medal and numerous European championships, briefly mentioned the tragedy.

Three days later, Walasiewicz was laid to rest at nearby Calvary Cemetery, the largest Catholic cemetery in Cleveland. There is no sign at Calvary directing visitors to the grave of the Olympic champion. There is no prominent gravestone marking the spot, so no one would stumble upon her by accident. The site is marked by a small, weathered, gray stone slab, slowly sinking into the soft earth. In the winter, snow covers the modest marker, fallen leaves hide it in the autumn, and in the summer the grass creeps up over it, almost obliterating the words.

The inscription "Olympic Champion" at the bottom of the marker is almost eroded away, a sober reminder of Walasiewicz's forgotten place in American sports history. The three names on the memorial hint at her complicated, multilayered identity. She was christened Stanisława Walasie-wiczówna in Poland,[2] but on a 1930 work permit application she gave her name upon arriving in the United States in 1912, as Stefania Walasiewicz. Her family called her Stasia, but she was known to friends and to the American public as Stella Walsh, and she often signed her sports memorabilia "Stella Walsh Walasiewiczowna." After a brief marriage to Californian Harry Olson in 1956, for many years she used the name Stella Walsh Olson. Any allusion to that curious episode in her life does not appear on the gravestone.

Walsh's story leads down intersecting paths of national allegiance, ethnic loyalty, and gender identity. She spent most of her life in Cleveland but lived in Warsaw in the 1930s and Los Angeles in the 1950s. She received financial support from numerous funding sources and represented more than a dozen

The inscription on Stella Walsh's gravestone.

Stella Walsh's modest grave marker in Calvary Cemetery in Cleveland. *Author photo.*

American and Polish athletic clubs. She was a Polish citizen for the first half of her life and a U.S. citizen for the second.

The prominence of the Olympic rings on the grave marker point to the central role that sports played in Walsh's life. The modern Olympics, reconstituted in Athens in 1896, was one of the first truly international institutions of the early twentieth century. Walsh was one of the first athletes, man or woman, to take advantage of this new, globalized world of sports. She competed in the Olympics in Los Angeles and in Berlin in 1936, and in hundreds of track and field meets throughout the United States and Canada. She competed for Poland in the 1932 and 1936 Olympics but was estranged from Poland's Communist government after the war. She never wore Polish colors at the Olympics again. Walsh was eligible to try for a spot on the U.S. Olympic team in 1956, but age caught up with her and she did not qualify for the Melbourne Games. Before and after World War II, she crisscrossed the Atlantic Ocean to run in competitions throughout Europe. Walsh was the original "Globetrotter."

Walsh was also a pioneer of women's sports, but the fame of her contemporaries—swimmer Gertrude Ederle, aviator Amelia Earhart, tennis great Helen Wills, and Babe Didrikson—dwarf Walsh's memory. Didrikson also won two gold medals and a silver at the Los Angeles Olympics. She went on to become the best female golfer of her time and the most recognizable name in American women's sports.

Few people outside of the Polish American community in Cleveland remember Stella Walsh, and that community is rapidly disintegrating. As *Washington Post* journalist Paul Farhi wrote in 2008, after Walsh's retirement in the late 1950s, she was "all but forgotten." After her murder in 1980, the memory of one of America's greatest female athletes was buried with her.

Walsh's life in Poland, Cleveland, and Los Angeles is remembered in these pages. It is a saga of Polish American immigrants, the Olympic Games, and women's struggle for a place in the world of sports.

From Russian Poland to Cleveland's Slavic Village

The teachers decided my name was a tongue twister, so they changed it.

—*Stanisława Walasiewicz, on teachers at South High School calling her Stella Walsh*

The search for Stella Walsh begins thousands of miles away from her lifelong home on Clement Street in the Polish section of south Cleveland. On April 3, 1911, in the tiny Russian-Polish village of Wierzchownia—about fifty miles east of Toruń and one hundred miles northwest of Warsaw—eighteen-year-old Weronica (Ucinski) Walasiewicz gave birth to her first child. It was a girl, christened Stanisława Margaret Walasiewiczówna. She was probably born in the Walasiewicz house without any doctor present. Most references list Poland as Stanisława's birthplace, but the Polish state did not exist at the time. She was born a subject of Russian tsar Nicholas II.

Weronica's husband was not there to witness the birth of his daughter. In the fall of 1910, twenty-year-old Julian Walasiewicz had taken a train bound for Germany, leaving his pregnant young wife behind. On October 28, in Hamburg, Julian boarded the *Graf Waldersee*, a steamship of the Hamburg-Amerika line. Łukasz Musial, the father of the greatest Polish American baseball player in history, Stanislaus Musial, had left Hamburg earlier that year on the same ship. After Germany lost World War I, the U.S. Navy took the liner as war booty, and the USS *Graf Waldersee* became a troop transport. Julian was on the ship's first voyage to the port of Philadelphia, where he disembarked on November 10. Julian's brother Bolesław had arrived in the United States a year earlier and was living in a small house on Warsaw Street in the heart of Cleveland's Polish "Warszawa" neighborhood. Julian boarded a train to Ohio and moved in with his brother.[1]

Julian and Bolesław Walasiewicz were among the hundreds of thousands of Poles who left the Russian Empire at the turn of the century. Life in Russia presented few prospects. The dream of all Poles before World War I was the resurrection of their once-great state, but that seemed a remote possibility. The seventeenth-century Polish–Lithuanian Commonwealth had been one of the largest and most important countries in Eastern Europe. Polish king Jan Sobieski is credited with leading an army that lifted the Ottoman siege of Vienna in 1683, ending the Turkish threat to Central Europe. Poland was also the proud Roman Catholic outpost sandwiched between Protestant Prussia and Orthodox Russia. By the end of the eighteenth century, however, the weakness of the Polish central government, noble privilege, and the great power intrigue had enabled Russia, Prussia, and Austria to carve up the Polish polity in three partitions (1772, 1792, and 1795). Poland was gone for nearly 125 years.

The link between the United States and Poland is the strongest of the countries of Eastern Europe. Polish Americans comprise the largest ethnic group from that region; Julian found a welcoming Polish community in Cleveland. Denied their political freedom at the same time the American colonies were gaining theirs from Great Britain, Poles looked to the American Revolution and French Revolution as inspiration in their quest for the return of the Polish state. Following the lead of the American and French revolutionaries, Poles identified themselves with a tradition of fighting against despotic rule. They touted the democratic character of the Commonwealth, although only the Polish nobility was represented in the Commonwealth's *Sejm* (parliament), and the lack of a powerful monarch and an effective central government were fatal weaknesses. The Polish state became an easy target for its expansionist neighbors.

Poles were also proud of the progressive Constitution of May 3, 1791, which was a desperate attempt to establish a stronger constitutional monarchy and fend off the complete dismemberment of Poland. After the Russian-Polish War of 1792 led to the Second Partition, Polish general Tadeusz Kościuszko, who had fought with the Continental Army in the American Revolutionary War, led a failed rebellion against the Russians.

The key roles played by Kościuszko and fellow Polish officer Count Casimir Pułaski in the American Revolutionary War cemented the close relationship between Poles and the United States. Chicago has the largest Polish American community in the country, and every March the city and the state of Illinois celebrate Casimir Pułaski Day. Cleveland also holds a Pułaski Day in the fall.

The many border changes in Eastern Europe in a span of two centuries created multilayered national identities among the people there, including the Walasiewicz family. Poles, whether Catholic or Jew, were also Austrian, Prussian, or Russian. Wierzchownia had been part of Prussia before Napoleon's defeat at Waterloo in 1815. At the Congress of Vienna, the great powers

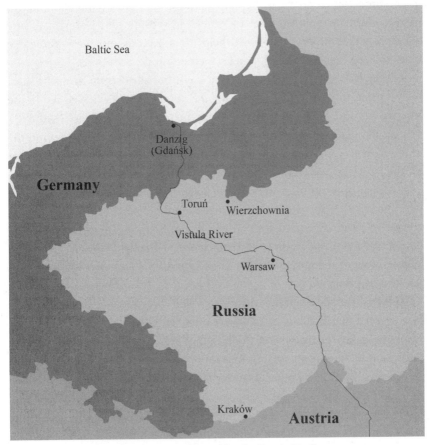

Russian Poland in 1911. *Map by Gracia Lindberg.*

changed the boundary of Prussia and Russia, and the village became part of Russian-administered Congress Poland. Congress Poland enjoyed a modicum of autonomy until the failed Polish uprising against Russia in 1830, when Wierzchownia and the rest of Congress Poland came under direct tsarist rule.

The changing borders and governments did not stifle a strong sense of Polish identity and patriotism; on the contrary, in the face of increasing German and Russian oppression Polish national consciousness deepened. In the 1870s, German chancellor Otto von Bismarck began a so-called *Kulturkampf* against the Catholic Church, giving free rein for Protestant Germans to discriminate against devout Catholic Poles. German instructors replaced Polish priests in schools, and in 1904, the government mandated that religious instruction be conducted in German, further antagonizing the Polish population. Berlin tried to Germanize Polish areas by providing subsidies for Germans to buy out Polish landowners. Polish self-help organizations mobilized to enable Poles to keep their land and maintain their cultural institutions.

Although Wierzchownia was only a day's horseback ride from the German border, life was much harder for the young Walasiewicz family in the Russian Empire. Polish peasants working the unyielding soil scratched out a meager living. Russian industrialization and urbanization lagged behind the other great European powers, limiting the opportunities for peasants to get off the land to work in towns and cities. Standards of living were higher and educational opportunities were much greater in Germany, where the GDP per capita in 1870 was double that of Russia. Only 15 percent of Russians were literate in 1870, compared with an 80 percent literacy rate in Germany. Julian Walasiewicz was an illiterate farm laborer with few prospects. Like Stella Walsh, most of the famous Polish expatriates in the early twentieth century fled Russian Poland.

Ruthless Russian repression forged a stiff Polish resistance movement that erupted in rebellions in 1830 and 1863. In the wake of the futile Polish "January Rising" of 1863–1864, thousands of Poles were exiled to Siberia. One Polish family housed the young Russian revolutionary Vladimir Lenin, who served time in a Siberian penal colony from 1897 to 1900. Poles were forced to learn Russian in school, classes conducted in Polish were prohibited, and the Russian language was used in public affairs. Warsaw University became a Russian institution in 1869. Conscription into the Russian Army was particularly onerous for Poles.

Following the revolution of 1905 and the shocking loss in the war with Japan, Tsar Nicholas II was forced to share power with a duma. The tsar's repeated dissolution of that parliamentary body was, in part, a reaction to persistent Polish calls for greater autonomy. A Russian police report from 1911, the year Stanisława was born, reveals the extent to which Russian agents monitored the Polish national movement. Polish teachers worked underground in so-called flying schools to keep Polish culture alive. "In the house of Pergricht," one Russian police report found, "a dangerous person by the name of Rusek is teaching. . . . In some of the schools, e.g., in Rusek's, Góralska's, or in that of the Drozdowska sisters, a considerable number of [Polish] children, up to fifty at a time, are taught in two shifts."[2]

The situation of Poles in Russia was typical of many oppressed minorities in Europe at the time. The lack of political rights and economic opportunity precipitated the greatest migration of peoples in history. Many Poles went to western Germany and France to work, but the lure of the United States—the "land of the free"—was particularly strong.

Julian and his young wife and child were among an estimated 4 million Poles who immigrated to the United States from 1870 to 1914. According to the 1870 U.S. Census, there were only seventy Poles in Cleveland, but because there was no Polish state, many ethnic Poles probably registered as Russians, Germans, or Austrians. Official visas and passports were virtually nonexistent. Passenger manifests had two categories for immigrants coming to the United States: "nationality" and "race or people." Julian and Weronica listed "Russia" in the first line and "Polish" in the second. After World War I, there were between 50,000 and 80,000 Poles in Cleveland, comprising 10 percent of the city's population. One Polish journalist visiting the Warszawa neighborhood of Cleveland was astounded by the number of Polish speakers. "This is not America!" he exclaimed.[3]

In the late nineteenth century, the United States became the world's premier industrial power, and there was work to be had in the burgeoning factories. Spurred on by demand from the U.S. Civil War, iron and steel mills popped up along the Great Lakes and throughout the Ohio River Valley. Chicago, Cleveland, Detroit, Pittsburgh, Cincinnati, and Buffalo were booming industrial cities in the late nineteenth century, and Poles came in droves to work in the factories.

Cleveland was a big steel town; Henry Chisholm built one of the first Bessemer mills in 1868, and by the 1890s, the Cleveland Rolling Mill Company had about 8,000 workers, the largest employer in Cleveland.[4] At the turn of the century, Ohio was second only to Pennsylvania in steelmaking. After World War I, about half of the workers in the American Steel and Wire factories in Cleveland were Polish.[5] Łukasz Musial found work at a steel mill in Donora, Pennsylvania, not far from Pittsburgh. Julian and Bolesław Walasiewicz went to work at the old Newburgh steel mill in Cleveland, which had been built in 1857.

In the summer of 1912, Weronica and little Stanisława left Wierzchownia to join Julian in the United States. On June 13, the two sailed from Bremen on the Norddeutscher Lloyd steamer *Chemnitz*, bound for Baltimore. Weronica did not speak English, had a thirteen-month-old baby in tow, and carried five dollars and a train ticket to Cleveland in her pocket. Weronica must have felt some additional trepidation in boarding that ship because the mighty *Titanic* had gone down on the Atlantic crossing only two months earlier.

In early July, Julian was reunited with his young wife and saw his infant daughter for the first time. They moved into a tiny house at 3932 East 67th Street, not far from Bolesław's house on Warsaw Avenue. The family easily transitioned into their new life. Julian had steady work, they had a house with the luxury of running water, and the neighborhood was full of Poles, so there was no need to learn English. Stanisława's two younger sisters, Sophia and Clara, were born there. In 1926, the family settled into a house a few blocks away on Clement Avenue, where Weronica lived until her death in 1991. Ninety years after the Walasiewicz family bought the Clement Avenue property, Clara's son Joe Battiato was still living in the dilapidated old house.

Polish immigrants found solace and support in their ethnic neighborhood, but prejudice and discrimination also limited their options to live and work elsewhere. At the turn of the century, Anglo-Saxon Protestants in the United States were alarmed that a critical mass of immigrants from Ireland, Italy, and Eastern Europe was threatening the cultural identity of the nation. These immigrants posed a challenge to the elites' idea of what it meant to be an American. The United States was supposed to be a "melting pot," but, in fact, it was difficult for these new immigrants—mostly Catholics, Eastern Orthodox, and Jews—to assimilate and identify with their new country. When the United States entered World War I in 1917, against Imperial Germany, German Americans fell into this "less desirable" ethnic category as well. Compounded by the fear of German and foreign "Bolshevik" elements, the

The first Walasiewicz house on Warsaw Avenue (top) and the Clement Avenue house, which was the family residence for sixty-five years. *Author photos.*

government began to demand passports and other identification papers to weed out suspect peoples.

In 1917, Congress passed an immigration law that increased the tax on immigration and called for anyone age sixteen or older to pass a literacy test. Congress had already set a precedent for the formal exclusion of certain immigrant groups with the passage of the Chinese Exclusion Act in 1882. The 1924 Immigration Act codified quotas of immigrants from certain countries, favoring those from the British Isles and Western Europe, while limiting newcomers from Southern and Eastern Europe. Poland's quota fell from 30,977 in 1923 to 5,982 in 1924.

Public schools expanded social studies curricula in U.S. history and politics to inculcate these immigrants with a strong sense of mainstream Anglo-American identity. Facing blatant discrimination, the newer immigrants from Ireland and Eastern Europe gravitated toward their own neighborhoods in the big northern industrial cities—New York City, Chicago, Milwaukee, and Cleveland. They struggled to overcome such stereotypes as the "drunken Irish pug" or the "dumb Polak." Poles in the German Empire were seen as second-class citizens, and German Americans were the particular purveyors of these slurs against Poles.

Prejudice against Polish Americans worsened after Leon Czolgosz, a second-generation Pole from Cleveland, shot President William McKinley on September 6, 1901, in Buffalo, New York. It was the third assassination of a U.S. president in four decades. Abraham Lincoln was killed in 1865, and James Garfield was shot in 1881. Czolgosz's family had left Prussian Poland in 1873, and Leon was born in Detroit shortly after the family arrived in the United States. In 1881, Paul Czolgosz moved the family to a small farm near Cleveland. Leon eventually worked at the same American Steel and Wire mill in Newburgh that employed Julian Walasiewicz.

Cleveland's power brokers had regarded the city's Slavic community with suspicion even before McKinley's assassination. At times, Poles were recruited to replace striking Irish iron workers, creating bitter hostility between the two ethnic communities. In 1882, Czechs and Poles were hired as strikebreakers at the Cleveland Rolling Mills. Three years later, they themselves went on strike for higher wages, but their violent takeover of the mills alienated other steelworkers. The depression of 1893 ruined the dreams of many migrant workers to rise out of their desperate condition, and Czolgosz moved from job to job and city to city to find work.

Czolgosz's parents raised him in the Polish Catholic Church, but he renounced religion and embraced anarchism. Friends and family said he had no close familial, social, or ethnic connections. Czolgosz was a troubled soul; at the time of the assassination he had taken the alias Fred C. Nieman, which means "no one" in German. He could not connect with the Polish American community, his new country, or even his working-class friends. His stepmother, who at the time was living with Czolgosz's father Paul on Fleet Avenue in the Slavic Village, told the press that Leon was insane: "I have always said he was crazy. . . . He must have been crazy or he would never have tried anything like that." Czolgosz's aunt Mary said that "he was a strange boy and an awful coward. He had few friends because he did not associate with anyone."[6]

Appalled at the harsh conditions for workers in U.S. factories, Czolgosz was radicalized by Marxist and anarchist literature. He became a blind follower of Emma Goldman, one of the most prominent anarchists in the United States at the turn of the century. Czolgosz went to see "Red Emma" speak in Cleveland on May 6, four months before he shot the president. "I do not believe in violence or in taking human life," Goldman declared.

> But desperate evils require desperate remedies, and in this country things are getting desperate. *We hear of the assassination of emperors and kings—the king of Italy falls, the president of France falls, and the hand that strikes the blow strikes in the name of outraged justice.* . . . I do not approve of violence or assassination; but when it does take place *the man who strikes the blow is a hero.* He has done what others who are suffering from oppression have not the courage to do.[7]

The timid, impressionable young man was smitten with Goldman's emotional denunciation of the exploitive capitalist class. Czolgosz had a brief audience with her after the speech. He was also inspired by Italian American anarchist Gaetano Bresci, who had assassinated Italy's King Umberto a year earlier. Bresci was sentenced to life in prison, but he died there in suspicious circumstances in May 1901, a few months before McKinley's assassination. Goldman eulogized Bresci in the leftist paper *Free Society.*

The press announced that the president was scheduled to appear at the Pan-American Exposition in Buffalo in early September 1901. Czolgosz took a train to Buffalo, rented a room at John Nowak's saloon, bought a .32-caliber revolver, and waited for McKinley to come to town. On September 6, Czolgosz stood in a reception line to shake hands with the president. When he got to McKinley, Czolgosz reached out and shot him twice at point-blank range, once in the chest and once in the stomach. Asked why he shot the president, Czolgosz replied simply, "I am an anarchist, and I did my duty."[8]

McKinley developed gangrene and died of septic shock eight days later. Modern-day antibiotic drugs would have saved him. The president was interred in his hometown of Canton, Ohio, about sixty miles south of Cleveland. Goldman did not lament McKinley's death but found kind words for her young anarchist follower: "My heart goes out to him [Czolgosz] in deep sympathy, and to all the victims of a system of inequality, and the many who will die the forerunners of a better, nobler, grander life."[9]

On September 23, Czolgosz went on trial in Buffalo. After three days of testimony, the twelve-man jury took thirty minutes to convict him of murder. Presiding judge Truman C. White addressed the defendant as follows: "Czolgosz, in taking the life of our beloved president you committed a crime

Polish American Leon Czolgosz lived and worked in Cleveland before assassinating President William McKinley in 1901. *Library of Congress.*

which shocked and outraged the moral sense of the world."[10] White sentenced him to death. Czolgosz expressed no remorse, saying, "I killed the president because he was the enemy of good people—the good working people. I am not sorry for my crime."[11]

Czolgosz spent his last days in solitary confinement at Auburn Prison in upstate New York. Justice was immediate in those days. In the United States today, it takes, on average, more than a decade to carry out a death sentence. One inmate in Florida spent thirty-three years on death row before being put to death in 2011. Czolgosz went to the electric chair on October 29, 1901, a little more than seven weeks after the assassination. None of his family members were there. Prison guards threw sulfuric acid on his face to make it unrecognizable, and he was buried at Soule Cemetery in the little town of Sennett, New York, about five miles north of Auburn. Edison Studios filmed a macabre reenactment of the death chamber scene, with officials hovering around an actor playing Czolgosz as electric current surged through his body. The opening scenes of the short film feature actual footage of Auburn Prison on the day of the execution.

Czolgosz had tried in vain to identify with the American working classes and the anarchist movement, which, by nature, was multiethnic, interregional, and disparate. He found no solace or comfort among the Polish neighborhoods in U.S. cities, which gave so many immigrants a sense of community and belonging, the Walasiewicz family included. Czolgosz was a disgrace to his family and Polish Americans throughout the Great Lakes area. According to an article in a September 1901 issue of the New York-based journal the *Literary Digest*, "A number of Polish societies and journals of this country have repudiated the idea of his Polish nationality, claiming that he is a Russian Hebrew." Many Poles pointed out that Goldman was Jewish. The Chicago daily *Dziennik Narodowy* [National Daily], one of the most important Polish American newspapers in the country, wrote that the name Czolgosz was likely Hungarian or Slavonian, not Polish. One Polish leader from New York told *Literary Digest* that the Czolgosz brothers and sisters "spat on all things Polish," and that Czolgosz had called himself "Nieman," a German name.[12] Cleveland's *Plain Dealer* quoted a resolution from Polish American demonstrators: "The Polish nation can boast of never having produced a man who would stain its reputation by attacking authority because [the Polish nation is] imbued with Christian principles."[13]

The image of Poles in the United States changed for the better when the United States went to war with Germany in April 1917. German Americans now became the target of suspicion, prejudice, and ridicule, shifting the focus off of Poles and other Eastern European immigrants. German-language books were removed from libraries, German-language newspapers closed, and German-language classes in public schools were eliminated. Many German Americans altered their names and enlisted in the U.S. Army to show their loyalty to the United States. One famous photo from the time shows several children standing at Edison Park in Chicago in front of a sign that reads, "Danger!! To pro-Germans." Beneath that is, "Loyal Americans are welcome to Edison Park." President Woodrow Wilson spoke out against so-called hyphenated Americans and declared that "every citizen must declare himself American—or traitor."[14] In 1918, Congress passed the Sedition Act, and after the war Ohio enacted a law mandating that school lessons be conducted in English. Both measures mainly targeted German Americans.

Julian Walasiewicz got out of Europe only a few years before the continent became embroiled in World War I. Poles in Russia found themselves fighting on the side of the Triple Entente, while German and Austrian Poles were conscripted into the armies of the Central Powers. If the Walasiewicz family had stayed in Wierzchownia, Julian might have perished with the Russian Army fighting against fellow Poles. Polish poet Edward Słoński wrote about this prospect of a Polish soldier in the German Army facing a Russian Pole across enemy lines:

> So when you catch me in your sights
> I beg you, play your part,
> And sink your Muscovite bullet
> Deep in my Polish heart.
>
> Now I see the vision clearly
> Caring not that we'll both be dead;
> For *that which has not perished*
> Shall rise from the blood that we shed.[15]

An old Polish prayer envisions the day when Poles would have the chance to fight for the independence of their country:

God of the Jagiellos! God of Sobieski! God of Kościuszko! Have pity on our country and on us. Grant us to pray again to Thee as our fathers prayed, on the battlefield with weapons in our hands, before an altar made of drums and cannons, beneath a canopy of our eagles and our flags.[16]

Cleveland's Polish community ran Red Cross fundraisers and organized Liberty Loan drives for the Allied war effort.

Some 1.9 million Poles fought in World War I, suffering 450,000 dead. In spite of this high price in blood, the war was a godsend to Poles' aspirations for the resurrection of their country. The division of Poles in three different empires seemed an insurmountable obstacle to the return of the Polish state, unless, as famous Polish poet Adam Mickiewicz once wrote, this prayer was answered: "Deliver us, oh Lord. For a universal war for the freedom of the nations, we beseech thee, oh Lord." World War I was just that "universal" conflict. The seemingly impossible happened when the partitioning powers lost the war, even though they fought on opposite sides. The tsar was overthrown in early 1917, and Lenin's Bolsheviks grabbed power that fall, promising Russians "peace, bread, and land." Lenin extricated Soviet Russia from the war, capitulating to the Central Powers at Brest-Litovsk in March 1918. When the Germans surrendered to the Western Allies in November, the Central Powers' victory in the east was rendered null and void. Germany and Austria were at the mercy of the Western Allies, and the Soviet Red Army could not prevent the creation of the new Polish state.

During the war, famous Polish pianist Ignacy Paderewski was instrumental in lobbying the Western Allies for the reconstruction of Poland. As a young man, Paderewski had used some of the money he made from winning music competitions to travel the Polish countryside, visiting towns and villages much like Wierzchownia:

I had heard many tales of suffering among the poor in Russian Poland. And I wanted to see for myself. I found conditions even worse than depicted, and the trip left an indelible impression on my mind, and to some extent altered the course of my life. I became convinced of the righteousness of the Polish cause, and understood fully, for the first time, the great longing of the Poles for liberty.[17]

By the outbreak of war, Paderewski was already a celebrity in the United States, having played hundreds of concerts in the previous two decades. In 1916, he met President Wilson at the White House and toured the country, calling for Poland's independence. In April 1917, Paderewski spoke at the Polish Falcon Convention in Pittsburgh, rallying Polish Americans to the war effort. The Falcons were a Polish American association that promoted Polish patriotism and physical education. It was at one of these clubs on Cleveland's Broadway Avenue that Stella Walsh got her first taste of athletic competition. When Wilson declared war on the Central Powers later that month, Paderewski induced many Falcons to serve in the U.S. Army. Others went to France to fight in Polish divisions under Polish general Józef Haller. After the war, some of these soldiers joined the army of the new Polish state.

In January 1918, Wilson outlined U.S. war aims in his Fourteen Points. Paderewski helped draft the thirteenth point, which called for an "independent [Polish] state." Poland was the only East European country that Wilson promised independence; he merely proposed "autonomous development" for the other nationalities in the Habsburg and Ottoman empires. At the end of the war in 1918, Poland returned to the European State System after a 123-year hiatus. Paderewski became prime minister and represented Poland at the Paris Peace Conference.

By default, Stanisława Walasiewicz was now a citizen of the new Polish state, but like so many American immigrants in the early twentieth century, she had dual allegiances. The Polish American community in Cleveland kept her connected to her place of birth, but there was no question about going back to Poland. She had no memory of that place. The new Poland was desperately poor anyway, and Julian and Weronica were not about to uproot the family to return to Wierzchownia.

While Paderewski was instrumental in burnishing the image of Polish Americans during the war, the specter of Bolshevism emanating from Russia prompted a "Red Scare" in the United States after the war. The government was especially suspicious of East European immigrants. U.S. attorney general A. Mitchell Palmer declared that the

> blaze of revolution . . . was eating its way into the homes of the American workman, its sharp tongues of revolutionary heat were licking the altars of the churches, leaping into the belfry of the school bell, crawling into the sacred

corners of American homes, seeking to replace marriage vows with libertine laws, burning up the foundations of society.[18]

There was an anti-Semitic element to Palmer's arrests and deportations, in part because Russian Jews like Emma Goldman were overrepresented in the ranks of anarchists and radical leftists. "Red Emma" was among the deportees.

Goldman had a Polish-Jewish counterpart in Rosa Luxemburg, one of the most prominent European Marxists of the early twentieth century. "Red Rosa" was born in Zamość, a Polish town in Russia. She left Russia in 1889, but returned to Warsaw for the failed 1905 Russian Revolution. She fled the country for Germany and became a leader of the German Social Democratic Party. Luxemburg demonstrated against World War I, which put her in the crosshairs of radical nationalists who blamed Jews and Communists for Germany's capitulation in 1918. Adolf Hitler's Nazis called it a "stab in the back." In January 1919, right-wing German soldiers shot Luxemburg and threw her body into a Berlin canal.

There were thousands of Poles (many of them Polish Jews) in the socialist movement in the United States, but there were no Poles in prominent leadership positions. Russian leftists were the main target of Palmer's raids, and Polish Catholics vigorously tried to distinguish themselves from their Slavic kinsmen. Many Poles had greater hatred for Russians than for Germans. One section of the Polish community in Cleveland was anti-Russian and supported General Józef Piłsudski. In 1920, Piłsudski led the Polish Army to victory against the Red Army in the so-called Miracle on the Vistula, saving the new Polish state. Another group of Polish immigrants supported the staunchly nationalist, anti-Semitic Roman Dmowski, who had rested his hopes for a new Polish state on tsarist Russia. The Bolshevik Revolution scuttled those plans and undermined his support. Piłsudski grabbed dictatorial power in Poland in 1926, and remains to this day a controversial figure in Polish history. There is no record of the Walasiewicz family's political leanings, although like most working-class Poles in the neighborhood, they probably voted for the Democratic Party.

Palmer's raids stemmed, in part, from fears among Anglo-Saxon Protestants that the influx of Catholic, Orthodox, and Jewish immigrants from Italy, Ireland, and Eastern Europe was changing American culture for the worse. In the late nineteenth century, "race" had become a social construct to distinguish between Caucasians: Anglo Americans were at the top of the hierarchy, with Irish, Italians, and Poles, for example, on lower rungs of the racial scale. Of course, African Americans were put into another racial category altogether, and now they were coming north to work in the urban factories in the so-called Great Migration. From 1910 to 1920, more than a half-million African Americans moved north, and in the 1920s, 750,000 more left the South. The black population of some northern cities doubled in the 1920s.

In 1922, Henry and Emma Owens, from Oakville, Alabama, put their family on a train to Cleveland, where Henry and three of his older sons went to work in the steel mills. They were among the 34,000 African Americans living in Cleveland in 1920. A decade later, that number had jumped to 64,000. The youngest of the Owens's ten children was named James Cleveland Owens, later known as Jesse Owens, one of the two greatest sprinters of the first half of the twentieth century. The other was fellow Clevelander Stella Walsh. Harrison Dillard won the gold medal in the 100-meter dash at the 1948 Olympic Games in London. Dillard also hailed from Cleveland, giving the city three gold medalists in the 100 meters in three consecutive Olympics.

Jesse was nine when the family moved to Cleveland. The Owens found a house on the east side of town, just a few miles from the Walasiewicz home. They lived in a predominantly Polish neighborhood as well. According to historian William J. Baker, "[The Poles] ignored his [Jesse's] strange color; he ignored their strange accents. They were 'peasants and strangers' all, newcomers to an alien environment."[19] Owens attended Fairmount Junior High, where comedian Bob Hope had joked around a few years earlier.[20]

The migration of African Americans to the North accelerated their calls for racial justice. Women were also challenging white men's political power and threatening traditional gender roles. In 1919, after a long fight, suffragettes finally convinced Congress to pass the Nineteenth Amendment, which gave women the vote. Spurred on by economic opportunities that opened up during the war, as well as gaining the franchise, some women in the Roaring Twenties were behaving in ways that made prudish conservatives shudder. Making matters worse in their minds were the Hollywood movies showing these women smoking, drinking, dancing, flashing more skin, and flaunting their independence. As an immigrant woman athlete, Stella Walsh did not fit into mainstream America's idea of bourgeois femininity.

The division of Poles into Germany, Austria, and Russia before 1918 magnified the importance of cultural institutions as keepers and purveyors of a shared Polish national experience. The Catholic Church, church schools, and *sokóls*—cultural and recreation centers in Polish communities in Europe and expatriate communities—kept alive Polish consciousness and the idea of a reconstituted Polish state. Julian and Weronica sent their eldest daughter to the neighborhood elementary school at the Immaculate Heart of Mary Church on Lansing Avenue. The cornerstone of the church was laid in 1914, and it had a four-room elementary school. Stanisława was one of the first students to attend the new sixteen-room classroom, which the church built in 1918. The dwindling Polish Catholic population in Cleveland's Slavic Village today has forced the diocese to close many of the old parishes, but Immaculate Heart of Mary still serves the community. Stanisława spoke Polish at home and learned English on the street and at school.

Walsh attended elementary school at Immaculate Heart of Mary Church on Lansing Avenue. *Author photo.*

After elementary school, Stanisława attended South High School on Broadway and Osage avenues, less than a mile from her house. It was her first foray into the public school system, where she received regular exposure to a community outside of Warszawa. At South, she encountered teachers who had difficulty pronouncing Stanisława Walasiewicz: "The teachers decided my name was a tongue twister," she said. "So they changed it [to Stella Walsh]."[21] Outside of her circle of family and friends, and in Poland, she would be known as Stella Walsh for the rest of her life. Walsh was a solid Anglo name that did not give away her Polish background, an ethnic tag that often drew bigoted ridicule. Eventually she learned perfect English. For those who did not know her, Walsh she was as Middle America as they came. She was unabashed about her Polishness, however; the signature on most of her sports memorabilia reads, "Stella Walsh Walasiewiczowna," one of the many variations of her name she used.

Walsh finished her high school years at Notre Dame Academy on 1332 Ansel Road, near Doan Brook. Locals called the school the "Castle on Ansel." The spirit of the great Stella Walsh no longer inspires students in these schools. Her alma maters have closed or moved. In 1963, Notre Dame moved to Chardon, Ohio, about thirty miles east of Cleveland. The Ansel location has been turned into an apartment building. Immaculate Heart elementary closed in 2003, and South High School shut its doors in 2010.

At an early age, Walsh discovered that she could outsprint both girls *and* boys. She began to train with the local Polish Falcon club on 7146 Broadway Avenue. The Falcons' gymnasium was half the size of a regular basketball court, but it was better than nothing. After leaving Immaculate Heart elementary school, the Falcons became a key connection to Walsh's Polish heritage and her homeland. In the late 1920s and early 1930s, the club subsidized her trips to a number of Falcon meets in the United States and Europe.

Walsh entered into a sporting world that was dominated by men; furthermore, Polish identity was fashioned around a masculine personification of the nation through such figures as Sobieski, Kościuszko, Pułaski, and Piłsudski. The one female icon for the devout Catholic country is the revered figure of the Madonna, and specifically the painting of the *Black Madonna of Częstochowa*, which hangs in the monastery at Jasna Góra in southern Poland. According to legend, in 1655, the Black Madonna miraculously saved the monastery from a Swedish siege and turned the tide of the Second

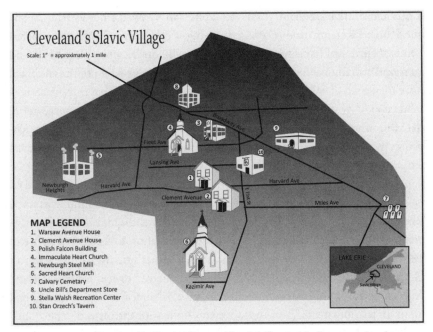

Cleveland's Slavic Village. *Map by Gracia Lindberg.*

Northern War. Some believers think her image appeared in the clouds over Warsaw during the Red Army invasion in 1920, once again saving the nation.

The most famous Polish woman of the time was physicist Marie Sklodowska. Born in Warsaw in 1867, Sklodowska also left the oppression of Russian Poland, traveling first to Kraków (under Austrian rule) and then to study at the Sorbonne in Paris. Together with her husband Pierre Curie, Marie Sklodowska Curie became world renowned for her pioneering work in radioactivity. The Curies won the Nobel Prize in Physics in 1903.

In 1912, the same year that Stanisława and her mother left for the United States, acclaimed Polish writer Henryk Sienkiewicz led a group of Polish professors to Paris to plead with Sklodowska Curie to return to Warsaw to head a new research laboratory. "We are losing confidence in our intellectual faculties," Sienkiewicz told her. "We are being lowered in the opinion of our enemies, and we are abandoning hope for the future. . . . Possessing you in Warsaw, we should feel stronger, we should lift our heads now bent under so many misfortunes." Sklodowska Curie was torn between her loyalty to Poland and her work in Paris. In 1913, she visited Warsaw for the opening of a new radioactive laboratory that would be run by two of her assistants. She condemned Russian rule of Poland, saying, "This poor country, massacred by an absurd and barbarous domination, really does a great deal to defend its moral and intellectual life. A day may come perhaps when oppression will have to retreat, and it is necessary to last out until then. But what an existence! What conditions!"[22] Walsh would face a similar dilemma twenty years later in deciding whether to run for the United States or Poland in the 1932 Los Angeles Olympics. But by that time Poland was an independent state and tsarist Russia was gone, making her decision easier.

A woman like Sklodowska Curie at the pinnacle of the scientific world was an anomaly. The Polish Falcon athlete, in most people's mind, was not a woman either. The Polish Falcons patterned themselves after the nineteenth-century Czech *sokol*, which was a sporting association founded in Prague in 1862. The Czech *sokol* got its inspiration from Father Friedrich Ludwig Jahn's German *Turnen* movement earlier in the century. *Turnen*, a term derived from an old Germanic word meaning warrior, intended to engender a liberal German patriotism and hone young men's bodies for the birth of a new, unified Germany. Jahn's *Turnen* had an explicit German national and egalitarian character, which the conservative authorities considered revolutionary. Jahn's movement was outlawed, and Jahn was imprisoned. The founder of the Czech clubs, Miroslav Tyrš, declared that "no club can unite Slavic youth and men by so natural and strong a means as the Sokol brotherhood."[23]

Every six years the Czechs held a *slet*—a big athletic event that attracted hundreds of Czech athletes from throughout the world. Participants often showed up in traditional Czech garb. These events had a nationalist agenda, namely to gain independence from the Hapsburg Empire. Worried about subterfuge, the Hapsburg authorities kept a close watch on *sokol* members.

The Poles formed their first *sokół* (in Polish) in the Austrian Galician capital of Lwów in 1867. In 1892, the Polish *sokóls* held their first *zlot* in Lwów. More than a thousand athletes came from Galicia, the Czech lands, and Prussian Poland. The prewar *zlots* were staged in Austrian Poland, where Poles enjoyed more cultural freedom than their fellow nationals in the German and Russian empires. After the 1905 Russian Revolution, a Falcon Alliance was formed in Warsaw, but it was outlawed two years later.

In 1887, Felix L. Pietrowicz founded the first *sokół* in the United States. He called the Chicago *sokół* a Falcon "nest." Pietrowicz wrote that "a 'Falcon' is

The Polish Falcon Nest on Broadway Avenue in 1945 (top) and today. Walsh began her athletic career at the club, which is about one mile from her house. *Cleveland State University.*

the modern transformation of an ancient man to a modern man and . . . into a 'new' and different, better Pole, and therefore better United States citizen."[24] In 1912, the Falcons moved their national headquarters to Pittsburgh, which was more or less equidistant from the largest Polish communities in New York City and Chicago. By the 1930s, the Falcons had some 10,000 members.

The Polish Falcons of America adopted the adage "*w zdrowym ciele zdrowy duch*" [a healthy spirit in a healthy body], which mirrored the British promotion of "muscular Christianity" and Max Nordau's idea of "Muskeljudentum" [muscular Jewishness]. The Polish *sokóls* borrowed gymnastic techniques from Turnen and Swedish sports clubs that connected sports with military drill. In this age of social Darwinism, a strong body was associated with a healthy, virile, masculine nation. To compete on Polish teams against other national teams maintained a sense of ethnic pride in the face of German and Russian discrimination. Winning was a way to compare favorably to other national groups.

In 1904, Poles established Falcon Nest 50 on the East Side of Cleveland, and in 1909, another nest (141) was started on the South Side. In 1911, the year Walsh was born, Nest 141 moved into a building at 7146 Broadway, where prospective Polish soldiers trained during World War I. Stan Musial began playing sports at his local Falcon Nest 247 in Donora, about 150 miles southeast of Cleveland. There was some division within the Polish community in the United States about whether the Falcon mission was training soldiers or grooming athletes, but in 1914, the Falcons affirmed their mission as furthering the "physical and spiritual rebirth of the Polish nation through all possible means." Facing discrimination against suspected leftist East Europeans after the war, Falcon president Teofil Starzynski emphasized loyalty to both the United States and the new Polish state. In a pointed reference to the Soviet Union, Starzynski said that Falcon culture and values were "rooted in Western civilization" and not in the "barbaric culture of the East."[25]

The Falcon Nest on Broadway was within walking distance of the Walasiewicz house, and in playing sports there Walsh had her second home. The Falcons were a strong tug on Walsh's Polish identity at the same time she was finding her niche in the Cleveland sports scene; athletics became her passion, her identity, and her one and only love.

2

Cleveland's "Twentieth-Century Flyer"

It wasn't so bad that she beat us, but did you see her turn half way down the track to see where we were?

—*Canadian sprinter Dallas Creamer, after losing to Walsh in the 220-yard dash*

By the time Stella Walsh entered high school in the fall of 1926, she had grown to nearly 5-foot-6, dwarfing her 4-foot-10 mother and topping her 5-foot-4 father. In her first race for the South High Flyers, she won the 50-yard dash. "Flyer" was the nickname given to virtually every sprinter of the time, so Walsh became the Flyers' "Flyer." Her first big track and field meet was the Junior Olympics in 1927, sponsored by the *Cleveland Press*, which advertised the event as "seeking Olympic athletes." Walsh won the 50- and 70-yard sprints, and came in second in the standing broad jump and baseball throw.

The odds were long for a young Polish immigrant girl from Russia to gain notoriety in American sports. In the early twentieth century, most avenues to fame and fortune for women were closed, including sports. Few women rose to prominence in big business or national politics, but some gained celebrity in the movies, dance, and literature. After World War I, women asserted themselves into male bailiwicks as never before, including the worlds of film and sports, but with strong push back from the guardians of mainstream bourgeois American culture.

Women's sports were not an important part of the cultural scene in the 1920s. Hollywood had far greater impact on American society. The most famous Polish American woman in the United States at the time was world-renowned film actress Pola Negri, born Barbara Apollonia Chalupec in 1897, in Lipno, a small Russian-Polish town about 30 miles southwest of Wierzchownia. Negri's film career paralleled Walsh's rise to the top of the track and field world. Negri also knew that her future in Russia was bleak. Her father had been thrown into a Warsaw prison for his involvement in the abortive 1905 Russian Revolution. Negri once said that "our people were ground down by the Russian, Austrian, and German oppressors, and nowhere was our lot worse than in the provinces governed by Russian officials."[1]

Like Walsh, Negri was not known by her given name. Pola was short for Apollonia, and she took the name Negri from famous Italian poet Ada Negri. Pola Negri first entered the theater scene in Warsaw, but she saw few prospects there. Near the end of World War I, she moved to Berlin to make films, where she worked with brilliant German director Ernst Lubitsch. For her 1987 obituary, the *New York Times* wrote that she was a "startlingly beautiful woman, with skin as delicately white as fine porcelain, jet black hair, and flashing dark-green eyes."[2]

Negri made many great silent films in Germany and Hollywood (some of them are lost), establishing herself as one of the first movie "vamps"—women who lured unsuspecting, helpless men into their irresistible clutches and to ultimate doom. Gloria Swanson was her main rival for these roles, and Greta Garbo and Marlene Dietrich followed in their footsteps. "I was the first," Negri bragged. "And I was the best."[3] Although the femme fatale was a familiar theatrical role, the movies exposed the masses to the dangerous idea that women could control men. "I was the star who introduced sex to the screen," she said, "but it was sex in good taste."[4]

Negri became a huge celebrity in Los Angeles in the decade before Stella Walsh arrived at the 1932 Olympics. Negri was the lover of the notorious lothario Rudolph Valentino, and she claimed to be engaged to marry the dashing film star, although he denied it. In June 1926, Hollywood's darling couple went to Grauman's Theater for the premier of Valentino's last film, *Son of Sheik*. Following a cast party at the famous Cocoanut Grove nightclub,

Poland's Pola Negri was one of the great silent film stars and Rudolph Valentino's lover. *Library of Congress.*

Valentino left on a publicity tour. In New York, he suddenly collapsed with a gastric ulcer and appendicitis. On August 23, Valentino died from peritonitis. He was thirty-one. Negri was crushed, at least in public. She went to New York for the funeral, where she wept inconsolably. The news of Valentino's death was plastered all over the August 24 edition of the *Plain Dealer*. Walsh, who loved to go to the movies, was undoubtedly following press accounts of Valentino's passing and Negri's funereal swoon.

For most of her film career, Negri's voice was never heard, and yet the Polish temptress exploded on the silent screen with an exotic Slavic sensuality that put her on the watch list of Americans who wanted to protect their image of a pure, chaste woman. One critic said that she seemed to "have a little dirt behind her neck."[5]Although the Hays Film Code of 1934 put a temporary end to the overt portrayal of the "bad girl" in Hollywood films, Walsh and other female athletes were also challenging the conventional gendered order of things—not as hypersexualized femmes fatales, but as women on a field of play that was dominated by men. Pola Negri titillated men, while Stella Walsh beat them.

The sophisticated, cosmopolitan, beautiful Negri seemed to be everything that Walsh, the modest, plain-looking, young sprinter from Cleveland, was not. But Walsh's métier was also a silent stage. She carved out her public persona on the track, the basketball court, and the softball diamond. On the field of play, few words were spoken; off it, media coverage of women's sports was negligible, so Walsh could compete with little fanfare. Walsh was a shy, private person anyway. In competition she could forget about any questions of her national allegiance and snide comments about her masculine looks. The one unambiguous, clear identity Walsh had was on the track, where the lanes were straight, the measurements exact, and the winners and losers clear. There she could be judged simply on the basis of how fast she ran.

Walsh was not a "looker"—in the parlance of the time—so the success she had running and playing games gave her newfound confidence. It was often a lonely existence for these women who lived on the frontier of a man's world—Goldman, Luxemburg, Sklodowska Curie, Negri, and Walsh. Awkward in social situations and troubled by her own sexuality, the adulation Walsh received on the track liberated Stanisława Walasiewicz.

The gradual rise in women's opportunities to compete in sports after World War I paralleled Stella Walsh's rise in the track and field world. Her victories on the cinders brought unlikely notoriety for the quiet, reserved immigrant girl. In the late 1920s, she competed in sports in and around the Cleveland area, but the teenager was unknown throughout the rest of the United States and Europe. The big names in American women's sports at the time were the great tennis player Helen Wills and all-around athlete Mildred "Babe" Didrikson. Didrikson was the same age as Walsh, and they both played softball and basketball, and did track and field.

Women faced stiff resistance to participating in "men's" sports. At the turn of the century, it was acceptable for women of leisure to play such genteel lawn games as bowling, tennis, and golf, but the gatekeepers of traditional gender norms judged strenuous exercise unladylike, uncomely, and dangerous to a woman's health. Maud Watson was one of the first English tennis champions in the late nineteenth century. In 1935, she told Helen Wills about the reaction to women playing the game in those days:

> When I began to play tennis, I hit balls against the wall in our garden. My father was a vicar and a very broad-minded man for those days. He let me and my sisters play in a match in Hurlingham, which we won. People thought it was scandalous that he should let us play in public! We enjoyed it, though.[6]

Women tennis players had to wear long dresses and broad-brimmed hats, making it impossible to do an overhead serve. High-heeled boots further restricted movement, but then volleying, according to one tennis manual, was off limits: "The volley game is not made for ladies. It is too quick, and is too great a strain on the system."[7]

Sweating was for men and manual laborers. There was an old saying that if a girl finished first in sports she would finish last in the race to find a husband. Walsh, along with many other courageous sportswomen, challenged these traditional gender norms. *Plain Dealer* sports columnist James Doyle wrote a little ditty that underscored the stigma facing women athletes: "Twinkle, twinkle, parva Stella. You run too fast for any fella."[8]

Harriet Fitzgerald, a top official in the northeast Ohio Amateur Athletic Union (AAU) in the 1920s, left the organization because of its increasingly liberal ideas about women participating in sports. Fitzgerald maintained that doing hard sports would irreparably damage a woman's body. Walsh's neighborhood friend Frances Kaszubski, who became one of the greatest shot putters and discus throwers in the United States after World War II, remembered that Fitzgerald "made it known throughout the Cleveland school system—in fact all northeast Ohio—that if you competed on such a level you could never have a child." Kaszubski said that one girl was such a good athlete that "her parents made her join a convent to prevent her from playing basketball."[9]

In the early Olympics, women were relegated to swimming and tennis competitions. Frenchman Pierre Coubertin, the pioneer of the modern Olympics, had lobbied hard to keep women out of the competition altogether. "The Olympic Games must be reserved for men," he declared. Although French enlightened philosophers and political theorists provided the foundation for the American Revolution and French Revolution, and the idea of equality according to law, women had to wait. After World War I, women in most West European countries and the United States got the franchise, while French women finally received the vote at the end of World War II. Coubertin once said that the "French would accept equality as long as it was not openly displayed and did not change deep-rooted traditions." Coubertin was not opposed to women exercising in private, but the spectacle of women running and jumping around in shorts in full public view was anathema to the conservative Frenchman. He warned that if there were women runners or soccer players in the Olympics, "would such sports practiced by women constitute an edifying sight before crowds assembled for an Olympiad?"[10]

Undoubtedly, the antics of famous French shot putter Violette Morriss, holder of the world record, appalled Coubertin. The imposing, stout, and muscular Morriss played all sports, and during World War I she was an ambulance driver on the western front. In 1921, she won the javelin and shot put at an international women's meet in Monte Carlo. She had a short-lived marriage in the early 1920s but was hardly the domestic type. Morriss smashed traditional gender roles by cross-dressing, chain-smoking, flaunting her bisexuality, and undergoing a mastectomy to better play sports and drive race cars. She often posed for photos behind the wheel of a sports car, dressed in a suit and tie, with pomaded short hair and a cigarette dangling from her mouth. It was a shocking image for the times. In 1927, Morriss won the prestigious Bol d'Or auto race.

In the 1920s, Frenchwoman Violette Morriss broke gender norms in athletics and auto racing, prompting outrage from male sport authorities. *National Library of France.*

Coubertin's persistent bias against women participating in the Olympics prompted Frenchwoman Alice Milliat to launch a parallel women's Olympic movement. Milliat helped form the Fédération Sportive Féminine Internationale (FSFI) in Paris in 1921. The FSFI held four women's world competitions in the interwar period, opposite of the Olympic years: the Women's Olympic Games in 1922 and 1926, and the Women's World Games in 1930 and 1934 (the International Olympic Committee [IOC] successfully lobbied against Milliat's use of the term "Olympics"). United States Olympic Committee head Avery Brundage said of Milliat, "She was active for years, and she demanded more and more. She made quite a nuisance of herself."[11] The first Women's Olympics in Paris, in 1922, attracted athletes from five countries to compete in eleven different disciplines. Walsh ran in the 1930 and 1934 Games.

Until the 1928 Amsterdam Olympics, women were only allowed to compete in swimming, tennis, and figure-skating events. The International Association of Athletics Federations (IAAF), the conservative governing body for track and field, finally bent to Milliat's constant pressure, and women were allowed to compete in official track and field events at Amsterdam, albeit on a temporary basis. Five events were staged: the 100 and 800 meters, the high jump, the discus, and the 80-meter hurdles. When some of the exhausted runners fell onto the cinder track after the 800-meter race, the New York Times wrote, "Even this distance makes too great a call on feminine strength."[12] The IOC took the event off the women's Olympic track and field program until the 1960 Rome Olympics. The 1,500 meters for women debuted at the 1972 Munich Olympics, and women did not run an Olympic marathon until the 1984 Los Angeles Games.

Milliat had to be diplomatic in her quest for equality for women's sports, knowing that the doyens of international sport were adamantly opposed to her movement. Violette Morriss went too far in confounding gender norms, even for Milliat. The French athletic federation banned Morriss before the 1928 Amsterdam Olympics. According to historian Jean Williams, "Morris [sic] was distanced by Milliat from 'respectable' FSFI competition in the late 1920s and failed in a much-publicized court case to have her competitor's license restored in 1929."[13] Evidently the Nazis invited the disaffected Morriss to the 1936 Olympic Games, where she was received by Hitler. She worked on and off for the German secret police before and during World War II, earning the moniker "Hyena of the Gestapo." French resistance forces assassinated her in 1944.

Coubertin, Brundage, and the other upper-class men on the IOC could tolerate women playing tennis and swimming, but they were vehemently opposed to the idea of women doing track and field. Brundage told the New York Times that the "ancient Greeks kept women out of their athletic games. They wouldn't even let them on the sidelines. I'm not so sure, but they were right."[14] The pope was of the same mind. "After twenty centuries of Christianity," Pius XI wrote in 1928, "the sensitiveness and attention to the delicate care due young women and girls should be shown to have fallen lower than pagan Rome."[15] Morriss confirmed their worst fears of what this uncivilized spectacle would become.

Halina Konopacka, the most famous Polish female athlete of the time, helped change attitudes toward women in the Olympics. Born eleven years before Walsh in Rawa Mazowiecka, in Russian Poland, Konopacka was a svelte, attractive, long-necked brunette. Like Morriss and Walsh, she dabbled in many different sports, including skiing, tennis, swimming, basketball, and team handball. She burst onto the Polish athletic scene by winning the discus throw at the 1924 Polish National Championships. Konopacka hoped to compete at the 1924 Paris Olympics, but women's track and field was not yet on the program.

Poland struggled to field a men's team for the first postwar Olympics in Antwerp, let alone a women's contingent. At a meeting in Kraków in 1919, Polish sports officials formed an Olympic Committee and looked forward to sending a team to Antwerp. The committee even made a poster dedicated to the event. But the new Polish government did not have the funds to adequately support an Olympic team. The fledgling state was recovering from the devastation of World War I and had to coordinate the bureaucracies and economies of the former German, Austrian, and Russian territories. About two-thirds of the population worked in the agricultural sector, and the land reform after the war only covered 6 percent of the land. Most Polish peasants were still desperately poor, small subsistence farmers.

Polish industry also lagged behind the rest of Europe. Many of Poland's trading connections that had existed before World War I were now cut off. For example, Łódz was a major textile center that had supplied the Russian Empire, but with the emergence of the new Soviet state that market dried up. In the interwar period, trade with the Soviet Union amounted to less than 1 percent of Poland's total trade. In the mid-1920s, shipments of Polish coal from the former Prussian region of Upper Silesia to Germany were blocked by tariffs. Commerce was further impeded by rail lines that often connected the three parts of Poland to the partitioning empires but not to other regions within the new Poland. Even the rail gauge between former Prussian and Russian Poland was different. Devastating inflation hit Poland in 1921, and in 1929, the Great Depression sent the Polish economy into a tailspin. From 1929 to 1932, industrial production fell by nearly two-thirds.

The recurrent economic crises unsettled the politics of the Polish Second Republic, and Marshal Piłsudski ended the political stalemate by taking dictatorial power in May 1926. The "May Coup" remains a controversial topic in Polish history. The political and social divide in Poland was so wide that one British historian observed, "If the Second Republic had not been foully [sic] murdered in 1939, by external agents [the Germans], there is little doubt that it would have soon sickened from internal causes."[16]

Poland sent its first Olympic team to the 1924 Paris Olympics. Sixty-five Polish athletes competed, winning two medals, a silver in team cycling and a bronze in equestrian. Polish sports authorities showed little interest in women's sports. Fencer Wanda Dubieńska was the lone woman on the team, and she lost all five of her matches. When Stella Walsh competed for Poland at the 1932 Los Angeles Games, there were still only nine women on the fifty-one-member Polish team.

Piłsudski was acutely aware of Poland's precarious geopolitical situation between revanchist Germany and the Soviet Union, and he made the strength of the Polish Army a top priority. Poland followed a long British and continental tradition of linking organized sports with the development of disciplined, healthy, and fit foot soldiers. As the Polish economy stabilized in the late 1920s, Piłsudski began to devote more resources to physical education in schools and sporting activities in general. In 1927, he formed the *Urząd Wychowania Fizycznego i Przysposobienia Wojskowego* [State Council of Physical Education and Military Training]. The effort was only marginally successful. From 1924 to the last interwar Olympics in Berlin in 1936, Poles won twenty medals in the Summer Olympics. Hungary, with half the population of Poland, won forty-nine.

Konopacka won Poland's first Olympic gold medal. At the 1928 Amsterdam Olympics, she took the discus, breaking her own world record by two and a half meters in beating American Lillian Copeland. "Halina of Gold" became a hero in Poland, which was desperate for international recognition and prestige. Polish president Ignacy Mościcki sent Konopacka a congratulatory telegram, and Piłsudski gave her a reception at the Belvedere Palace in Warsaw. She won two consecutive "Great Sport Award of Honor" trophies, the top sport prize in interwar Poland. Stella Walsh won the award in 1930, 1932, 1933, and 1934.

Konopacka became one of Poland's best tennis players in the 1930s. She also gained fame as a poet, publishing in such prestigious Polish literary journals as *Wiadomości Literackie* [Literary News]. In December 1928, she married Poland's minister of finance, Ignacy Matuszewski. Matuszewski served on the Polish General Staff and, after Germany overran Poland in September 1939, organized a daring operation to move gold from the Bank of Poland through Romania, Turkey, Syria, and Lebanon, and eventually to France. The gold finally ended up in the hands of the exiled Polish government in London. By some accounts, Halina was involved in the operation, but that seems to be a fabrication. Early in the war, Matuszewski and his wife escaped Europe to the United States.

Halina Konopacka was Poland's first great female athlete, winning a gold medal in the discus at the 1928 Amsterdam Olympics. *Kurier Codzienny, Narodowe Archiwum Cyfrowe [National Digital Archive].*

When the Soviets imposed a Communist regime on Poland after the war, Konopacka Matuszewski, like most Polish exiles, did not return to Poland, but lived out her life in the United States. She died in Florida in 1989, and her remains were interred in Brodnowski Cemetary in Warsaw. She outlived Stella Walsh by nine years. In 2013, Macek Petruczenko, writing in the main Polish sports journal, *Przegląd Sportowy* [Sports Review], called her the "most interesting figure in our interwar sport, and taking into wider consideration her participation in Warsaw salons and in the cultural field, she was surely one of the most interesting Polish women."[17]

While Halina Konopacka Matuszewski was celebrated in Poland for her Olympic victory, Walsh was still an unknown there. She had lived almost her entire life in Cleveland and was just beginning to compete in meets in other parts of the country. The Walasiewicz family did not have the wherewithal to finance her running career, especially after the Great Depression hit in 1929. Like many other Poles in the Slavic Village, Julian's hours and wages at the Newburgh steel mill shrank. The economic crisis was especially hard on African Americans who had come to northern cities to work. Writer Langston Hughes, Walsh's fellow Clevelander, noted, "The Depression brought everybody down a peg or two. And the Negro had but a few pegs to fall."

Walsh turned to the Polish Falcons to subsidize her track and field career. Through her connections to the Falcons in the United States and abroad, she became an international star. She felt deeply indebted to the club, which strengthened her bond with the Polish community in Cleveland and her native Poland. Nonetheless, Walsh fully expected to get U.S. citizenship when she turned twenty-one in 1932, and to compete for the United States at the Los Angeles Olympics.

In the spring of 1928, Walsh boarded a New York Central Railroad (NYCRR) train at Cleveland's Union Terminal on her way to Syracuse, New York, to compete in the Polish Falcon's quadrennial *Zlot*, a track and field meet of athletes from *sokóls* throughout the country. Running outside of Cleveland for the first time, the seventeen-year-old surprised everyone by winning the all-around track and field championship.

Clevelanders thought that Walsh was a serious contender for a spot on the 1928 U.S. Olympic team. Funds to travel to these meets were always in short supply in those days, and the *Plain Dealer* called for contributions to send

Walsh to Newark for the Olympic trials. Running under the name Walsh and speaking English, few people outside of her neighborhood knew that she was not a U.S. citizen. On July 4, she tied for first in her 100-meter quarterfinal heat but came in third in the semifinal heat. Only the top two finishers advanced to the finals. Walsh was chosen as an alternate for the 4 × 100 U.S. relay team, but it was soon discovered that she was not eligible to run for the United States. "They started measuring me for a uniform, and I had to fill out some cards," Walsh later recalled. "They had a blank for my birthplace, and I was honest. I didn't know up to then that it made any difference." At age seventeen, Walsh was too young to apply for naturalization anyway.[18] Years later, she claimed that her disappointment at not making the 1928 U.S. Olympic team influenced her decision to run for Poland at the 1932 Los Angeles Games.[19]

The Syracuse *Zlot* and the Olympic trials established Walsh as a world-class athlete, and in March 1929, she anchored the NYCRR Athletic Association's (NYCRR AA) "famous girls' 440-yard relay team" to a victory in the Cleveland Athletic Club's annual track meet.[20] Her next stop was the 1929 world *Zlot* in Poznań, Poland. The Polish Falcons again raised funds to send their star sprinter abroad. Walsh arrived in Poznań in late June, nearly seventeen years after she had left Russian Poland as a one-year-old. It was a remarkable journey back to Poland for Walsh, competing in a city only about 160 miles from her birthplace. Few in Poland had heard of Stanisława Walasiewicz, as she was known there.

This trip to Europe was the first of many for Walsh. Globalization is a phenomenon that many people associate with such recent technologies as the cell phone and the Internet, but the rapid movement of people, capital, goods, services, and ideas throughout the world really began in earnest in the latter half of the nineteenth century, with the advent of the railroad, the steam engine, steamships, electricity, the internal combustion engine, the telegraph, and the telephone. Walsh had immigrated to the United States on one of those oceangoing vessels, and she would traverse the Atlantic many more times in her lengthy running career.

The Poznań *Zlot* was set to begin on June 28, exactly ten years to the day after the signing of the Versailles Treaty. Surely the Germans noted the timing of the event. Polish notables like politician Roman Dmowski, World War I general Józef Haller, and pianist and diplomat Ignacy Paderewski were on hand for the meet. Before World War I, Poznań (Posen in German) was an

agricultural trading and financial center in the German Empire. The population of the city was about 60 percent Polish, and on this basis the Versailles
Treaty awarded the entire Poznań province to the new Polish state.

Germans could stomach the loss of Alsace-Lorraine to France in the
west, but the loss of this Prussian land to Poland was a bitter blow. The
so-called Polish Corridor to the north of Poznań separated East Prussia
from Germany proper and left 1 million Germans in Poland. Poles called
the acquisition of this predominantly German area the "Vistula [River's]
wedding to the Baltic Sea." German right-wing nationalists, Hitler's Nazis
among them, made the return of the Corridor and the German-populated
port of Danzig a centerpiece of their revanchist foreign policy. With a
hostile Soviet Union to the east, interwar Poland was in an impossible
geopolitical position.

Walsh's complete dominance of the Poznań *Zlot* instantly made her a
name in Polish sports circles. She won five events: the 60, 100, 200, and
400 meters, and the broad jump. She also took the all-around championship. Polish track and field officials were so impressed that they invited
Walsh to join the Warsaw sports club Sokół Grażyna. In a meet that July,
in Chorzów, a predominantly German city in Upper Silesia that had been
awarded to Poland in a disputed plebiscite, Walsh competed with the Polish national team against Australia, winning gold medals in the 60, 100,
and 200 meters, as well as the broad jump. She won those events again in
a meet against Czechoslovakia. Walsh became an overnight sensation in
Poland, and she basked in the accolades. She took home a box full of medals and a photo of Piłsudski, which her parents displayed prominently in
their house.

Walsh was now famous in Cleveland, and sports fans eagerly awaited her
Olympic debut for the United States. One Ohio newspaper wrote, "Miss
Walsh's big thrill came last summer, when she returned to Poland, where she
was born, and there ran the native girls breathless. . . . Her one ambition is to
run for America in the 1932 Olympics at Los Angeles (she will have become
an American citizen by that time)."[21]

Walsh was clearly one of the best sprinters in the world. That fall in
Newark, Walsh led an 880-yard relay team to an AAU record. The association then invited her to the 1930 Millrose Games, the signature indoor track

meet in the country. Rodman Wanamaker, heir to New York's Wanamaker department store company, had organized the first Millrose Games in 1908 (Millrose was the name of Wanamaker's estate). He was also instrumental in creating the Professional Golfers Association (PGA) in 1916, and the PGA championship trophy bears his name to this day. Held every February at New York City's famed Madison Square Garden, the Millrose Games was the most prestigious indoor track and field meet in the country. Ireland's Eamonn Coghlan, who won the "Wanamaker Mile" seven times from 1977 to 1987, commented that "it was regarded as the Olympics of track and field. The stars were household names, attracting fans who may not have even had a close interest in athletics."[22]

Walsh qualified for the final in the 50-yard sprint. The other finalists were Canadians, with Canada boasting a reputation for producing world-class women athletes. One historian called the 1920s the "Golden Age of Women's Sport" in Canada, when women began to play basketball, ice hockey, and baseball, and curled, bowled, speed skated, rowed, and ran track. The University of Toronto and McGill University in Montreal spearheaded the women's athletic movement; by 1908, both schools had a physical education degree for women. There was pushback to these women playing sports. Dr. A. S. Lamb, the Canadian representative on the IAAF, tried unsuccessfully to keep women's track and field off the Olympic program. Even after the Amsterdam Olympics, where women competed in these events for the first time, Lamb again voted to drop them.

The Canadian women's 1928 Olympic team, nicknamed the "Matchless Six," surprised everyone at the Amsterdam Games. Canada had some of the best sprinters in the world; three of the six finalists in the 100 meters wore Maple Leafs on their uniforms. Canadians won four out of the eighteen medals awarded at Amsterdam and two of the five gold medals. Jane Bell, who anchored the gold medal 4 × 100-meter relay team, remembered the huge crowd that greeted them on their return to Toronto: "We were the toast of the town. . . . We were on everybody's tongue."[23]

Although Walsh was not yet a U.S. citizen, her coach, Dr. Dan Griffin, appealed to her sense of national pride as the only American in the Millrose field: "I don't know whether you know it or not," he told Walsh, "but there are four girls in this race and three of them are Canadians. One or the other of them has won this event for the last five years. Suppose you bring the championship back to the United States."[24]

Walsh was overwhelmed by the sense that she was running for the entire country:

> I didn't just feel like Stella Walsh then, but as if I was part of every girl in the United States. I can't describe that feeling. I wanted so much to win, but I can say honestly that this time I didn't have a thought for the personal glory that would go with it. I was just one American girl against these aliens, and it has never seemed so important that I win a race as it seemed then. There were millions of girls in the United States, and I was the one chosen to run this race. That was the thrill.

Walsh blew away the Canadians in a world record time of 6.0 seconds. The *Plain Dealer* wrote that "she was bound to win—because she was Stella Walsh, American girl."[25]

Walsh was named the Millrose Games' top athlete, the first woman to win the award. A few days later, she beat one of the Canadians—Dallas Creamer—again, at the Meadowbrook Games in Philadelphia. Walsh broke the 220-yard dash world record by two seconds. "It wasn't so bad that she beat us," remarked Creamer. "But did you see her turn halfway down the track to see where we were?"[26] Walsh's winning streak ended in Buffalo in March, with a loss in the 75 yards to Kay Griffith, one of the Canadians Walsh had beaten at the Millrose Games. After one false start, a cautious Walsh got out slowly and never caught up to Griffith. That summer, Walsh bounced back to become the first woman to run the 100-yard dash in less than eleven seconds (10.8).

The national news media followed the exploits of the sensational new sprinter as she set world records, but Walsh kept her quiet, reserved demeanor. Coach Griffin told the press that "not one victory, not a single achievement on the track turns her head in the slightest. She goes to bed each night before ten, and she has never had a boyfriend." Griffin did say that Walsh liked to go to the "talkies"—the new sound movies.[27]

Walsh claimed that she never drank, but that was against the law as she came of age in the 1920s. The Eighteenth Amendment (1919) prohibited the production and consumption of alcohol, and Ohio was at the center of the crusade to ban the "lawless contraband." The Women's Christian Temperance Union was founded in Cleveland in 1874, and the Anti-Saloon League was formed in Oberlin in 1893. Operating out of Cleveland, Wayne Wheeler was a leader of the Anti-Saloon League and the driving force behind the "dry laws" in Ohio and throughout the nation. Upon the passage of the Eighteenth Amendment, evangelist Billy Sunday declared that "men will walk upright now, women will smile, and the children will laugh. Hell will be forever for rent."[28]

Protestant America was behind Prohibition, and in their view, women doing sport was one way to steer the fairer sex away from the "evil elixirs." Walsh often said that she did not hoist a beer because she was in training. According to the press, she was not interested in the nightlife anyway: "She plans to keep on running for at least four or five years in the time she can spare from her duties in a railroad office," one Ohio newspaper reported. "She is in bed by ten, never later, and therefore finds no time for such entertainment as movies, bridge parties, or dancing."[29]

Walsh's Polish community energetically circumvented the law, however. The barkeep was a respected person in Catholic Polish American neighborhoods, and as one historian pointed out, "[I]mbibing was traditional [for Poles]. Peasants drank for recreation and hospitality, and in the new world the tavern continued its old function as a place of repose and sociability. . . . Roman Catholic teaching condemned drunkenness, not drinking per se."[30] After her Olympic career was over, Walsh was known to frequent the many pubs in the Slavic Village and worked at one for a time.

The Cleveland press anticipated that Walsh would lead the U.S. women's team at the 1932 Los Angeles Olympics. The *Plain Dealer* reported that she was going to night school to pass her citizenship test. After her twenty-first birthday on April 3, 1932, it would take three months for Walsh to become officially naturalized, making her eligible for the Los Angeles Games in August.[31] On March 6, 1930, the newspaper ran an article and a big cartoon of "Stella Walsh—Cleveland's Spring Queen" kneeling at the starting line, surrounded by smaller drawings of her favorite things: a leggy pose sitting in an easy chair reading a "Wild West" story, a couple of apples (her favorite fruit), and standing in a dress at a filing cabinet next to the caption, "She is a clerk at the New York Central R.R. offices." In the right corner of the cartoon is a newsboy hawking papers with the headline, "Stella Walsh Breaks World's Record!" He remarks, "It's a good thing that she changed her name—the newsies would have choked on the real one—Stella Walasiewicz." The paper also published a photo of the "world's two fastest humans," Walsh and Ohio State University sprinter George Simpson, who had set a world record in the 100 yards in 1929. That mark was not recognized because he had used starting blocks.

On April 7, 1930, Walsh submitted her "Declaration of Intention" to the Naturalization Service to become an American citizen in 1932. The application read,

> I will, before being admitted to citizenship, renounce forever all allegiance and fidelity to any foreign prince, potentate, state, or sovereignty. . . . I am not an anarchist; I am not a polygamist. . . . It is my intention in good faith to become a citizen of the United States of America and to reside permanently therein.

Walsh had no qualms about giving up her Polish citizenship. Although it is not clear whether she had legally changed her name from Stanisława Walasiewicz, she signed the document "Stella Walsh."[32]

On April 17, Walsh left Union Station on the New York Central 5204 bound for the AAU National Indoor Championships in Boston. Probably because she was an employee of the NYCRR, the *Plain Dealer* was able to get a shot of her in a stylish knee-length black dress standing on the locomotive's cowcatcher. Walsh's rise to national sprinting prominence had prompted the railroad's Cleveland office to give her a job in the billing department in 1929, and she began to run in track meets in the jersey of the NYCRR, one of the oldest and biggest railroad companies in the country. Shipping magnate Cornelius Vanderbilt had taken over the railroad in 1867, building a vast rail network from the Northeast to the Midwest.

As Walsh's fame grew in Cleveland, the railroad's bosses used her for publicity. One took Walsh to the kitchen of his house to take pictures of her cooking—with flour on her face and all—to show that she not only worked and played sports, but also could carry out domestic activities. A woman who could outrun guys was an oddity, so Walsh became somewhat of a novelty act at company picnics and events. Other male employees were given a head start, but Walsh beat them anyway.

In 1930, the Cleveland press dubbed Walsh the "Twentieth-Century Flyer," after the railroad's most famous train—the "Twentieth-Century Limited"—a sleek, steel, gray steam locomotive that ran between New York and Chicago.[33] The train was already well known before it was featured in the 1934 hit comedy of the same name starring John Barrymore and Carole Lombard. The entire movie was shot on the Twentieth Century traveling from Chicago to New York City, with the failing theater producer (Barrymore) trying desperately to seduce his former lover and ingénue-turned-Hollywood star (Lombard). Alas, after World War II, the passenger train and the Twentieth Century succumbed to the American auto industry. The NYCRR merged with Penn Railroad in 1968, and the new Penn Central Railroad went bankrupt two years later, at that time the largest bankruptcy in U.S. history.

In Boston, Walsh added to her growing national reputation by winning the 220 yards and narrowly beating Babe Didrikson in the broad jump. Walsh confirmed her bona fide status as an international track star at the Women's World Games in Prague in September 1930. This was the third of Alice Milliat's international women's athletic track and field meets. The last one was held in London in 1934. In spite of Milliat's efforts to legitimize women's track and field, in 1929, the IOC voted to take women's athletics off the program of the 1932 Los Angeles Games. Pressure from the AAU and the American representative from the IAAF forced the IOC to rescind the edict. Nonetheless, the IOC told the AAU not to send a team to the Prague Games, but the AAU allowed Walsh to accept an invitation to run for Poland. Her departure was delayed for a time because there was some question that if she ran for Poland in Prague she would be ineligible to compete for the U.S. team at the 1932 Olympics. The Women's World Games was not an IOC-sanctioned meet, however, so Walsh got the go-ahead to run for Poland. Walsh completely dominated the Prague Games, winning gold medals in the 60, 100, and 200 meters, and a bronze in the 4 × 100 relay. She was named the "World's Greatest Woman Athlete."

That fall Walsh helped the Polish national women's track and field team soundly beat Japan in a dual meet in Warsaw. The featured matchup was Walsh against Japan's star Hitomi Kinue. Kinue was a graduate of Tokyo's Women's College of Physical Education, and like Walsh, she was an outstanding all-around athlete. She dominated the 1926 Japanese National Track and Field Championships and was sent to the 1926 Women's Olympics in Gothenberg, Sweden, as Japan's only entrant. The nineteen-year-old was the first woman to represent her country in an international meet.

Stella Walsh at the 1930 Women's World Games in Prague, wearing the uniform of the New York Central Railroad, although she ran for the Polish team. *Kurier Codzienny, Narodowe Archiwum Cyfrowe [National Digital Archive].*

Kinue took the Trans-Siberian Railroad on her way to St. Petersburg, where she got on a ship to Sweden. Despite the long and arduous two-week trip, she was a sensation in Gothenburg, winning the running broad jump, the standing broad jump, a silver medal in the discus, and a bronze in the 100 meters. Halina Konopacka won the discus and came in third in the two-handed shot put, but Kinue won more medals than any other competitor and was named the Women's Olympics' "outstanding athlete."

Kinue led the Japanese women to the 1928 Amsterdam Olympics. After finishing a disappointing fourth in the semifinals of the 100 meters, she decided to try the 800 meters, a distance she had never run. Japanese spectators in the stadium cried for joy when their countrywoman took home the silver medal, the first ever for a Japanese woman.

Walsh met Kinue for the first time at the Women's World Games in Prague in 1930. Kinue finished third in the 60 meters at Prague. After the meet, the Japanese women toured Poland, Germany, France, and Belgium. Running for Poland against the Japanese team in Warsaw, Walsh broke her own world record in the 100 meters, again beating Kinue with ease in that race and in the 200 meters. The *Plain Dealer* tagline put Walsh's victories in typical indelicate fashion: "Stella Wins Two Races from Japs."

After the tour, Kinue fell seriously ill on the ship from France to Japan. Her family was shocked at her wan appearance as she disembarked in Kobe. Hitue Kinue, Japan's first great female athlete, died of respiratory failure on August 2, 1931. She was only twenty-four years old. Years later, Walsh reflected on her friend and rival:

> I'll never forget her. At the awards dinner [in Prague] she made a speech, predicted I would be the new Olympic champion two years later, and that I would break the world's record in the games. Then she presented me with enough spikes for a pair of track shoes. I had a special pair of shoes made with those spikes and used them for the first time at Los Angeles when I won the 100-meter dash.[34]

That fall Walsh established another world record in the 60-meter dash. By that time she was a national hero in Poland. *Przegląd Sportowy* named Walsh Poland's most popular sportsperson. The Polish government was so proud of its native daughter that it awarded her the prestigious Silver Cross of Merit,

Walsh beats Japanese sprinter Hitomi Kinue in the 100 meters in Warsaw, 1930. *Kurier Codzienny, Narodowe Archiwum Cyfrowe [National Digital Archive].*

an unprecedented honor for a Polish athlete. The *Plain Dealer* wrote that "[the medal] came all the way across the Atlantic to repose yesterday on the running jersey of Stella Walsh, Cleveland's world champion sprinter."

Walsh left Europe in early October. The NYCRR AA gave her a resounding reception when she arrived in New York. A big crowd of fans greeted her at Union Terminal in Cleveland, and Mayor Edward A. Weigand organized a banquet and dance in her honor. Another throng cheered Walsh at City Hall, although many were there queuing up to register for park improvement jobs, highly sought-after positions in the economically strapped city.

In 1930, the IOC put women's track and field on the Olympic program for good, just as Walsh was emerging as the world's top woman sprinter. She was a shoo-in to win a place on the 1932 U.S. Olympic team.

Stanisława Walasiewicz Runs for Poland

I'm not trying to duck the United States, but I've got myself to look out for. If a big company like the NYCRR can't give me a job, where can I get one?

—*Stella Walsh, on her decision to run for Poland at the Los Angeles Olympics*

Workers worldwide were in desperate straits after the onset of the Great Depression in 1929. The economic crisis hit the northern U.S. industrial cities particularly hard. By 1933, nearly a third of Cleveland's labor force and half of the city's industrial workers were out of work. The Newburgh steel mill was in trouble, and with Julian Walasiewicz relegated to part-time work, he could not support his wife and three daughters.

Walsh was fortunate to have a clerking job with the NYCRR, and her paycheck was a crucial source of income for the Walasiewicz family. Walsh could not capitalize on her greatest talent, however. She could not play sports for money and remain eligible for the Olympics. Coubertin not only wanted to keep women out of the Olympic Games, but also he was determined to keep professional athletes out of it too. Coubertin was heavily influenced by the amateur tradition of English sports, which favored those who had the wherewithal to play just for fun, and to finance their own training and travel to competitions. Amateur sport was the purview of the rich.

Britain's Harold Abrahams won the 100 meters at the Paris Games in 1924. Although the movie *Chariots of Fire* (1981) plays up Abrahams's confrontation with anti-Semitism among England's Oxbridge elites, Abrahams's hiring of a "professional" running coach was, in fact, a bigger issue. In 1930, the AAU briefly barred Babe Didrikson from competition because a photo appeared of her running the hurdles in a car advertisement. Didrikson denied knowing anything about it and was exonerated.

The most famous case of a breach in the Olympic amateur code involved Native American Jim Thorpe. In June 1912, Thorpe and the U.S. Olympic team boarded the SS *Finland* in New York, bound for the Stockholm Olympics, at the same time one-year-old Stanisława Walasiewicz and her young mother Weronica were on a ship in the Atlantic headed in the other direction. Like Walsh, Thorpe was not a U.S. citizen. He was a ward of the federal government (Native Americans became citizens in 1924).

Thorpe had few ways to make a living except through sports. Pop Warner, Thorpe's famous football coach at Carlisle Indian School in Pennsylvania, observed that "unfortunately, amateur athletics is not for the poor and the friendless."[1] Thorpe scrounged enough money to compete in Stockholm, where he won gold medals in the pentathlon and decathlon. He was the most famous Olympic athlete in the United States.

Soon after the Stockholm Games, the IOC discovered Thorpe had taken money for playing baseball in the Carolina League and promptly stripped the athlete's medals and struck his name from the Olympic record book, the first time that had ever happened. In 1982, twenty-nine years after Thorpe's death, the IOC overturned the decision and recognized his victories. A year later, IOC president Juan Antonio Samaranch presented facsimiles of the gold medals to two of Thorpe's children.

Walsh had to turn down any monies she might have been offered to run track meets or play basketball and softball, although one of her softball coaches admitted to the *Plain Dealer* in 1981, that she "would try to slip them something whenever possible." There were no AAU or Olympic rules, however, barring athletes from working for a company and playing on its sports teams. Funds from the NYCRR AA and the Polish Falcons enabled Walsh to compete in meets throughout North America and Europe. Without her job at the NYCRR, Walsh's opportunities to run would have been limited, and her family would have struggled to make ends meet.

Walsh also formed her own basketball team, dubbed the "Stella Walsh Flyers." Walsh was the team's leading scorer, although three to four points was often her total in low-scoring games that barely made it into double figures. She even had to be careful not to take any money for playing in one game of a doubleheader if the other game on the bill included a professional team.

Walsh's popularity in Cleveland was at its zenith in the early 1930s. With the Cleveland Indians mired in the middle of the American League baseball standings, Walsh was a source of pride for the depressed city. Clevelanders could follow her sports career in the *Plain Dealer*, but reporters did not have much to write about her life off the track. There was no romantic connection in her life. She was a frequent subject of sports columnist James Doyle, who wrote that Stella Walsh "stays at home nights, is a good time gal only when she's stepping out against the clocker's watch."[2] After work, Walsh spent much of her time on the track, going to the movies, and driving around in her car. She enjoyed the few luxuries that her job afforded her and had no qualms about flaunting them. In the winter, she wore huge, ostentatious fur coats that were in vogue.

Walsh loved the celebrity of being a star athlete, but she did not seem happy. According to the March 12, 1930, installment of Chicago's *Daily Times*, she "smiled rarely and spoke only when spoken to, but in her complete self-possession there was no hint of the sullen." Aside from her own personal issues, in those days women athletes were targets of societal scorn; Walsh's success on the track did not inoculate her against ridicule of her muscular looks. Some people in her Polish community called her "Bull Montana," a cruel comparison to a swarthy professional wrestler and bit-part actor. Montana (Luigi Montagna) played such characters as the Ape Man in *The Lost World* (1925) and Bullfrog Kraus in the Buster Keaton short *The Palooka from Paducah* (1935). "Stella the fella" was another insult tossed about in the neighborhood.

Barred from taking money for track, basketball, or softball, Walsh decided to capitalize on her notoriety by entering a local popularity contest. In the summer of 1931, the city ran a "Queen of Cleveland" competition as part of the festivities commemorating the 135th anniversary of the founding of the city and the completion of the new 80,000-seat Municipal Stadium on Lake Erie. Walsh seemed an unlikely candidate for this beauty contest. One *Plain Dealer* reporter commented that "girls with lots of dimples and personality usually become queens in this sort of thing." But Walsh was after the prizes that went with the title, including a new car: "After all of the running I've done," she told the *Plain Dealer*, "I haven't anything to show for it. Just some cups and medals lying around the house. They don't get me anything. I want that car." Walsh hit the pavement and worked tirelessly to garner votes. She admitted that she "had never broke training so badly before."[3] With overwhelming support from the Polish community, she polled 327,400 votes, 126,500 more than second-place finisher Anna Griffith. Walsh got her car. Now she set her sights on competing at the Los Angeles Olympics in 1932.

Walsh decided not to run on the indoor circuit that winter. Instead, she began training for the U.S. Women's Olympic Trials, scheduled for July in Evanston, Illinois. She worked on four events: the 100 meters, the 80-meter hurdles, the discus, and the broad jump. In a practice throw, she set the U.S. discus record, making her a favorite to qualify for that event and the 100 meters. On June 5, Walsh ran in the Northeast Ohio Association Track and Field Meet in Cleveland, winning the discus and the 50 and 100 meters. She was in top form for the trials. Fifteen-year-old Cleveland sprinter Jesse Owens was going to the Olympic tryouts too, but he would not qualify.

Walsh's main competition in the sprints at the trials was expected to come from Betty Robinson of Riverdale, Illinois, Eleanor Egg from Paterson, New Jersey, and Babe Didrikson from Port Arthur, Texas. Robinson was four months younger than Walsh, and like Walsh she played all sports. Legend has it that a track coach from her Harvey, Illinois, high school saw her dashing to catch an Illinois Central train, and her running career began. "I had no idea that women even ran then," she recalled later. "I grew up a hick. That is when I found out that they actually had track meets for women."[4]

Three days a week, Robinson made the long train and bus ride from Harvey to work out at the Illinois Women's Athletic Club on Chicago's North Side. In 1928, competing in only her second track meet, she broke the world record in the 100 meters at Soldier Field in Chicago, although it was wind-aided and went unrecognized. Many of these reports of records set were premature, because the meets were not always officially sanctioned, and the AAU and the IOC did not recognize the records. The club paid Robinson's way to the U.S. Olympic Trials in Newark in July, to try to qualify for the 100 meters at the Amsterdam Olympics. Walsh was there too but did not make it out of her semifinal. Robinson won her semifinal heat, but twenty-year-old

Eureka, California, native Elta Cartwright beat her in the final. Both Robinson and Cartwright qualified for the team.

"Cinder-Elta," as the press nicknamed Cartwright, was a known entity in track circles. She won her first AAU Championship in Pasadena, California, in 1925, beating Egg in the 50-yard dash. Cartwright won three straight AAU titles in the 50 yards and added the 100-yard championship in 1927, so her win at the Olympic Trials in Newark came as no surprise. What happened in Amsterdam was. Cartwright got seasick on the ship to Amsterdam, never found her form, and did not make it to the 100-meter final. She was left off the relay team as well. Later she hinted that the coach had favored the athletes from the East Coast. The U.S. relay team finished second to the Canadians. Nonetheless, when Cartwright returned home, Eureka greeted her with a big parade. That was it for Cartwright on the cinders; she retired from running, became a schoolteacher, and got married in 1932. She and her husband honeymooned in Los Angeles, where they watched Stella Walsh run in the Olympics.

The Amsterdam Olympics was Robinson's fourth track meet. She was only sixteen. Canadian world record holder Myrtle Cook was the favorite in the final of the 100 meters, but she had two false starts. Cook was devastated and fell sobbing onto the infield grass. Robinson nipped Cook's teammate Bobbie Rosenfeld to win the first U.S. women's gold medal in Olympic history. *Chicago Tribune* journalist William L. Shirer, soon to be famous for his reporting from Nazi Germany, wrote that an "unheralded pretty, blue-eyed, blond young woman from Chicago, Elizabeth Robinson, became the darling of the spectators when she flew down the cinder path, her golden locks flying, to win . . . in world record time." The president of the American Olympic Committee, Major General Douglas MacArthur, gushed that her "sparkling combination of speed and grace . . . might have rivaled even Artemis herself."[5] MacArthur was taken with Robinson and asked her to join him at various functions for the rest of the Games. Years later, Robinson recalled the moments after her victory: "I started crying like a baby. . . . Just talking about the awards ceremony gives me duck bumps when I think of my standing in the middle of the stadium with all these people there and the *Star-Spangled Banner* playing because I had just won the hundred meters."[6] Robinson and the other gold medal Olympians received a ticker-tape parade down Broadway in New York City.

For several years after the Amsterdam Olympics, Robinson was one of the top sprinters in the United States. She won both the 50- and 100-yard dashes at the 1929 AAU Championships in Chicago. In a much-anticipated final in the 100 yards at the 1930 AAU Championships in Dallas, Walsh beat Robinson by a nose, and then Walsh won the 220 handily. Robinson's Illinois Women's Athletic Club wanted a rematch and finally got one on February 23, 1931. The press called it a "match race"—like two horses—although there was a third starter. Robinson won that race, setting up a dual with Walsh for a berth on the 1932 U.S. Olympic team.

That summer Robinson trained at Northwestern University to prepare for the AAU Championships in Jersey City. July 28, 1931, was a steamy, hot Sunday, but Robinson worked out anyway. Afterward Robinson's coaches would not let her cool down in the swimming pool for fear that she would exercise the wrong muscles, which could affect her speed on the track. That absurd notion almost cost Robinson her life, as she recalled later:

> The day of the accident . . . I was training. It was so hot, and we weren't allowed to swim as runners. I decided to ask my cousin, who was part-owner of a plane, to take me up. That's why I went up, to cool off. I was hoping to make the 1932 Olympic team. But I made the mistake of flying. I was destined to go to Los Angeles and would be expected to win.[7]

The Waco biplane had mechanical problems and went down in a marshy field in Harvey, about ten miles south of downtown Chicago. Ironically, Harvey is where Robinson had gone to high school. A passerby pulled her from the wreckage and put her mangled body into his trunk. Robinson remembered that he drove her to an "old people's home because he had a friend who was there who was an undertaker, and he thought I was dying." The mortician realized that she was still breathing and took her to a local infirmary. Robinson had suffered a severe concussion and a broken arm and leg. Robinson's nephew Jim Rochfort said that a doctor and nurse there saved her life: "At first they said she wouldn't live, then they said she wouldn't walk, and then they said she'd never run again."[8] Robinson speculated that "if I had not been in such good physical condition, I would not have lived through it." A pin was inserted in her left leg, making it a little shorter than her right leg. She was out for the Los Angeles Olympics, and it looked like her running career was finished.[9]

Several years later, Robinson began to run again for exercise and decided to try out for the 1936 Berlin Olympics. Her injuries still prevented her from a crouching start, so running a leg in a relay was her only chance. The 24-year-old made the Olympic team in the 4 × 100-meter relay, and she ran the third leg on the team that took gold, beating the favored Germans. Another ticker-tape parade awaited Robinson in New York City.

Eleanor Egg, Walsh's other main competition in the sprints, was born two years before Walsh. Egg had sports in her genes. She came from a family of vaudeville acrobats known as the "Three Spauldings." At an early age, her father engaged her in such stunts as balancing a ten-foot pole on his chin with little Eleanor sitting in a chair on top. Egg said, "I was billed all over the country as the smallest acrobat in the world."[10]

Dr. L. Raymond, head of the Paterson, New Jersey, Recreation Department, formed the Paterson Girls' Recreation Association (PGRA) in 1923, which helped launch Egg's track and field career. She attended Paterson Eastside High School, where Larry Doby went to school. Doby was the first African American to play baseball in the American League, only a few months after Jackie Robinson broke the color barrier with the Brooklyn Dodgers. Although Doby endured the same cruel treatment and racist slurs as Robinson, he, like Walsh, has remained in relative obscurity.

Egg soon became one of the most recognized women athletes on the East Coast, running sprints, high jumping, and throwing the discus and shot put. In 1924, in Pittsburgh, Egg competed in her first of seven consecutive AAU outdoor championships, finishing second in the high jump. The *Paterson Evening News* raved that she was "one of the finest specimens of womanhood that any city in this meet can boast of." The PGRA and the city galvanized support for the Paterson women to make the long trip to the 1925 AAU Championships in Pasadena, where Egg finished third in the 50-yard sprint and the high jump. The 4 × 100 relay team came in second. In 1926, she ran on a 4 × 100-yard relay team that set a world record and a year later established another world record with a Paterson relay team.[11]

Egg was the pride of Paterson. The city anticipated that she would qualify for the 1928 U.S. Olympic team, but in early 1928, Egg tore ankle ligaments and failed to qualify in the high jump or the 100 meters. Elta Cartwright lobbied to put Egg on the team, arguing that she would be a valuable member of the 4 × 100 relay team: "If I can do anything or say anything, Miss Egg will be a member of the team for I know she can help us win points if she gets to

Amsterdam." Egg was grateful but said that the injury was too serious for her to run in the Olympics.[12]

Egg was to Paterson what Walsh was to Cleveland: a much-needed morale booster for a city that was devastated by the Depression. Paterson was the center of the silk industry in the 1920s, but with the substitution of rayon for silk, manufacturing was already in decline. When the Depression hit, two-thirds of Paterson's silk factories were shuttered.

Egg met Walsh for the first time at the 1930 AAU Championships in Dallas. Walsh beat Egg handily in the 100-yard dash and the broad jump. A year later, Egg was fully recovered from her ankle injury, and in September she registered the biggest win of her career, when, at the AAU Championships in Jersey City, she upset the heavily favored Walsh in the 100-yard dash. Egg downplayed the victory because she had run 0.2 seconds slower than Walsh's world record. "Had I broken the record when I beat her," Egg said years later, "I would have gotten excited about the race."[13] Furthermore, Walsh was shaken by a bizarre prerace incident in the discus competition. Walsh was in the outfield retrieving throws from the other competitors. On one toss back to the throwing circle, she hit a 28-year-old New Jersey man in the head, knocking him unconscious. He had to be taken to the hospital. Egg said that Walsh was not herself when the race began:

> I don't count that race like everybody else does. They all get mad at me, and they say I shouldn't tell anybody. Well, I'm sorry, it's the way it is. She had been in the discus throw just before our race. The discus slid out of her hand and she fractured a man's skull, and for a while there was talk of her being brought up on charges.[14]

Walsh was arrested but later released. The man lived.[15]

The city of Paterson celebrated their young star. One of Egg's trainers compared her importance to the city to what famous football coach Knute Rockne meant to Notre Dame and Babe Ruth to Major League Baseball. The city leaders held a dinner in her honor and commissioned local sculptor Gaetano Federici to forge a bronze plaque of Egg to be hung in the city's new 10,000-seat stadium. Mayor John V. Hinchliffe said that the bas relief was "not merely an honor to Paterson's outstanding daughter . . . [but she] exemplifies for Paterson in the highest and most ennobling degree the dynamic spirit of American youth."[16]

The 1931 AAU Championships was the last time Egg ran against Walsh. The ankle injury flared up again before the 1932 U.S. Olympic Trials, and once again she failed to qualify. It is a cruel reality that the Olympic Games come only every four years, and many great athletes, for one reason or another, miss their small window to compete. Later in 1932, the same injury caused Egg to bow out of the first-ever meet at Paterson's new Hinchliffe Stadium, but she was there for the dedication of her plaque. Dr. Thomas E. Manly, head of the Paterson Civic Pride Commemorative Committee, declared it was "fitting that such a marvelous victory [over Walsh], which has gained nationwide praise not only for Miss Egg, but for Paterson as well, should be honored."[17]

Egg's injury made Walsh a shoo-in to qualify for the U.S. Olympic team, along with the brash young Didrikson. Didrikson entered eight of the ten events at the Olympic Trials, winning five, although the Olympics had only five events on the women's program. Before the Olympics began, Didrikson boasted, "I'm going to win the high jump Sunday and set a world's record. I don't know who my chief opponents are and anyway, it wouldn't make any difference." Evelyne Hall, who was Didrikson's main competition in the 80-meter hurdles, called her "selfish, loud, and annoying."[18] With Walsh running the sprints and throwing the discus, and Didrikson running the hurdles, high jumping, and throwing the javelin, the U.S. women were the favorites to dominate the track and field events.

The Olympic bid that went to Los Angeles in 1923 was a controversial choice. Most Olympic teams came from Europe, and the Atlantic crossing and 3,000-mile train ride to California would be long and costly. On the way to the Los Angeles Games, one member of the German Olympic team was astounded to find out that when their train stopped in Kansas City, they were only halfway across the country. The last Olympic Games in the United States had taken place in St. Louis in 1904, and few foreign athletes came. Of the 687 competitors, 525 were American and 41 Canadian. With Los Angeles in the throes of the Great Depression in 1932, many of those in Southern California also thought that the Olympics were an unaffordable luxury. President Herbert Hoover had done little to revive the economy, and by the end of his term, one in four American workers was unemployed. He did not show up for the Olympics, sending the vice president, Charles Curtis, instead.

The Los Angeles Olympic organizers argued that the Games would be an economic and psychological boost to the depressed region. The city's power brokers saw the Olympics as an opportunity to put people to work and showcase a modern American metropolis and its leisurely, sun-drenched Southern California lifestyle. Businessmen, corporate lawyers, and bankers, among other private interests, enthusiastically backed the Games. Olympic organizers consciously put an American stamp of commercialism on the Games. The head of the Los Angeles Olympic Organizing Committee, William May Garland, promised that the region would get $10 million in free publicity. Hollywood movie stars were enlisted to promote the Games, and newspapers, radio, and movie newsreels brought the spectacle to more people than ever before.

Clevelanders eagerly awaited Walsh's appearance at the Olympics, but the dire economic situation in the country in 1932 had a direct impact on her decision not to run for the United States. The stock market crash of October 1929 foreshadowed the most serious economic crisis in the nation's history. By mid-November, the Dow had lost more than a third of its value, and by the spring of 1930, 4 million Americans were out of work. The Depression gutted industrial output throughout the Great Lakes region; in 1933, half of Cleveland's industrial workforce was sidelined. A third of American families depended solely on income from women.

Demand for the NYCRR's freight trains collapsed, and the railroad was forced to downsize. Walsh's life took an unexpected turn in early July, when the NYCRR furloughed her indefinitely from her clerk's job at the passenger agent's office. The entire department was let go. Any job was a blessing in those days, especially for women; the 1933 Federal Economy Act even prohibited a husband and wife from both holding civil service jobs. Many state and local governments followed suit, as did many private businesses.

Walsh's dismissal was a devastating blow to the Walasiewicz family, which was dependent on her wages. Nonetheless, on July 8, the *Plain Dealer* reported that Walsh would receive her citizenship papers the next day, even though she had lost her job: "Miss Walsh stated definitely last night that she would go through with her naturalization."[19]

Polish sports authorities pounced on the opportunity to enlist their favorite daughter to run for Poland. After all, she was a citizen of Poland after the collapse of the Russian Empire at the end of World War I. On July 8, Walsh was leaving her house for the U.S. Federal Building to take her oath of citizenship when a telegram arrived from the Polish Consulate in New York, offering her a job and an education scholarship to study in Warsaw if she would join the Polish Olympic team in Los Angeles.

Clevelanders knew the importance of employment in those tough times and were reluctant to fault Walsh if she decided to run for Poland. The press was more critical of the fact that American authorities did not come up with a means to keep her on the U.S. squad. "Poland, like most other European nations," wrote the *Plain Dealer* on July 9, "'does something' for its athletes who need financial help. America does not. . . . No one can criticize her if she elects to run for her native land." The newspaper even pointed to gender discrimination as the reason for Walsh's lack of support:

> Any young man one-quarter as capable in athletics would have no difficulty at all financing a college career with attendance at the Olympics provided as an essential part of his academic advancement. But such opportunities are not for the girls. At women's colleges athletics are "kept in their place" in practice, as well as theory.[20]

In defining the "amateur athlete," Coubertin and his cronies overlooked the way these college scholarships compromised the idea. During the Cold War, Western countries ignored these stipends, while complaining about the subsidies that Soviet-bloc governments gave their athletes.

Coubertin had envisioned an Olympics of individual athletes competing without any national designation or national teams, and in the first few Olympic Games athletes did not have an official affiliation. The identification of athletes with their country was just too strong, and by 1908, athletes participating in the London Olympics were part of a national team and countries kept track of their ranking on the medals table. French author Charles Maurras was sitting with Coubertin at the first modern Olympic Games in Athens in 1896, when Greek fans went wild about their kinsman's win in the marathon. Maurras commented sarcastically, "I see your internationalism does not kill national spirit—it strengthens it."[21]

Walsh now had to choose between putting on the uniform of the Stars and Stripes or the Polish Eagle. Immigrant communities in the United States have always had divided loyalties between their country of origin and their adopted homeland. Walsh was torn: "I'm not trying to duck the United States, but I've got myself to look out for. If a big company like the NYCRR can't give me a job, where can I get one?"[22]

Coach Griffin tried to convince Walsh to sign the citizenship papers, but she said that finding work would be the deciding factor and that she was "ready to run for the country which presents the most attractive opportunity."[23] Walsh had taken night classes in physical education administration, so Cleveland mayor Ray T. Miller offered her a job in the Cleveland Recreation Department if she became a naturalized U.S. citizen. But that was a job Walsh could not take; the IOC prohibited athletes from making money in any career related to sports. The chairman of the women's AAU, Fred L. Steers, telegraphed Walsh that she would be ineligible for the Olympics if she took the position. Given the circumstances, the NYCRR would have given her job back, but seniority rules prevented the company from doing so.

Walsh's decision hung on finances more than her loyalty to Cleveland, the United States, or Poland. One way or the other, she would run at the Olympics. On July 12, Walsh took the offer from the Polish Consulate. Calling it the "most important decision in my life," she joined the Polish Olympic team.[24] The *Washington Post* wrote the next day that "Uncle Sam's talented adopted niece, Stella Walsh, of the cinder track, went back to the home folks today and henceforth will do any Olympic record-breaking for the glory of her native Poland." The newspaper exaggerated Walsh's prospects, predicting that there was "virtual certainty of victory in the discus, 100-meter dash, and 400-meter relay."[25]

"I am going to run for Poland," Walsh told the *Plain Dealer*. "But I will always have a warm spot in my heart for Cleveland. I sure do hate to leave this place." She expressed gratitude for the support she had received from the Polish Falcons to become an international star: "I am running for Poland because I am a Pole. Polish people, both in this country and in my native land, were the first to give me help to go to big meets, and for them I will compete again."[26] Walsh pointed out that her amateur status circumscribed her work prospects: "The way it looks to me I can't have any kind of job because I'm in athletics."[27] Walsh also mentioned that she had been disappointed to be left off the U.S. Olympic team in 1928, although she had only been an alternate in the 4 × 100 relay and at the time was too young to be naturalized.[28]

The press called for the U.S. government to match Poland's offer. On July 12, 1932, the *Plain Dealer*'s James Doyle appealed to Democratic presidential candidate Franklin Roosevelt to give Walsh her own New Deal: "Hey there, Mr. Roosevelt! . . . Forget about the Forgotten Man for a few minutes, will you, and give a thought to the Forgotten Woman. . . . Dig up a job, I mean, for Stella Walsh so she can put on the steam for your country and mine in these Olympics." In an article titled "Any Pork in the Barrel for Olympic Fund, Mr. Garner?" conservative *Chicago Tribune* journalist Westbrook Pegler appealed to Texas congressman John Nance Garner—who Pegler charged was "very liberal with the public money" anyway—to subsidize the U.S. Olympic team. Pegler wrote that the unemployed Walsh had gone "shopping for a country": "Miss Walsh, who is Polish and robust, was on the point of becoming a bread-and-butter American, which is something on the order of the Chinese rice Christian." He suggested that "but for some jowl and greens," Walsh would be running for the United States. "The United States was outbid," he lamented, "and by a new or newly reorganized and struggling nation." He pointed out that high school football players were sometimes lured by monetary incentives to attend college and that the old English amateur tradition had been repeatedly subverted anyway.[29]

The *Los Angeles Times*, in its July 13, 1932, edition, called for Walsh to be barred from the Games for taking payment from the Polish government to run for Poland: "If the International Athletic Federation does not take some drastic action against Miss Walsh or her advisers for the act of brazen professionalism it means the death of the Olympic Games in years to come." The issue of what constituted an amateur athlete confounded the IOC for decades until professionals were allowed to compete at the 1992 Barcelona Olympics.

The IOC's byzantine rules prevented Stella Walsh from taking a job in Cleveland related to sports, so Walsh joined the Polish Olympic team in Los Angeles. That momentous decision changed her life. Now Walsh was committed to not only competing for Poland, but also studying in Warsaw. What Walsh knew of her place of birth came from her parents, the Polish community in Cleveland, and a short trip to Europe. Poland was, for her, a strange and foreign place. Griffin was hurt by the loss of his once-in-a-lifetime athlete but graciously wished her the best. "I believe Stella is making a very serious mistake in not representing the United States in the Olympics," he told the *Plain Dealer*, "but I trust for her sake that everything will work out ok."[30]

For a young woman from an old industrial city, and one who loved the movies and sports, Walsh was enthralled with the ethos of Los Angeles. On the surface, the City of Angels seemed the perfect place to host a sporting event that had been inspired, in part, by the ancient Greeks' cult of the body. Coubertin was a big enthusiast of the warm place. After devastating floods in Paris in 1923, which put the 1924 Olympics in jeopardy, he had even asked Los Angeles if the city would host the Games if Paris could not. Los Angeles was the only city to bid for the 1932 Olympic Games, and Coubertin whole-heartedly endorsed it.

The 1932 Olympics contributed to the emerging culture of sport and leisure in Southern California, epitomized today by such sports as surfing and skateboarding. In a way, the cult of the suntanned, muscular, beach-body beautiful mirrored the Greek ideal of the human form. The region invented the term "laid-back lifestyle."

Southern California was the land of eternal summer, blue skies, sandy-white beaches, and unlimited opportunity. Hollywood films served up stunning starlets and suave leading men. Los Angeles had an exuberant, youthful feel, and sports and the "talkies" were a welcome diversion from the hardships of the Depression. With an eye on landing the Olympics, the city built the Los Angeles Coliseum in 1923. The head of the Los Angeles Olympic Organizing Committee, William May Garland, was also a member of the Community Development Association, which built the stadium. It was the largest sports arena in the world at the time.

In the 1920s, city planners began a beautification effort by planting tens of thousands of nonnative palm trees along the city's broad boulevards. Los Angeles promoted itself as a tourist attraction, featuring the "cool Pacific" and "Hollywood nightlife," in the "atmosphere of old Spain."[31] If, as some historians have argued, that avant-garde Weimar Berlin was *the* city for urbane sophisticates in the 1920s, a case could be made for Los Angeles as the high artists' mecca in the 1930s, attracting such famous writers as William Faulkner and F. Scott Fitzgerald, and the great German directors Fritz Lang and Ernst Lubitsch.

In 1927, the *New Republic* wrote, L.A. was "a civilization that will not need to hang its head when the Athens of Pericles is mentioned."[32] In the 1920s, it was the fastest-growing city in the world. Before the city gained its reputation as the car and freeway capital of the world, Los Angeles had a vast, 200-mile

Los Angeles Railway (LARY) streetcar system. The beautiful "Huntington Standard" cars, often seen in Hollywood films, ferried people throughout the burgeoning metropolis. In the 1920s, the LARY carried some 250 million passengers annually. Sadly, in the 1930s, busses and then automobiles began to replace the streetcars, and by the 1950s most of them were no more.[33]

The Olympians would not see the dark side of the sunny city. Orson Welles called it a "bright and guilty place." Three years before the Olympics, the city was rocked by the sensational double murder of Hugh Plunkett and Ned Doheny, the son of oil magnate E. L. Doheny, at Ned's fabulous Greystone mansion on the east end of Beverly Hills. The case was never solved, although it appeared to be a murder-suicide. After the Great Depression hit, 1,500 desperate Midwesterners were coming to the city each day. Los Angeles became "America's suicide capital," registering 750 in 1931.[34] Some demonstrators picketed the state capitol in Sacramento, protesting the cost of the Olympics given the hardships that Californians were facing in these tough times.

The 1932 Los Angeles Games were a turning point in the Olympic movement. For the first time, the Olympics was promoted as a business proposition and a way to showcase the booming metropolis. The oil and film industries were fueling rapid economic growth, and the population of the city more than doubled in the 1920s. By the end of the decade, Hollywood was making 80 percent of the world's movies. Despite corruption surrounding the Los Angeles water, oil, and film industries the city had a progressive side: Southern California was in the forefront of the movement for the women's vote and passage of the Nineteenth Amendment.

Olympic organizers marketed the event like never before, enlisting the support of Los Angeles business elites and signing on sponsors the likes of Coca-Cola. Los Angeles ushered in the Americanization of the Olympic Games as mass entertainment. The Germans were overwhelmed and wondered if they could put on such a show four years later in Berlin: "The beautiful coliseum . . . the crystal clear swimming pools, this organization! What contests, what performances, what hospitality! . . . In our opinion the advertising for the Olympic Games was simply unimaginable."[35] The Games were a huge financial success, in no small part because the main Olympic venue, the Los Angeles Coliseum, had already been built. The Los Angeles Olympics set a record for spectators and emerged with a profit of $1.5 million. For the first time, the Olympics were broadcast on radio, and newsreels sent coverage of the Games throughout the world.

Hollywood went all out for the Olympics. Fox Studios prepared a luncheon for the women athletes; the Marx Brothers threw parties; and Mary Pickford and Douglas Fairbanks hosted a reception for Olympic officials at their famous Beverly Hills mansion, where Charlie Chaplin and Pola Negri had frequently dined. Pickford and Fairbanks were avid Olympic fans; they had even accompanied the U.S. Olympic team to the 1924 Paris Games. Pickford told a radio audience that the women athletes would be an important part of the Los Angeles Olympic spectacle: "While their records have not yet equaled the men's—notice, I say 'not yet'—they have accomplished wonders in the short time in which they have been competing . . . our cheers will be their inspiration."[36] Pundits Grantland Rice and Will Rogers posed for photos with the athletes, and famed flyer Amelia Earhart attended several events. The Olympic Games had become a Hollywood commercial spectacle.

The Olympic Organizing Committee knew it would be a financial hardship for teams to get to Los Angeles. The state of California offered Los Angeles a $1 million loan to put on the Games, and when the Depression hit, the committee offered the Olympic athletes reduced rates on ocean liners and trains coming to Los Angeles. Team members were charged two dollars a day for housing and food. The Olympic Organizing Committee picked up the rest. As U.S. high jumper Jean Shiley put it, in those difficult economic times, "I was just glad there was something on the table. I didn't care *what* it was."[37]

Olympic organizers also decided to build the first Olympic Village to reduce the cost of housing. Still, only forty countries sent teams to Los Angeles, with 1,332 total competitors. The U.S. team was the largest, with Japan coming in second. Forty-six countries had sent teams to the 1928 Amsterdam Olympics, where 2,883 athletes competed, and of those 277 were women. Stella Walsh was among the 126 female athletes in Los Angeles, but Poland's team had only nine women, down from eleven at the Amsterdam Games.

In the immediate postwar period, Poland had few resources to devote to its Olympic teams and had to rely on donations from the well-to-do. The IOC recognized the Polish Olympic Committee (POC) in 1919. Its first president was Prince Stefan Lubomirski, a member of one of the oldest and most venerated Polish aristocratic families. The Lubomirski family served the new Polish state in various capacities. Stefan's cousin, Kazimierz Lubomirski, took over the presidency of the POC in 1921, and was Poland's representative on the IOC until 1930. Ignacy Matuszewski, Halina Konopacka's husband, was an IOC member from 1928 until the outbreak of World War II in 1939. The Olympic Organizing Committee for the 1920 Olympic Games in Antwerp extended an invitation to the POC, but engulfed in the desperate war with the Bolsheviks in 1920, many of Poland's top athletes were in the army. Poland did not send a team to the first postwar Olympics.

American Polonia helped subsidize the Polish Olympic team's long trip to Los Angeles. On July 2, the contingent left Gdynia on the Polish liner *Pułaski*. The ship took eleven days to reach New York City, giving the Polish athletes little opportunity to work out. Many got seasick. The German team had the same problems, but their ship, the *Bremen*, made a faster Atlantic crossing. Stella Walsh and a large group of fellow Polish Americans, with Poland's flags waving, were waiting for the Polish team in New York City. Still, a long cross-country train ride to Los Angeles awaited them.

Poland's top long distance runner, Janusz Kusociński, took a French ship that crossed the Atlantic in only five days, giving him more time in Los Angeles to train. He had already been in Los Angeles for five days when the Polish team arrived on July 19. In a photo of the Polish team's arrival at Los Angeles' Union Station, Walsh is front and center in Poland's colors—in a white skirt and red blazer with the Polish White Eagle on the jacket breast.

The Olympic Village, in Baldwin Hills, housed the male athletes. Some people thought it was a bad idea to put men from various nations together in one place, where fraternization might undermine their competitive nature. The official 1932 Olympic Report found that there were

> evidences of jealously guarded training secrets, and theories opposing the leveling touch that comes from intermingling. As self-discipline is fundamental in the development of an athlete, so it follows that nationalistic discipline is necessary in preserving the athletic perception of a country.[38]

However, Baldwin Hills was an overall success and set a precedent for future Olympic Villages. "I'll never forget the elation of living at the Olympic Village in 'Baldwin Hills,'" recalled U.S. sprinter Frank Wycoff. "Being able to visit throughout the village trying to overcome the language differences with representatives of fifty-six nations was a rare delight."[39]

The stodgy old IOC members would have objected to coed dorms, so the Los Angeles Olympic Organizing Committee found other accommodations for the women. The women stayed at the five-story Chapman Park Hotel on Wilshire Boulevard, near famous Los Angeles hot spots like the Brown Derby restaurant and the Ambassador Hotel, where Hollywood stars came to be seen. The Ambassador opened in 1921, with the claim that it would turn Los Angeles into the "Paris of the West." That boast was not far off. Pola Negri used to parade around the hotel grounds with her pet cheetah. Marilyn Monroe signed her first contract with the Blue Book Modeling Agency at the Ambassador, and Soviet premier Nikita Khrushchev stayed there during his groundbreaking visit to the United States in 1959.

The Ambassador housed the famous 1,000-seat Cocoanut Grove night-club, a favorite watering hole of such film stars as Marlene Dietrich, Cary Grant, Jean Harlow, and Clark Gable. The papier-mâché palm trees in the club had been used in Rudolph Valentino's famous movie *The Sheik*. The Cocoanut Grove hosted many Academy Awards ceremonies and was the set for George Cukor's acclaimed film *A Star Is Born* (1954). The assassination of presidential candidate Robert F. Kennedy at the Ambassador in the summer of 1968 accelerated the decline of the iconic hotel, and it closed in 1989. It fell to the wrecking ball in 2005.[40] The former arts editor of the *Los Angeles Times*, Charles Champlin, lamented its passing: "The Ambassador was the last outpost of nightly glamour in Los Angeles. I don't think anything has come along to take its place."[41]

During the second week of the Olympics, the Ambassador threw a "Ball of All Nations" for the athletes. Olympic organizers also offered them a symphony concert at the Hollywood Bowl and a Los Angeles Angels base-ball game at Wrigley Field in South Los Angeles. If the athletes wore their Olympic uniforms they could ride the streetcars for free. It was a once-in-a-lifetime experience for most of them. U.S. hurdler Evelyne Hall recalled that a hairdresser on Western Avenue even gave the women free haircuts: "This was the first time I had ever been in a beauty shop and had my hair cut and my eyebrows tweezed, so it was quite an experience for me."[42] Grace Walker, the women's chaperone at the Chapman, commented on the atmosphere at the hotel, saying, "It's great. It's splendid. It seems to be youth calling to youth over the barriers of language, custom, and rivalry."[43] Evidently Walsh and the other Polish women were on their best behavior. Walker said, "If I had as much trouble with all of the teams as I had with the Poles, I would have had little to do."[44]

The opening ceremonies of the Xth Olympiad began on July 30. Motorcades brought the male athletes from the Olympic Village and the women from the Chapman Park Hotel to the Los Angeles Coliseum. The weather that day was spectacular, and it stayed that way for the entire two weeks. The Polish team, including Stella Walsh, marched into the stadium dressed in dark blazers and white slacks or skirts. Los Angeles was a long way from the little Polish village of Wierzchownia and the congested feel of Cleveland's Slavic Village. Walsh loved the weather, the city, and the hoopla surrounding the Games. After running at the Coliseum Walsh gushed, "I've never run on such a fast track as that at the stadium. And the climate's been ideal. You take those two things—climate and good track—and they're hard to beat."[45] Walsh was so enamored of Southern California that twenty years later she would leave her parents behind in Cleveland and move there. For a woman who loved sports, there was no better place.

4

Winning Olympic Gold and a Challenge from Missouri

I have always felt Polish, I have fervently desired, in order that for me and my countrymen who emigrated to America [that] the *Mazurek Dąbrowski* was played and the Polish flag was raised.

—*Stella Walsh, after winning the 100 meters at the Los Angeles Olympics*

Polish newspapers in the interwar period devoted scant space to sports, including the Olympic Games. The country's sport scene was in its nascent stages. Soccer was by far the most important sport in Poland, but even that game got little coverage in the mainstream press. The Polish media in the summer of 1932 was not focused on the Olympics, but on the frightening news coming out of Germany, where Adolf Hitler's Nazi Party was on the rise. Hitler was a direct threat to the very existence of the Polish state. The Nazi platform explicitly called for revision of the Versailles Treaty and a rollback of Poland's territorial gains along the German border. On July 31, the Nazis won 230 seats, the largest single bloc in the history of the Reichstag. Soviet leader Josef Stalin was worried too; on July 25, he signed a Nonaggression Pact with Warsaw, a seemingly impossible diplomatic development after Poland's victory in the Polish-Soviet War twelve years earlier.

The Polish press barely took notice of the Olympics until Janusz Kusociński's victory in the 10,000 meters. *Kurjer Warszawski* [Warsaw Courier] wrote that Kusociński's gold medal was a huge boost for Poland's image: "Whoever knows the relationship of America to sports must understand that the victory of our runners in the competition for Olympic laurels is the best propaganda for Poland abroad." Kusociński's biggest rival, Finland's legendary long-distance runner Paavo Nurmi, did not run at Los Angeles. Before the Olympics, the Germans had challenged Nurmi's amateurism, and the day before the opening ceremonies the IOC determined that he was a professional and banned him. One wag wrote that the Olympics would now be "like Hamlet without the celebrated Dane in the cast."[1] After Kusociński's win, the Germans and Finns questioned the Pole's amateur status as well, charging that he had also taken money to run.[2] That protest came to nothing.

On August 1, *Kurjer Polski* [Polish Courier] listed the Polish medal hopefuls at Los Angeles, but Stanisława Walasiewicz, who was favored in the 100 meters, was curiously not mentioned. The women's 100-meter preliminaries began that day. Just as Kusociński did not have to run against Nurmi, Walsh's main rival was also not in Los Angeles. After suffering severe injuries from the plane crash a year earlier, defending 100-meter Olympic champion Betty Robinson was unable to compete. Walsh's competition was expected to come from Californian Wilhelmina (Billie) von Bremen and Montreal native Hilde Strike, who, at 5-foot-1 and 105 pounds, was nearly a head shorter than Walsh. Strike's father was a professional hockey player, and she was exposed to sports at an early age. Like Walsh, Strike loved to play softball. Strike was in top form, having tied the Olympic mark in the 100 meters in May.

Walsh won her first two heats, the second in a world record time of 11.9 seconds. No other sprinter in the qualifiers came within three-tenths of a second of Walsh's time, which is light-years in a sprint. Strike and von Bremen moved on to the final as well. Walsh was confident that the final on August 2 was just a formality. "I expect I can do even better tomorrow," she said. "My cold bothered me a little at the first of the races today."[3]

Walsh had a distraction. The discus was scheduled for the same day as the 100-meter final. This was not her best event, but Polish women were dominant in early discus competitions (women's shot put debuted at the 1948 London Olympics). Walsh was inspired by 1928 Olympic discus champion Halina Konopacka, who was the first Pole to win a gold medal. Konopacka also finished first in the 1926 and 1930 Women's World Games. Konopacka was not in Los Angeles, but Walsh's teammate Jadwiga Wajs was another world-class discus thrower. Wajs was born two years after Walsh in Pabianickie, near Łódź. Her ancestors came from Westphalia. Their German name Weiss was of Jewish heritage. Wajs won the bronze medal at Los Angeles, gold at the 1934 Women's World Games, and the silver medal at the 1936 Berlin Olympics. After the war, she took third at the 1946 European Championships in Oslo and fourth at the 1948 London Olympics.

The favorite in the discus in Los Angeles was American Lillian Copeland, who had finished second to Konopacka at the Amsterdam Games. Ironically, Copeland, like Marie Sklodowska Curie, Pola Negri, Konopacka, and Walsh, had a Russian-Polish background. Copeland's mother, Minnie Drasnin, was born and raised in the old Jewish-Polish section of Grodno (today Hrodna in Belarus). Lillian was born in New York City in 1904. After Lillian's father died, Minnie married Abraham Copeland, and the family moved to Los Angeles, where Lillian attended Los Angeles High School and the University of Southern California. The Los Angeles Coliseum, where the Olympic track and field events were held, was in Copeland's backyard.

It was yet another warm and sunny day in Los Angeles, as Copeland set an Olympic record and won the event. Walsh finished a disappointing sixth, seven meters behind Copeland's throw. Discus was not Walsh's best event, and she might have been thinking about her loss in the 100 to Eleanor Egg a year earlier, when before that race Walsh had accidently plunked a spectator on the head with an errant toss and faced possible criminal charges.

Walsh now had to refocus on the 100-meter final. She was the only Pole in the field, but she was the odds-on favorite. She had gone to church the previous Sunday and said later, "I am sure it helped me." The Olympics was not yet the spectacle it has become today, and the stadium was half empty. The few thousand spectators focused on the starting line as the sprinters dug out their holes in the cinder track.[4]

At Walsh's coming-out party at the Millrose Games two years earlier, her competition had come from Canadian sprinters. Now Hilde Strike stood in the way of her Olympic gold medal. They barely knew one another, because Walsh did not spend much time at the Chapman Park Hotel hobnobbing with the other athletes. "She didn't stay at the hotel with us," Strike noted. "She was with her male coach all alone, all the time. She would come in her sweat suit and leave like that. . . . We never spoke more than ten to twenty words to each other the whole time we were in Los Angeles."[5]

American Mary Carew, who ran the opening leg of the gold medal–winning 4 × 100-meter relay team, had met Stella Walsh many times. Her portrayal does not square with most characterizations of the shy, reserved Pole: "I don't think I ever beat her in hundred meters outdoors," Carew recalled. "I ran against her a lot. She wasn't friendly. People don't like pushy women; she seemed so big and aggressive, and didn't know her place, according to us girls. . . . Young, unsophisticated kid was competing against this manly woman."[6] Walsh's fluid running style also raised eyebrows.

Strike was not confident heading into the final. She thought that the track was too hard and did not feel comfortable in the California heat. "The climate bothered me," she told reporters. "I've felt sick ever since I came."[7] Strike was in the third lane of the final. Walsh was two lanes to her right, in lane five. At the report of the starter's gun, Strike broke from the line first and Walsh last. Polish officials later blamed the starter for waiting too long between saying "get set" and firing his gun. Von Bremen fell off the world-record pace as the Canadian struggled to hold off the bigger Pole. Walsh's long strides caught Strike at the halfway mark, and they hit the tape in a near-dead heat. Strike lifted her arms toward the tape, while Walsh thrust out her chest to break it. The timers clocked both in 11.9 seconds. The so-called "Kirby camera"—an "electric and motion-picture timing device"—was used for the first time at Los Angeles. Although it was not official, the photo helped the judges declare Walsh the winner. Von Bremen finished third. The camera was also used to resolve the men's 100 meters, which American Eddie Tolan won by a hair over teammate Ralph Metcalfe.[8]

At the awards ceremony, the three women climbed onto the perches of the medals podium, Walsh on top, Strike on her right, and von Bremen on her left. This was the first time the podium was used at an Olympics, along with the raising of the victor's national flag and playing of the country's anthem. Contrary to Coubertin's vision of individual athletes competing to promote international cooperation and world peace, the Olympics had become a symbol of a nation's power. The winner was announced as Poland's Stanisława Walasiewicz; the 21-year-old stood on top of the platform with a gold medal and a world record in hand. Poland was ecstatic. Walsh expressed pride in her heritage and made reference to the hardships of Poles and Polish Americans:

I have always felt Polish, I have fervently desired, in order that for me and my countrymen who emigrated to America [that] the *Mazurek Dąbrowski* [the Polish national anthem] was played and the Polish flag was raised. For us, for Polish Americans, it was a matter of honor and reward for the many tough times that we repeatedly lived through in exile.[9]

Polish foreign minister August Zaleski sent a telegram congratulating Walsh for the gold medal. *Kurjer Polski* called Walsh's victory a "heroic" effort. It was the only gold medal in women's track and field that did not go to an American, and the Polish press made no mention that Walsh had lived all but the first year of her life in the United States. If Walsh had run for the U.S. team in 1932, she would have won two gold medals. Five days after Strike's narrow loss to Walsh in the 100 meters, Strike's Canadian relay team again lost by a nose to the United States in the 4 × 100-meter relay, with both teams clocking the same time (47 seconds). Mary Carew led off the gold medal–winning relay team, and von Bremen anchored. Other than Walsh, the Poles could not find three other world-class sprinters to field a competitive relay team.

Kusociński and Walsh were the most renowned athletes in interwar Poland. The POC concluded that their athletes' showing at the Olympics was "tremendous for Polish propaganda abroad, and likewise electrified all of Poland."[10] Born three years before Walsh, also in Russian Poland, Kusociński became known as the "Father of Polish Distance Running." When Germany attacked Poland in September 1939, to start World War II, Kusociński fought with the Polish Army, earning Poland's *Krzyż Walecznych* [Cross of Valor]. After Poland went down to defeat, Kusociński joined the Polish resistance. In 1940, the Gestapo caught the Olympic champion. One historian contends that the "largest single massacre of the [German] AB-Aktion [Extraordinary Pacification Operation] took place at Palmiry, when 348 men and women were shot on 20 and 21 June [1940]. Kusociński was among the victims."[11] Every year the northern Polish city of Szczecin holds the Kusociński Memorial Track and Field Meet. In 1969, IOC president Avery Brundage went to Poland to commemorate the fiftieth anniversary of the formation of the POC. One of his stops was to visit Kusociński's grave in Palmiry.[12]

In 1932, the Polish government honored Walsh with the distinguished Gold Cross of Merit, and *Przegląd Sportowy* again named her Poland's most popular athlete. Cleveland was happy for its native daughter but regretted that Walsh had not run for Uncle Sam. The *Plain Dealer* wrote, "Fleet Stella Walsh . . . deserted Cleveland's unemployed to run and work for Poland."[13] W. J. Nowak, publisher of the Polish American paper *Polish Daily Monitor*, said, "I doubt if there will be such celebrations as have taken place before. We are glad to see Stella win, of course, but we would have been more glad [*sic*] if she had finished her nationalization and won as an American. We are Americans." *Plain Dealer* columnist James Doyle joked, "Stanisława Walasiewicz of Poland seems to run even faster than did Stella Walsh of Cleveland."[14] One letter to the editor criticized the newspaper for questioning Walsh's choice to run for Poland:

> The law of self-preservation is first; by making contact with Poland, her first fatherland, her future is secure, and why should we begrudge her that? The United States seems to be none the worse for Stella's absence, as the United States is in no danger of losing first place at the Olympics.[15]

Walsh's gold medal in the 100 meters was the most coveted at the Olympic Games, because she could claim to be the "world's fastest woman." Americans won the other gold medals in the five women's events at Los Angeles and half of the total medals. Babe Didrikson won gold medals in the 80-meter hurdles and the javelin, and a silver medal in the high jump. She became an instant celebrity in Los Angeles. "It was a good meet, and everything was swell," she told the *Los Angeles Times* for its August 14, 1932, edition. "The only thing that bothered me was so many people coming out to see me. I like people, but I didn't get any rest. One night I just had to take a car and ride around until I was sure that lobby [of the Chapman Park Hotel] was clear and that nobody would try and telephone me."

In fact, the publicity did not really bother Didrikson, but it rankled some of her teammates. She was brash, boastful, and self-promoting. Olympic high-jump champion Jean Shiley recalled, "If you [or the press] weren't paying any attention to her she would reach in her pocket and get out her harmonica and start to play, and she played it *very well.*" When Didrikson was told of U.S. swimmer Helene Madison's gold medal–winning time in the 50 meters, she boasted, "I did it in three seconds less one day and wasn't even tryin'." Didrikson claimed there was no sport she could not do. She told U.S. diving gold medalist Georgia Coleman, "You haven't seen me get goin' yet, have you? Nope, they won't let me enter the swimming events, but I can show you all."[16]

Evelyne Hall thought she had nipped Didrikson in the 80-meter hurdle final, but after huddling up the judges awarded the gold medal to Didrikson. After the race, as the judges were trying to determine the winner, Didrikson told Hall matter-of-factly, "I won."[17] Years later, Hall still thought that she had at least tied for the gold medal. "At the tape," she said, "she put her arm up and turned her shoulder, and that was how the race was decided. I had a real cut, and my neck was bleeding in a semicircular pattern from the finish line." Hall contended that Avery Brundage and other U.S. track and field officials had agreed that the race was a dead heat, and promised they would give her an unofficial second gold medal. That never happened.[18]

Walsh with U.S. Olympic gold medalists in Los Angeles, 1932. From left to right, high jumper Jean Shiley, Walsh, discus thrower Lillian Copeland, and hurdler Babe Didrikson. *University of Southern California Special Collections.*

Didrikson was the victim of some questionable judging in the high jump, however. Shiley said that some of the other competitors had wanted to claim a foul on Didrikson from the start of the competition, but Shiley declined to question the legality of Babe's "western roll." In a jump-off with Shiley, the judges disqualified one of Didrikson's jumps because she led with her head, and Shiley was awarded the gold medal. Didrikson finished second.[19] Shiley said later, "The fact is that the rules were very rigid on how you could jump. . . . Your shoulder could not precede your body over the bar." She acknowledged that it was a "very bad time to call a foul."[20]

Didrikson's victories were among her many athletic triumphs. At the AAU Championships in Dallas in 1930, she won the baseball throw and javelin. The next year at the championships in Jersey City, where Eleanor Egg upset Walsh in the 100 yards, Didrikson took the 80-yard hurdles. Didrikson entered every event at the 1932 U.S. Olympic Trials at Evanston, winning five (not all of the events were on the Olympic program). Olympic rules limited her to competing in only three events.

Muscular, athletic women like Didrikson and Walsh were still considered abnormal. After the prelims and the final, Walsh did not shower with the other women or with her teammates. She immediately left the Coliseum for the Chapman Park Hotel, leaving some to wonder what she was hiding. Famous sports reporter Paul Gallico called Didrikson a "muscle moll . . . a hard-bitten, hawk-nosed, thin-mouthed little hoyden from Texas."[21] Didrikson was criticized for stepping outside of the assigned bounds of women's proper place in society; she was even charged with being a homosexual. Gallico wrote, "Everybody in Los Angeles was talking about the Babe. Was she all boy? Or had she any feminine traits?"[22] One college physical education teacher remembered her mother warning her about playing softball: "I just don't want you to grow up to be like Babe Didrikson," her mother had said.[23]

Many sports officials still thought that women's track and field should be dropped from the Olympic program altogether. At a meeting of the National Athletic Federation at the Los Angeles Biltmore Hotel a week before the Olympics began, Agnes R. Wayman of Barnard College declared, "The women's division feels that for the school or college girl, or girl of like age, the intense, intercompetitive [sic] program is not productive of better girls or better women."[24] One journalist wrote that women did not belong on the field of play, but in the water to swim.[25]

In 1932, Canadian sports editors selected Hilde Strike as Canada's greatest female athlete. Canadian women's Olympic team manager Alexandrine Gibb contrasted the petite Strike with the "big, husky Polish girl [Walsh] with the mannish frame."[26] One reporter lauded the Canadian women for their beauty and femininity, saying, "They constitute a denial in the flesh of the general idea that a woman athlete must be built like a baby grand piano and have a face like a hatchet."[27]

Poland was no more progressive in promoting women's sports. Eugeniusz Piasecki was one of the prominent Polish figures in youth physical education and sports during the interwar period. Piasecki began his career as a gym teacher in Lwów in Austrian Poland, and after the war he became a university professor in Poznań. Piasecki pioneered the Boy Scout movement in Poland but had no time for women running in shorts: "The loss of one of the most precious virtues of women," he declared, is "namely the feeling of shame."[28]

Women who challenged the normative gender roles were often ridiculed. When Dutch sprinter Fanny Blankers-Koen won four gold medals in the 1948 London Games, her neighbors bought her a bicycle "so she wouldn't have to run so much."[29] Blankers-Koen was well aware of these rigid parameters, saying, "People applaud me because I do my training and winning between washing dishes and darning socks.[30] Hurt by the criticism of her manliness, Didrikson tried to project a more feminine profile. On her way to the 1932 U.S. Olympic Trials in Evanston, the press reported that she had bought her first hat—a pink one at that.

Didrikson left track and field to take up the more refined game of golf. She began wearing makeup and lipstick, and married a professional wrestler. "I know I'm not pretty," said Didrikson. "But I try to be graceful."[31] Didrikson excelled in golf too, winning fourteen straight championships in 1946–1947. After she beat Grantland Rice in one round, he said he had never seen a woman hit a ball like that.

Walsh's mannish face and figure also caused her to be labeled a "tomboy" and resulted in bullying. One reporter noted, "She has a somewhat masculine form, and her legs are well developed."[32] Walsh later told the *Plain Dealer* that the one observation that she "prized above all others" came from University of Southern California track coach Dean Cromwell, who coached numerous Olympic champions. Said Cromwell,

> It would be wrong to say that Miss Walsh runs like a man. Most men run the wrong way, and the Polish sprinting lady runs right. When I say right, I mean easily, keeping well relaxed and showing little effort. [Olympic gold medalist] Eddie Tolan runs that way, and he's a pretty good sprinter too.[33]

Polish authorities did not care about the looks of Poland's new champion. After all, a 100-meter Olympic gold medalist did not come along every day. After recognizing Walsh in 1930, the National Physical Education and Military Training Office gave her the Greatest Honor in Sport Award for three straight years from 1932 to 1934.

Walsh's first exposure to the Olympics and Los Angeles left a powerful impression on the young woman. "The Olympic Games were wonderfully handled," she told the *Plain Dealer* on August 13, 1932. "I do think some of the Polish team would have done better except for the heat." According to an official POC report of the Los Angeles Games, the Polish team "left Los Angeles with sadness . . . [their days there] probably constituted the greatest time of their lives. California was, for them, the best coast of the 'promised land' of America."[34] On August 14, the *Los Angeles Times* reported that Jadwiga Wajs was in tears when she had to leave Los Angeles after the Games, saying, "I like it so much I don't want to go home. I ask everybody where I can get a job, but I don't find one. So I must go." The Polish team's chaperone told a reporter, "We're not sure we can get her on the train, she wants to stay here so badly. We tell her to go see if she cannot find a husband and stay," the chaperone joked. She might have been talking about Walsh, because she also loved the city.

On the train ride back to the East Coast, the Polish team made stops at the Grand Canyon, in Chicago, and at Niagara Falls. During the trip, the team was feted by Polish American delegations. The Polish Consulate threw a reception for the team in Chicago, and the city hosted a track meet. Kusociński won the 5,000 meters. In one of the few meetings between the world's two greatest female athletes, Walsh bested Didrikson in the 100 meters, tying her world record of 11.9 seconds. Walsh also set a new world record in the 200 meters and won the broad jump. Didrikson took the high jump. Her second-place finish in the discus (to Wajs) was the only event in which Didrikson beat Walsh, who finished fourth. On August 29, the *Plain Dealer* claimed that "Stella Walsh, Polish girl from Cleveland, stole the show from Babe Didrikson of Texas, star of the women's branch of the Olympics."

In early October, the Polish Olympic team boarded the *Pułaski* in New York for the trip back to Poland. In a team photo taken on the bow of the tugboat *Macom (NY)*, which took the team to the ship, a somber Walsh is sitting in the front row in a dress and her Olympic blazer. Wajs is next to her wearing a white hat and white gloves. To her right is the dapper, suntanned Kusociński in an unbuttoned white shirt.

For the first time since she had left Wierzchownia as a one-year-old, Stella Walsh was going back to live in Poland. As part of her deal to run for Poland at the 1932 Olympics, she received a scholarship for a three-year course of study in journalism and physical education at the Warsaw Institute of Physical Education. Walsh had lived in Cleveland for nearly her entire life, but the twenty-one-year-old Olympic champion thought she would easily adapt to living in Warsaw. She spoke Polish at home, and the Polish American community in Cleveland had nurtured her education and athletic career. Walsh's sense of Polishness was strong, and she had run races in Poland before. But this would be the first time that she would be away from home for an extended period of time. For the next four years, she lived on and off in Warsaw, running for Polonia Warszawa, Sokół Grażyna, and Klub Sportowy Warszawianka.

Walsh had blossomed from a shy, young immigrant girl from Cleveland into a globetrotting celebrity. No other female athlete of her time traversed the world as much as Stella Walsh, not even the great tennis player Helen Wills, who won seven U.S. and eight Wimbledon singles titles in the 1920s and 1930s. Wills won gold medals in singles and doubles at the 1924 Paris Olympics, but tennis was taken off the Olympic program until 1988. In the decade before the outbreak of war in 1939, Walsh competed in meets throughout North America and Europe, and she was the first foreign woman to run in a competition in Japan.

German heavyweight boxer Max Schmeling was the only male athlete to rival Walsh's number of transatlantic voyages. He became the darling of the Nazis after beating Joe Louis in 1936, but Schmeling made most of his money fighting in the United States with a Jewish trainer and Jewish promoter. Schmeling did not care who was handling him as long as he cashed in on his fights. The cover of the March 1929 German boxing magazine *Boxwoche* had a drawing of Schmeling standing on top of a U.S. silver dollar.

Walsh was excited about the opportunity to study in Poland. A *Los Angeles Times* reporter detected a newfound confidence in Walsh from the time she had arrived at the Olympics:

> Then, she resembled a big, scared, harassed, bewildered jackrabbit, scurrying for cover. She was afraid to open her mouth, mistrustful of everyone. Yesterday, she was beaming. . . . "Going to be a reporter, Stella?" "Ya—ah," she replied. "I've had to meet so many of 'em that I kind of took an interest in their work. Maybe my experience in being interviewed will help me to interview."[35]

In October 1932, Stella Walsh and the Polish Olympic team arrived in the Polish port of Gdynia, not far from the contested city of Danzig (Gdańsk in Polish). Danzig was the port at the northern end of the "Polish Corridor," a swath of German territory the Versailles Treaty awarded to Poland for "free and secure access to the sea," as Woodrow Wilson put it in the thirteenth of his Fourteen Points. The Versailles Treaty did not give Danzig—a predominantly German city—to the new Polish state. It was administered by the League of Nations, and Warsaw feared that the league would eventually return the city to Germany. Poland decided to build an alternative port of its own twenty miles north of Danzig, at Gdynia, with Poland maintaining complete control. Gdynia and neighboring Oksywie had a population of 200 in 1914, but this number had grown to 120,000 by 1939. By that time, Gdynia handled more tonnage than any other Baltic port, with some fifty oceangoing companies sailing out of the harbor. The biggest was the Gdynia-Ameryka Line, which had ten liners by 1939. Walsh sailed on all four flagships, named for Poland's greatest heroes: the *Kościuszko*, the *Pułaski*, the *Batory*, and the *Piłsudski*. Germany's naval bombardment of Westerplatte, near Gdynia and Danzig, and the Wehrmacht's invasion of Poland on September 1, 1939, marked the beginning of World War II. By that time, Walsh was safely back in Cleveland.

Walsh anticipated that she would be a major celebrity in Poland. After all, she and 1928 Olympic discus gold medalist Halina Konopacka were the most famous female athletes in Poland. Walsh was soon disappointed at the lack of attention. Soccer and other men's sports dominated the media, and Walsh went unrecognized in public. She had already been to Poland several times, but as an athlete traveling with a visiting team she had received first-class treatment. Now she was just a poor student living in Warsaw. She was surprised at the poverty of the Polish people. The Depression was hard on the country, especially given the monumental task of building the new Polish state after World War I. The real value of the economy fell by 25 percent from 1929 to 1933 (in contrast, Britain's economy contracted by 5 percent). By the mid-1930s, 450,000 Poles were out of work. Ethnic divisions exacerbated the dire economic situation. The population was one-third Jewish, Ukrainian, German, and Lithuanian. Poland's politics were hopelessly divided. Poland's treatment of these minorities in the interwar period was hardly exemplary, especially after Piłsudski died in 1935.

Poland's economic problems were complicated by its precarious diplomatic situation. The country had potential enemies on all sides. The Soviet Union, Lithuania, and Germany lost territory to Poland after World War I, and the countries remained estranged from Poland throughout the interwar period. After the surprise victory over the Red Army in 1920, Poland annexed the former Russian territories of Belarus and part of Ukraine in the Treaty of Riga (1921). Lithuania would not accept Poland's incorporation of Vilnius, a Polish city surrounded by a Lithuanian-populated countryside. Germans bitterly resented the cession of former German territories to Poland, cutting off East Prussia from Germany proper. Czechoslovakia had nabbed a portion of the predominantly Polish city of Czieszyn (Tešín in Czech) in 1920, souring relations between those two countries as well. The Piłsudski regime brought a semblance of political and economic stability to Poland in the late 1920s, but the Depression brought renewed domestic and international troubles. The modest gains the economy had made in the 1920s were rolled back.

Shortly after Walsh arrived in Poland, Adolf Hitler came to power in Germany. Five years earlier, a Nazi chancellorship had seemed impossible. In the 1928 Reichstag elections, Hitler's Nazi Party received a paltry 2.6 percent of the vote. The Depression sent voters to the Nazis in droves. By the fall of 1930, Hitler's share of the vote had increased to 18.3 percent, reaching a high of 37.4 percent in July 1932. German conservatives handed Hitler the chancellorship in January 1933, hoping to co-opt him in a right-wing assault on the German left. Hitler had other ideas and destroyed the Weimar Republic altogether. In

Interwar Poland. *Map by Gracia Lindberg.*

October, he signaled a new direction in foreign policy by leaving the League of Nations.

Hitler's denunciation of the Versailles Treaty was a direct threat to Poland. His demand for the "unification of all Germans" was an unmistakable reference to the 1 million Germans in Poland. Nothing united Germans more than Hitler's call for the return of Danzig and the Polish Corridor. "So long as this treaty stands there can be no resurrection of the German people," Hitler railed. "The treaty was made in order to bring 20 million Germans to their deaths and to ruin the German nation."[36] Piłsudski was so alarmed by Hitler's chancellorship that he approached France for a preventive war against Germany. With the carnage of World War I still fresh in French minds, and without support from London, Paris was in no mood to join Warsaw in a war against Germany. Germany was in no shape to fight either, and in a defensive move of his own, Hitler signed a nonaggression pact with Poland in 1934. He could tear up that piece of paper later.

Walsh had more trouble adjusting to the economic hardships of life in Poland than any culture shock. "It's hard to get along in Europe once one has been brought up in the American standard of living," she said.[37] The Walasiewicz family was struggling to make ends meet in the early 1930s, but Walsh was surprised by the meager living standards for a student in Poland. She missed the comforts of home. She had to tell the cooks at Warsaw University how to make the American food and drink she loved, for instance, toast and orange juice for breakfast. Although she knew spoken Polish, she found taking classes in the language the "worst part" of her studies.[38]

The cinder track had always been a place for Walsh to forget about any personal troubles. Shortly after her arrival in Warsaw, she set the Polish record in the 800 meters, a new distance for her and one that was no longer on the Olympic program for women. The *Plain Dealer* kept track of her exploits in Poland: "And here's Stella Walsh of Cleveland setting a new fast-foot record at Warsaw. It's useless," the paper quipped, "for her to try to hide her identity by calling herself Walasiewicz," which is, of course, how she was known in Poland.[39]

The refuge of the track was denied to Walsh in early 1933, when she suffered a severely sprained ankle. Various reports had her tripping over a railroad track in Lwów or turning an ankle walking to the post office while on vacation in Zakopane, a ski resort in the Tatra Mountains in southern Poland. The Associated Press sent out a release that her career was over, citing a Warsaw doctor's prognosis that "it was doubtful if she would be able to run again."[40] The *New York Times* reported that her career was "imperiled" and that she "might be permanently disabled."[41] The reports were erroneous. A month later the newspaper wrote that she had fully recovered.

Walsh was completely disillusioned with the Poles' lack of concern for her well-being after the injury. "I'd hate to say what I think about this incident," she griped to the *Plain Dealer*. "I don't intend to run in Poland while I'm finishing my course at the Institute of Athletics. I'm going to the United States when I'm through." Walsh was particularly angry with the "lack of consideration" by the Polish doctors. She said that her spirits had been injured as much as her ankle. The newspaper reported that she was "disillusioned and embittered by her life in her native Poland."[42]

Walsh on a Warsaw street, 1934. *Kurier Codzienny, Narodowe Archiwum Cyfrowe [National Digital Archive].*

Some solace came in February, when the Polish government gave her its highest annual honor for an athlete, the Grand National Sports Prize. Stefan Lenartowicz, director of the Polish Rada Organizacyjna Polaków z Zagranica [Council of the Organization of Poles Abroad], sent Walsh a letter of congratulations: "The award attests to the fact that through your fame Poland's reputation abroad has been enhanced. . . . Polish sport generally, and Polish sport abroad in particular, has you to thank for one of the most glorious chapters in its history."[43]

James Doyle of the *Plain Dealer* announced that it came with a $1,100 award and commented on the lack of U.S. financial support for Walsh before the Los Angeles Olympics, which had resulted in her running for Poland: "Over in Poland," he wrote, "amateur athletes are apparently paid off under the lights rather than in the alley, as is the United States custom."[44] It turns out that Doyle's Associated Press source was wrong; the sports prize did not come with cash.[45] Walsh would have been ineligible for the next Olympics if it had.

Homesick for family and friends in Cleveland, Walsh took any break in her studies to return to the United States, even if only to run in a few races. That summer, she was on a ship back to the States, and in July, she won four gold medals at the National Polish Falcons Track and Field Championships. Still upset by her decision not to run for the United States at the Los Angeles Olympics, the *Plain Dealer* put her Polish name first and Stella Walsh in parentheses, and wrote that she was "formerly of Cleveland."

In August, Walsh returned to Europe for a meet in Brussels. The ankle was still bothering her, and she lost the 100 and 200 meters to Tollien Schuurman of the Netherlands.[46] By the fall Walsh had fully recovered. Running for the sports club Polonia Warszawa, Walsh set two world records in the 60 and 100 meters at a meet in Poznań. At the end of September in Lwów she broke her own world record in the 60 meters, and two weeks later she set world records in the 80 and 100 meters in a meet in Katowice. After the ankle scare, Walsh was again at the top of the world of track—the unquestioned "Queen of the Sprints." In 1934 Walsh won Poland's Grand National Sports Prize for the second year in a row. It seemed that no one stood in the way of her winning gold again at the 1936 Olympics in Berlin.

Walsh was a familiar customer for the Gdynia-Ameryka line. Studying in Europe allowed Walsh to leave Warsaw for lengthy periods of time. Most courses of study in European universities consist of preparing for and passing exams, which the student can schedule. Attending lectures is often not mandatory. It is not clear, however, if Walsh ever finished a degree in Poland. In October 1933 she set sail again for New York. President Ignacy Mościcki gave Walasiewicz an official send off. In its coverage of the event, the *Los Angeles Times* joked about the difficulty in pronouncing their names, ignoring the fact that they were in Poland: "Just pity the guy who had to introduce them."

The *Plain Dealer*, which now called her Stella Walsh again, reported that she was returning to Cleveland to begin a two-year college prep course at Notre Dame High School, although she had yet to finish her studies in Warsaw. Walsh went back to her old familiar routines, starring for Cleveland's Vivian Beauty Shoppes' basketball team and for Kroger Stores' softball team. In April 1934 she took the 50 and 200 meters at the AAU Indoor National Championships in Brooklyn. Betty Robinson was there, running in her first big meet since her horrific airplane crash in 1931. She was relegated to the 4 × 100 relay because she could not bend her injured knee at the starting line. Robinson's team did not win a medal.

In May 1934 Walsh went back to Poland to prepare for the World Women's Games in London. This would be the last of Alice Milliat's all-women track and field events. The IOC had finally admitted women's athletics into the Olympic Games on a permanent basis, and the "Women's Olympics" was no longer needed. Few spectators showed up in London. Nonetheless, debate would continue for decades about which track and field events were "suitable" for women. The 200 meters, which was probably Walsh's best race, did not get on the Olympic program for women until the 1948 London Olympics. The 800 meters, which had been run at the 1928 Amsterdam Games, was taken off because some of the runners fell to the ground in exhaustion after the race. Canadian Jane Bell said that the "people who ran the 800 didn't think it was difficult. I'm sure no one thought it was hard. It was just those officials who thought so." Teammate Myrtle Cook claimed that the story about the women collapsing at the finish was "grossly exaggerated."[47] Women did not run the 800 meters in the Olympics again for 32 years.

Walsh's winning streak in the Women's World Games came to an abrupt end in London. Germany's Käthe Krauss was a music teacher at the Dresden Conservatory, but she also had a strong physique and the gift of speed. Walsh won the 60 meters, but Krauss whipped Walsh in her two specialties, the 100 and 200 meters. Walsh did not take the defeats too seriously because she had injured her leg training for the broad jump. In 1935, she set a recognized world record in the 200 meters, which was not broken for seventeen years, when Australia's Marjorie Jackson won the event at the 1952 Helsinki Olympics.

In December, Walsh was on another ship bound for the United States. That winter she played basketball for the Cleveland sporting goods company Blepp-Coombs but ran into trouble with a new AAU rule against an amateur team playing a game on the same program with a pro basketball team. The AAU suspended her for thirty days, and there was some question as to whether she would lose her amateur status permanently. "If I wanted to turn professional I could have done it long ago," Walsh huffed, "and made plenty of money in the process."[48]

A new sprinting phenom hit the sports scene in 1935. Helen Stephens, standing at six feet tall, was an unknown seventeen-year-old farm girl from the small town of Fulton, Missouri. Stephens's victories on the track brought a modicum of fame to the town in the mid-1930s, but Fulton would gain greater notoriety after World War II, when former British prime minister Winston Churchill made a visit to Westminster College in March 1946, to give a speech on the state of affairs in Europe. Churchill warned that the Soviet Union was building an "Iron Curtain" to divide Europe. He put a city in Walsh's Poland at the northern end of a line of Communist dictatorships in Eastern Europe: "From Stettin [Szczecin] in the Baltic to Trieste in the Adriatic," Churchill declared, "an iron curtain has descended across the Continent."[49] Churchill's memorable observation contributed to President Harry Truman's hard-line containment policy and the emerging Cold War. "Behind the Iron Curtain" became synonymous with the Soviet bloc.

Stephens and Walsh had their own hot war on the track and cold war off it, the latter spurred on by the Missouri press. Although both women had grown up in the United States, they took vastly divergent paths to the cinders. Stephens had little formal training, running on the farm: "From the time I was a small child I was in training, only I didn't know it," she recalled. "I was walking, running, doing chores, building up my body, my lung capacity, my wind, my endurance, everything that people have to train for today."[50] She told one reporter that she just chased rabbits all over the farm. Stephens was aware that women had run for the first time at the 1928 Amsterdam

Olympics. At one point she promised her mother, "I'm going to run in the Olympics someday."[51]

Stephens's high school track coach, Bert Moore, recalled the first day he saw her as a neophyte sophomore with pig tails:

> She came out where the boys were practicing one day and said she wanted to run. Well, that was all right with me. . . . One time I casually took out my stopwatch and timed her on a dash. I could hardly believe my eyes. . . . Do that dash again, I suggested. Again she came close to a record in the women's time in that sprint.

Moore turned out to be an excellent coach, honing Stephens's starting and running techniques. But he was also concerned that the young girl would be physically harmed by pushing her too hard: "I never let her run a race in competition until the following year. She was still growing like a weed. I let her tag along and run some exhibition races with the boys. No girl should be allowed to do any hard running until she is past sixteen."[52] Although Moore's opinion reflected the conventional wisdom of the time about overtaxing female athletes because of their supposedly fragile bodies, he was probably right about the damage of overtraining of *any* young athlete, male or female, which is rampant in the sporting world today.

Walsh spent all but the first year of her life in the big city and had formal training with coaches from the Polish Falcons, South High School, the Polish Olympic team, and Polish athletic clubs. She had traveled the world and now considered herself a sophisticated cosmopolitan urbanite. The confident twenty-four-year-old was an Olympic champion and seasoned veteran of many big international meets in North America, Europe, and Asia. Walsh liked to dress the part. Getting off the train from New York after one trip, one *Plain Dealer* reporter noted that she sported a "raccoon coat, a blue tam, a blue georgette dress, blue socks with white stripes, white kid slippers with blue trim, and several beautiful dinner rings."[53] Aside from the track, in public Walsh was always nattily dressed.

Stephens raced Walsh for the first time at the AAU Indoor Championships in St. Louis in March 1935. Stephens tended to exaggerate her rivalry with Walsh, and much of what she said later fudged the truth. She claimed that before the race she had put up a picture of Walsh on her wall to throw darts at it. A few years after Walsh's death in 1980, Stephens recalled that when she heard that she was to race the Olympic champion, she said, "So what? She can eat dirt as far as I'm concerned."[54] Walsh was equally dismissive of the young Missourian. Before the race, Walsh called Stephens "that greenie from the sticks."[55] Walsh was more worried about facing 1928 Olympic gold medalist Betty Robinson, but Robinson did not attend the meet.[56]

Walsh's nemesis, Helen Stephens. *Library of Congress.*

Walsh thought the race would be an easy win, but Stephens beat her in the 50 meters. The Missouri crowd went wild. Upon being congratulated for beating the "fastest woman in the world," Stephens supposedly replied, "Who is Stella Walsh?" When Walsh heard about Stephens's comment, she called it a "fluke" and claimed that Stephens had jumped the gun: "I don't like to complain," Walsh said. "But I was robbed." At a high school pep rally after the meet, Stephens once again delighted the crowd by repeating, "Who is Stella Walsh?"[57] The Missouri press dubbed their new star the "Missouri Express" and the "Fulton Flash."[58]

The loss to Stephens was a psychological blow to Walsh. Although she had been beaten in a few races before, Walsh had been the best woman sprinter in the country for several years. Stephens was nearly six inches taller and simply faster than Walsh, and there was nothing Walsh could do about it. A sprinter's psyche is fragile. Sports like sprinting or jumping rely on sheer physical gifts; as much as one might train, there is a limit to how fast one can run or how high one can jump. Sprinters can work on their starts and technique, but ultimately speed depends on genetics. Distance runners can put in more road work, discus throwers can lift weights and improve technique, and athletes in team sports can rely on teammates to improve chances of winning. Sprinters are alone in their pursuit of the finish line. There is no strategy in a race that is finished in seconds, so extraneous factors assume greater importance.

Before the institution of photo finishes and electronic timing, competitors were encouraged to wear a white top to stand out at the finish line. Before a race, competitors often study the starter to detect a pattern in his or her cadence. Some athletes have a quicker reaction time, which is a big advantage in the dashes. West German Armin Hari, who won the 100 meters at the 1960 Rome Olympics, was known as the "Thief of Starts."

Sprinters want to remain cool and calm before the start, and combine explosion off the start and a relaxed, steady acceleration. The speediest runners are able to combine supreme effort with a governor on their emotions. Seeing a rival in front can discombobulate the most veteran runner. Walsh worked as hard as anyone to maximize her sprinting talent, and she had built a life of fame and some financial reward around her unparalleled speed. There were no longer distances on the women's Olympic program at the time, so the stakes for Walsh the sprinter were high. Stephens was a problem.

A few months later, Walsh was scheduled for a rematch against Stephens at an AAU meet in St. Louis, but Walsh declined to run, claiming that the meet conflicted with her exams at Notre Dame Academy, which she was supposed to finish in June.[59] "I can beat her any time I try," Walsh boasted.[60] Upon hearing that, Stephens challenged, "Swell! Tell Miss Walsh I shall be delighted to race her any time—anywhere—even over plowed ground." Years later, Stephens said that Walsh "avoided racing me after that, but she couldn't duck out of the [1936] Olympics. I blew her doors off there, too."[61]

The Missouri press howled that Walsh was obligated to race Stephens again. The Jefferson City *Daily Capital News* wrote, "She says she is going to her native heath, Poland, to train girls in athletics. All right, if Stella has cold feet and refuses to meet our Helen, we'll just pin the muslin on the Missouri girl and let it go at that."[62] Dr. Noram Bothert, head of the St. Louis Girls Athletic Club, asked the AAU to suspend Walsh. Walsh was incensed, reiterating that she had to go back to school. "But instead of turning these facts over to the public," Walsh charged, "the St. Louis officials continued to advertise me for the meet until the last minute, when they gave out the information that I had 'run out' on them."[63]

Even without Walsh to push her, Stephens beat Walsh's world record in the 100 meters. That summer, Walsh returned to Poland on the *Kościuszko*, again vehemently denying that she was afraid to run against Stephens. They would meet again at the 1936 Berlin Olympics, under the curious gaze of Adolf Hitler.

5

Stella Walsh and
Helen Stephens at the
Nazi Olympics

[Stephens] could not have been more comfortable running around in Berlin, even if the Olympics had been held in the time of Frederick the Great: Without any doubt she would have been drafted into the grenadier's regiment. Miss Stephens does not betray femininity. She has broad shoulders, fully masculine arm muscles and legs, and runs like men.

—*Polish newspaper* Kurjer Warszawski *[Warsaw Courier], after Helen Stephens beat Stella Walsh in the 100 meters at the Berlin Olympics*

In August 1935, Stella Walsh was in Warsaw for the Polonia World Olympics. The mood that summer in the Polish capital was gloomy. The Depression was grinding onward, and Marshal Piłsudski had succumbed to cancer in May, leaving the country without its revered helmsman at a most crucial time. Adolf Hitler was stirring up German nationalism and rebuilding the Wehrmacht. His long-term expansionist plans were directed eastward, against Poland and the Soviet Union. One ode to Piłsudski after his death recalled his role in the resurrection of Poland:

> Out of the prison—grief of hopeless years,
> Out of the bloody travail—pangs of war,
> A nation to outsoar,
> The proudest vaunting of an earlier age.[1]

The author could not have imagined that in four years his country would be crushed again in another world war.

Walsh reportedly set a new world record in the 100 meters at the Polonia Olympics, and that fall, in the Silesian town of Czeladź, she set another world record in the 250 meters, one of the peculiar distances that padded Walsh's tally of record-setting marks. The number of Walsh's world records is unverifiable. Some races were wind-aided, and timekeepers with stopwatches had to rely on visual starts and finishes. Meet organizers often claimed that world records had been set because it was good publicity. Furthermore, the 250 meters was one of the many world records that Walsh set in such unusual distances as 40, 75, and 80 meters (or yards). The IAAF did not sanction many of these meets or recognize these record times. Nonetheless, Walsh was in top form heading into the 1936 Olympics.

After the Czeladź meet, Walsh left for a tour of Japan. Her ship went through the Suez Canal, where she stopped to see the pyramids in Egypt. Walsh established another unofficial world record in the 200 meters in Osaka, and in Tokyo, she set a new mark in the 500 meters, another odd distance. Japanese sports fans remembered Walsh because of her friendly rivalry with Japanese sprinter Kinue Hitomi in the early 1930s. Walsh was highly complimentary of the warm reception: "I never heard them make a bad remark about the United States," she said. "They were good friends. Large crowds, sometimes as many as 20,000 saw the meets—which is quite a lot for a women's meet. I was the only foreigner there."[2] The *Plain Dealer* kept tabs on "Stella the Traveler": "All races, including the yellow," as the newspaper put it about her races in the Far East, "are the same to Stella Walsh, who is currently showing a lot of heels to the speediest gal sprinters over in Japan."[3]

This was a delicate time for Japan's relations with the United States. Japan was bent on becoming the preeminent power in the Far East. Japan had joined the Western powers in World War I, hoping to take German possessions in the Shantung Peninsula and islands in the western Pacific. At the Paris Peace Conference after the war, Japanese emissaries asked the Western powers to agree to a resolution declaring the Japanese the racial equal of Caucasians. Woodrow Wilson, David Lloyd George, and Georges Clemenceau ignored them. The Japanese leaders also thought it was an affront when the Western powers, at several postwar disarmament conferences, would not agree to parity in naval tonnage. In the 1930s, militarists gradually took over the Japanese government.

By 1931, the Japanese Army was in Manchuria and poised to impose its will on the rest of China, threatening U.S. interests in the Far East. In 1934, Babe Ruth, the New York Yankees' famed "Sultan of Swat," led an All-Star team to Japan. Fellow Yankee great Lou Gehrig went along. American officials hoped that the "diamond diplomats" would marginalize the militarists and embolden the doves in the Japanese government. The American press commented on Japan's reverence for the Babe:

> In the newsreels we see him walking the narrow streets of Tokyo, Osaka, and Nagasaki, and as he walks, round-headed children swarm in his wake. Their elders line the curbs with shining eyes. . . . Ruth's fame has spread, undoubtedly, to every little rice village in the Land of the Rising Sun.

Japanese fans' rousing reception for the American stars prompted tour manager Connie Mack to exaggerate the political importance of Ruth's appearances:

> [This is] one of the greatest peace measures in the history of nations. . . . The parley on the naval treaty was on, with America blocking Japan's demand for parity. There was strong anti-American feeling throughout Japan over this country's stand. Things didn't look good at all. And then Babe Ruth smacked a home run, and all the ill feeling and underground war sentiment vanished just like that.[4]

That was not quite so. The home runs Ruth hit on the tour and Walsh's appearances on the track did little to change the course of Japanese imperial policy. Extreme anti-Western attitudes were still rampant in the country, as was evident when a radical Japanese nationalist knifed the baseball tour organizer and well-known publisher Matsutaro Shoriki. In 1937 Japan launched a full-fledged attack on China, and four years later the Japanese bombed Pearl Harbor.

In late 1935, Walsh returned to New York on the *Piłsudski*. She bowed out of the AAU Indoor Championships, scheduled for February 1936. "I am not taking part in indoor meets because of the Olympics," she explained. "There is a chance I might 'go stale.' I don't want to train too early." She also said that she was studying for another round of final exams at Notre

Dame and declared that this was her last year of competition.[5] It was not the first or last time Walsh would announce her retirement, only to renege again and again.

Walsh did not show up to race Stephens at another AAU meet in Chicago in March 1936. "I'll meet her in the Olympics," she told the *Plain Dealer*.[6] For some reason, Walsh was in Chicago at the time and personally congratulated Stephens on her new 50-meter world record of 6.6. A *Polish American Review* photo shows Stephens receiving an award from meet officials. A dour Walsh is in the background, looking smart in a white skirt, dark blazer, and feather hat, but obviously indifferent to the proceedings. The tagline reads, "Stella Walsh, foremost sprint star of the world."[7] Walsh claimed that Käthe Krauss and another German sprinter—Marie Dollinger—would give her more trouble than Stephens in Berlin, but after Stephens's decisive defeat of Walsh in 1935, Walsh knew in the back of her mind that she could not beat the big Missourian.

There was a chance Walsh and Stephens would not meet in Berlin, as a boycott of the Olympics loomed. Hitler's bellicosity increased in the mid-1930s, and the tyrannical character of the Third Reich was laid bare. In March 1935, Hitler announced that Germany was rebuilding its army and air force in contravention of the Versailles Treaty. In September, the Reichstag passed the Nuremberg Laws, which made marriage between Aryan Germans and Jews illegal, and formalized legal discrimination. Political opponents were being thrown into concentration camps, and the overt persecution of Jews increased.

Walsh personally witnessed the Nazi campaign against the Jews at track meets in Germany. In 1935, she told the *New York Times* that Germany's treatment of Jews was "very bad indeed." At a dual meet between the Polish and German national teams in Dresden in August, she said that one of her Jewish teammates, hurdler Mary Friewald, had endured humiliating denunciations from German athletes and fans. "Like every other athlete," Walsh said, "I'd hate to have anything prevent the Olympic Games. I hope things can be straightened out. Yes, there are anti-Jewish signs up. The Jews have to compete against themselves in their own clubs."[8]

Fascist understanding of the value of sport, first championed by Italian dictator Benito Mussolini, was rooted in nineteenth-century European sporting culture. Fascist images of a virile, brave, and disciplined male paralleled the aims of the YMCA's "muscular Christianity" and the lessons learned through German Turnvater Jahn's gymnastic drill. The Olympic movement had deviated from Coubertin's vision of individuals competing in a peaceful, cosmopolitan atmosphere to a test of national strength. Italian Fascists and German Nazis took the medal count as an objective measure of where the nation stood in the racial hierarchy. Fascist sport was largely a masculine endeavor. If women were allowed to do sport at all, it was to prepare them to bear healthy, strong children to replenish the racial stock.

The ideal of the blonde, blue-eyed, Spartan-like German athlete fit into the party's mythology connecting Greece and the Aryan race. The Nazis accused the Jews of injecting "sensationalism" into sport and bringing foreign sports to Germany solely for profit. After initial indifference to sport, the Nazis began to promote physical exercise as a means to perfect the body and a way to strengthen the vigor of the nation.

In 1931, the IOC awarded Berlin the 1936 Olympics. When Adolf Hitler became chancellor in January 1933, the IOC set a precedent by allowing the Olympics to stay in Berlin; the IOC has since awarded the Games to other such undemocratic regimes as Moscow in 1980 and Beijing in 2008. At first, the Nazis had little interest in the Olympics, but propaganda chief Joseph Goebbels realized that Germany had much to gain by putting on a successful show. Los Angeles had commercialized the 1932 Olympics by engaging the local business community and the Hollywood film industry. The Nazis did not put on the Olympics for economic gain, but to rally the German people behind the regime, confirm Nazi ideology about the superiority of the Aryan race, and assure the rest of the world that Germany was a peaceful country. The Nazis inaugurated the first "torch relay" from Athens through the Balkans to Berlin to connect the Third Reich to the ancient Olympics. The neoclassical architecture of the Berlin Olympic Stadium further connected the Germans to the Greeks.

The Olympics would also serve Hitler's short-term foreign policy goal of assuring the world that Germany was a "normal" state and that he had no aggressive designs on his neighbors. Of course, Walsh's homeland was one of Hitler's targets. The Wehrmacht was not yet ready for a major war, so Hitler had to bide his time, especially after he had gambled by remilitarizing the Rhineland in March 1936. If the French and British had acted to oust the Germans from the Rhineland, Hitler had planned to retreat.

Shortly after the Nazis came to power in early 1933, they imposed a boy-cott on Jewish businesses. Theodor Lewald, head of the German Olympic Committee, was sacked because he was half Jewish. The 1935 Nuremberg Laws codified discrimination against German Jews. The *Washington Post*, the *Los Angeles Times*, and the American Federation of Labor declared in favor of a boycott. When judge Jeremiah T. Mahoney, head of the AAU and a member of the American Olympic Committee (AOC), argued against sending a U.S. team to Berlin, the boycott movement gained momentum.[9]

AOC president Avery Brundage was adamantly opposed to the boycott, pointing out that during a fact-finding tour of Germany he had found nothing amiss in the state of German athletics. German handlers care-fully managed the tour, designated which sports facilities the delegation could visit, and convinced Brundage that the German government was not discriminating against Jewish athletes. He declared that the Berlin Games would go on as planned. Critics of the AOC pointed to a pamphlet that the Nazi Party had sent to German sports organizations about the Berlin Olympics, warning that we "can see no positive value in permitting dirty Jews and Negroes to travel through our country and compete in athletics with our best." Confronted with evidence that the Nazi regime was indeed discriminating against Jews, athletes or not, Brundage charged that there was a "Jewish–Communist conspiracy" to keep the United States out of the Olympics.[10] He warned about the disproportionate influence of Jews in both countries and the possible need for anti-Jewish laws in the United States:

> As it was in Germany, a great deal of the German nation was led by the Jews and not by the Germans themselves. Even in the U.S.A. the day may come when you will have to stop the activities of the Jews. They are intelligent and unscru-pulous . . . they must be kept within certain limits.[11]

Most American Olympians were opposed to the boycott. Eleanor Holm, the 1932 gold medalist in the 100-meter backstroke, declared, "The United States should not withdraw from the 1936 Olympics. Why should I, or any other athlete, be penalized for the action of Joe Zilch, or anybody else named Hitler who has nothing whatsoever to do with us?"[12] Helen Stephens received many letters imploring her to sit out the Berlin Games. She recalled AOC officials saying, "We don't want to get involved." Stephens wanted to run in Berlin, and polls showed that a clear majority of Americans opposed a boycott.[13]

A number of American athletes of Jewish heritage decided against going to Berlin, including Lillian Copeland, the U.S. gold medalist in the discus at the 1932 Los Angeles Olympics. Copeland was the daughter of a Polish Jew from Grodno. She was still a world-class discus thrower in 1936, having won several U.S. national championships in the early 1930s. As one of the two women on the American team at the 1935 World Maccabiah Games in Tel Aviv, Copeland won the discus, shot put, and javelin. The German team of 184 Jewish athletes was by far the largest at Tel Aviv, and Copeland heard from them firsthand about the Nazis' anti-Semitic policies. Copeland accused Brundage of "intentionally concealing the truth" about the nature of Hitler's regime. Although Copeland did not go to the Berlin Olympics, she was not an outspoken advocate for the boycott. Evelyn Furtsch, Copeland's teammate at the 1932 Los Angeles Olympics, went public in her support of it.[14]

Other top athletes also boycotted the Berlin Games, including Tulane University sprinter Herman Neugass and Harvard University teammates Milton Green and Norman Cahners. Basketball was on the Olympic program for the first time in Berlin, but the Long Island University basketball team, one of the favorites in the qualifying tournament at Madison Square Garden, decided against participating. The tournament came at the end of a long college basketball season and conflicted with players' classes, and several of the Long Island players were beginning baseball season. But with four Jewish players on the team, the anti-Semitic Nazi regime was a decisive factor in their decision to stay home.

Jesse Owens was torn about what to do. In November 1935, he declared in a radio interview, "If there is discrimination against minorities in Germany then we must withdraw from the Olympics."[15] Walter White, secretary of the NAACP, wrote Owens a letter pleading with him to stay home: "I am sure that your stand will be applauded by many people in all parts of the world," White argued, "as your participation under the present situation in Germany would alienate many high-minded people who are awakening to the dangers of intolerance wherever it raises its head." Owens's coach urged him to compete, and in early 1936, Owens changed his mind.[16]

Poland's great discus thrower Jadwiga Wajs was of Jewish heritage, but she decided to go to Berlin. Sprinter Tollien Schuurmann of the Netherlands, who had beaten Walsh twice in 1933, joined many other Jewish athletes in boycotting the Olympics.

Walsh and Wajs did not have to worry that the Polish government would stand in the way of their team going to the Berlin Olympics. Poland's boycott movement was among the weakest in Europe. At first Jews had been optimistic about their future in the new Poland. The first Congress of Jewish Poles pledged their allegiance to the state in 1919: "The Poles of the Jewish faith, penetrated with a sincere feeling of love for Poland, will, in spite of the difficult conditions of their existence, serve their country as devoted sons, and will always be ready to sacrifice their lives and fortunes of its benefit and glory."[17] Polish Jews would be disappointed. The parties on the right were openly anti-Semitic, and as the Depression worsened in the 1930s, the left became indifferent to Poland's minorities. Although the Polish parliament never passed racial laws, discrimination against Jews in the population was the norm. Most Polish Catholics had little sympathy for the plight of Polish Jews, let alone German Jews.

The Polish government also had a difficult balancing act between Nazi Germany and Soviet Russia. Both countries were mortal enemies bent on retaking territories lost after World War I. The specter of Bolshevism brought shudders throughout Europe; for many, Fascism and Nazism seemed to be the lesser of two evils. The European right coined the phrase "Better Hitler than Stalin." Josef Beck, the Polish foreign minister in the 1930s, was also of this mind, and Polish diplomacy leaned toward Nazi Germany. Each winter, Hitler's right-hand man, Hermann Goering, went on a hunting trip to Poland. Aside from retaking Danzig and the Polish Corridor, Hitler was unsure about what to do with the rest of the Polish state. His big target was the Soviet Union, and for a time he imagined Poland as a puppet state much like Slovakia became shortly before the start of World War II.

As Jewish organizations throughout the world were calling for a boycott of the Summer Olympics, the success of the 1936 Winter Games in the Bavarian resort of Garmisch undermined their cause. The Nazis carefully toned down their anti-Semitic rhetoric during the Winter Olympics and took down any anti-Jewish signs that visitors to southern Germany might see. The Berlin Olympics would go on as planned, and the Nazi regime was afforded an opportunity to prove it could organize the best Olympics ever, show off the superiority of its athletes, and present a peaceful Germany to the rest of the world. The Berlin Games proved to be a spectacular success for the Nazi regime.

The big news in European newspapers as the Olympics neared was the Spanish Civil War, which broke out in July. Italian and German forces came to the aid of General Francisco Franco's right-wing nationalist rebellion. London and Paris were reluctant to support the increasingly leftist Spanish Republic, especially when Stalin began sending it supplies. The Western powers stayed on the sidelines as the Spanish Republic went down in flames in April 1939.

Forty-nine national teams went to the Berlin Olympics, the most ever. Unlike the Los Angeles Olympics, it was much cheaper for European teams to make it to Berlin. The Polish team consisted of 127 men and only seventeen women (three in track and field). Walsh arrived in Poland on July 10. One Polish periodical wrote, "She is our hope in the 100-meter sprint at the Berlin Olympics, where she will be involved in a sensational duel with Canadian Stephens."[18] Of course Stephens was from Missouri.

From left to right, Polish Olympians Maria Kwaśniewska, Jadwiga Wajs, and Walsh on the train from Warsaw to the 1936 Berlin Olympics. *Kurier Codzienny, Narodowe Archiwum Cyfrowe [National Digital Archive].*

Walsh and Wajs were Poland's only favorites to win medals in track and field. Janusz Kusociński, the gold medalist in the 10,000 meters at Los Angeles, had retired from competition. Walsh was ready. The Polish journal *Polacy Zagranica* wrote, "As much as we know from America, Walsh is in excellent form and should take first place in the 100 meters."[19] *Polish American Review* declared, "Walsh Walasiewicz [*sic*] is burning up the cinder path. . . . This Mercury-footed miss . . . announces herself to be in the best physical and mental condition for the strenuous events in which she will participate."[20]

Walsh beat her own world record in the 80-meter dash at the Polish Women's Championships in mid-July. At a meet in Warsaw a week before the start of the Olympics, she equaled the world records in the 50 and 100 meters, the latter time in 11.6, which was Stephens's unofficial record. Although none of these times were recognized by the IAAF, Walsh seemed primed to defend her 100-meter Olympic title. In its July 29, 1936, installment, the *Plain Dealer* predicted that the Stephens–Walsh race would be the biggest "feminine feud" in Berlin.

The Nazis were determined to improve on the embarrassing showing of the German team at the 1932 Los Angeles Games. After finishing second to the United States at the 1928 Amsterdam Olympics, Germany fell to fourth at Los Angeles, winning only three gold medals. The German women's Olympic team at Berlin was the most formidable in the world, and its sprinters were expected to challenge Stephens and Walsh for gold in the 100 meters and win the 4 × 100 relay. One American reporter wrote, "With this fine pair [Marie Dollinger and Käthe Krauss] running against Helen Stephens and Poland's veteran, Stella Walsh, there should be fun at Berlin."[21]

The Nazis kept most of the German-Jewish athletes out of the Berlin Games. Everyone knew that Gretel Bergmann was one of the best high jumpers in the world, so it would be difficult for the German Olympic Committee to keep her off the team without risking a boycott from the Americans. Other countries might follow suit. Worried that the boycott movement was gaining momentum, the German Olympic organizers designated the regional championships in Stuttgart in late June and the German championships in Berlin on July 11 and 12 as the last chances to make the German Olympic team. In Stuttgart, Bergmann equaled the German high-jump record of 1.60 meters.

On July 15, the U.S. Olympic team set sail for Europe on the SS *Manhattan*. The boycott threat was over, and the Germans named their Olympic team on the same day. Although Bergmann was ranked as one of the top five high jumpers in the world, she was left off the team, allegedly for "recent levels of performance." "Damn it, I was one of the four best high jumpers in the world," Bergmann fumed. "And now because I came into the world as a Jew, they threw me away like an old shoe."[22] Three days after the Olympics ended, Bergmann went to the U.S. Consulate in Stuttgart to apply for emigration. In 1937, she left Germany for good.[23]

Bergmann vowed never to return to Germany, although the postwar West German Federal Republic was a democratic state and a NATO ally. In 1986 she declined an invitation to come to the fiftieth anniversary of the Berlin Games. "Although fifty years have passed since my exclusion from the German Olympic team in Berlin," she said, "My disappointment and bitterness have only slightly abated." In 1999 she finally accepted an offer to attend the opening ceremony of a Berlin sports arena named in her honor.[24]

The Nazis allowed one "half-Jew" on its women's Olympic team, fencer Helene Mayer. Mayer had been studying at Mills College in California, and she ignored pressure from American Jewish organizations not to return to Germany to compete. She did not think of herself as Jewish and at first was not particularly fond of sunny Southern California. After she and the other German athletes fared poorly at the Los Angeles Olympics, she offered this excuse: "Possibly, after I have been here longer, I will enjoy it very much, but now I find myself getting so tired in the afternoon. It has not been good for our team. I am not alone in my defeat. Our whole team had troubles. Something here is not so good for us."[25]

The Nazis warned the German press not to cover Mayer's arrival in Hamburg, but she was a favorite among German fans. Shops were selling little figurines of her. Evidently she liked the cold, gray weather in Berlin better, because she won a silver medal. In one of the most memorable images of the Berlin Games, Mayer proudly gave the Nazi salute on the winners' podium. On the top rung was Hungarian gold medalist Ilona Elek. She was Jewish but evaded Adolf Eichmann's deportation of Hungarian Jews to Auschwitz in 1944. At the 1948 London Olympics, Elek successfully defended her Olympic championship. Mayer returned to the United States after the Olympics, changed her name to Meyer, and became a U.S. citizen in 1940. In the early 1950s, she went back to West Germany and got married but was dead of cancer three years later, at the age of forty-two.

The big story on the SS *Manhattan* was the controversy surrounding Holm, one of the world's best backstrokers. She was only fourteen when she took fifth in the 100-meter backstroke at the Amsterdam Olympics. The comely Holm worked with the Ziegfeld Follies for a short time but left the revue to train for the Los Angeles Games. This time she won the gold medal in her specialty. Holm and fellow swimmer Helene Madison were the darlings of the press at Los Angeles. In qualifying for Berlin in 1936, Holm was the first U.S. woman to make three Olympic teams.

Holm was the life of the party on the Atlantic crossing, although she was married to bandleader Art Jarrett at the time. Invited to one all-night party with some sportswriters, she got stinking drunk. Brundage warned her about breaking curfew, but at a stopover in Cherbourg, France, Holm allegedly got so inebriated that Brundage threw her off the team. "All I did was drink a couple of glasses of champagne," she complained. She claimed that Brundage was exacting revenge because she had repulsed his romantic overtures: "I was everything Brundage hated. I had a few dollars, and athletes were supposed to be poor. I worked in nightclubs, and athletes shouldn't do that."[26] Holm was devastated at the time, but the incident made her a celebrity. "I got more publicity than Hitler," she quipped.[27] Holm went on to act in a few Hollywood films, most notably in the role of Jane in the B-movie *Tarzan's Revenge* (1938), which costars 1936 Olympic decathlon champion Glenn Morris as "Tarzan the Ape Man."

The Polish team arrived in Berlin on July 29. The 3,638 male athletes at the Berlin Games were housed in the Olympic Village on the western edge of Berlin, ten miles from the Reichssportfeld, the site of the track and field events. The Nazi goal of revising the Versailles Treaty was revealed in the naming of the Olympic Village houses. Each was identified by a German town, some of which had been in German territories lost to France and Poland after World War I. Much to the dismay of the Polish team, one house was called "Danzig," the German port city that had been ceded to the League of Nations. Poles feared the loss of the city they called Gdańsk would begin the dismemberment of their country. Indeed, World War II began on September 1, 1939, when a German gunboat shelled Polish naval installations near Danzig. During the Berlin Games that seemed to be a mad nightmare.

At the 1932 Los Angeles Olympics, Walsh and her fellow female Olympians had stayed at the Chapman Park Hotel, far away from the men at the Olympic

Village. In Berlin, the 328 women athletes were again housed separately at the Friesenhaus on the Reichssportfeld. While in Los Angeles, some athletes had complained that the Chapman was too far from the training facilities, but the Friesenhaus was situated in the shadow of the Olympic Stadium, a short walk to most of the Olympic venues. The women were assigned a roommate, but as usual, Walsh insisted on having her own room.

The Germans organized a memorable event. They wined and dined their foreign guests; added pageantry to the festivities; and introduced such new innovations as the torch relay, electronic timing, and photo finishes. The podium medal ceremony, first used at the British Empire Games in 1930, and adopted at the 1932 Los Angeles Olympics, was now exploited to exhibit German athletic superiority. One French journalist gushed about the impressive opening ceremony: "Never was the war threat on the Rhine less than during these moments. Never were the French more popular in Germany than on this occasion. It was a demonstration, but one of comradeship and the will for peace."[28] Approximately 1 million spectators attended the 1932 Los Angeles Games, while Berlin drew 3.7 million. Another 300 million listened to the Olympics on the radio.

The Berlin Games were a huge propaganda success for the Nazi regime. After Germany's political and economic troubles of the early 1930s, the Nazis seemed to have righted the ship, and the Olympics further legitimized the Nazi dictatorship. For a regime that was trying to establish its credentials at home and abroad, merely having the top teams in the world competing on German soil was a victory. Holm said that she and her teammates "were just amazed with the Nazis' organization."[29] According to historian Arnd Krüger, the "German people liked their Olympic Games. This was the way Germans liked to see themselves: open to the world, tolerant, splendid hosts, perfect organizers. It was a complete sell-out." For decades after World War II, Germans refrained from criticizing what others were calling the "Nazi Olympics."[30]

The Nazis had purged Berlin of its edgy, cosmopolitan feel. In the 1920s, the city was in the vanguard of modern art, architecture, theater, and movies, exemplified by Josef von Sternberg's acclaimed film *Der Blaue Engel* [The Blue Angel] (1930), in which upstanding school teacher Dr. Immanuel Rath's life is ruined when he falls for Lola Lola (Marlene Dietrich), a singer in a sleazy nightclub. Now all of that was considered culturally decadent. Expressionism was replaced by kitschy classicism. The Nazis pulled works of modern art by Jews and others, and created an exhibition called "degenerate art." Philistines agreed that these unintelligible works were un-German. During the Olympics, the Nazis took down anti-Semitic signs and pulled anti-Semitic newspapers and magazines off the newsstands. The overt persecution of Jews, homosexuals, Social Democrats, Communists, and other "undesirables" was temporarily halted.[31] The Nazis could not tamp down all the anti-Semitic demonstrations. Betty Robinson recalled seeing swastikas on Jewish stores in Berlin, and Nazi street thugs were heard chanting, "Wenn die Olympiade sind vorbei, schlagen wir die Juden zu brei" [When the Olympics are over, we will beat the Jews to a pulp].[32]

No one paid much attention to the notorious concentration camp of Sachsenhausen, located about thirty miles north of the German capital. Pierre Coubertin said that Berlin lived up to the highest ideals of the Olympic Games and thought that Rome and the Italian Fascists should get the 1940 Olympics. Responding to some French journalists who claimed that the Games had been "disfigured," Coubertin praised Hitler directly for holding an event that had "magnificently served, and by no means disfigured, the Olympic ideal."[33] "What's the difference between propaganda for tourism—like in the Los Angeles Olympics of 1932," he asked, "or for a political regime?"[34]

August 3 was a typical gray, overcast day as the women's 100-meter preliminaries began. The contrast between the blue skies in Los Angeles four years earlier and cold and rainy Berlin was stark. The weather in Germany was miserable for most of the Olympics. The women nicknamed the Friesenhaus—their residence during the Games—the "Freezin' House." The men's 100-meter final was scheduled for the same day. Fellow Clevelanders Walsh and Owens, a Pole and an African American, were running in the capital of the Third Reich in front of Hitler, his entourage, and thousands of Germans, trying to embarrass the Aryan master race and Nazi theories about the inferiority of Slavs and black Africans. Owens blew away the competition to win the first of four gold medals.

For at least the next twenty-four hours, Owens and Walsh—the 100-meter champion four years earlier—could claim to be the "fastest man" and the "fastest woman," respectively, on earth. Owens was the sensation of the Berlin Games, taking home three more gold medals, in the 200 meters, the 4×100-meter relay, and the broad jump. Much has been made of Hitler's refusal to congratulate

Cleveland's Jesse Owens at the 1936 Berlin Olympics. *Library of Congress.*

Owens on his victories, but the story is fabricated. After Hitler had personally congratulated some German gold medalists in his private box, the IOC warned him against repeating this breach of protocol with any athlete. Hitler obliged, although he continued to receive athletes in a room beneath the stands, including Helen Stephens after her win in the 100 meters. Although Owens was certainly an embarrassment to Nazi racial theorists, they explained it away as a manifestation of the animal-like traits of the Negro race. The German press gave Owens's exploits full front-page coverage. Even the radically anti-Semitic Nazi party organ *Völkischer Beobachter* [Folkish Observer] published photos of Owens, along with articles on his gold-medal performances.

Goebbels financed filmmaker Leni Riefenstahl's groundbreaking documentary of the Berlin Games. *Olympia* (1938) is not an overtly political film, but rather an attempt to link Nazi Germany to ancient Greece. Riefenstahl did not include the women's 100 meters in her film or the women's discus competition, although she did incorporate a montage of an ancient male Greek discus thrower with the nude German Erwin Huber in the famous coiled, ready position. Her camera fawns over the male athletes' bodies, especially in the nighttime pole vault competition and the mesmerizing diving sequence at the end of the film. Despite Goebbels's objection, Riefenstahl documented Jesse Owens's wins as well, prompting some critics to highlight her Fascist infatuation with the perfect human male form and the implicit rejection of the physically handicapped.

Stephens, Walsh, and Krauss easily won their first preliminary heats. Stephens beat Krauss in the semifinals, running an 11.5. Dollinger edged out Walsh in the second semi, with both timed in 11.7. No one seemed capable of challenging Stephens. In sprinting, two-tenths of a second is an eternity, and deep down Walsh knew that unless Stephens was disqualified, fell down, or got injured, she would not repeat as Olympic champion. Walsh had to be healthy to have any chance, but the Polish press reported that she was suffering from a right thigh injury. German doctors told Walsh that she could not run in the final with the bad leg, but four Polish doctors said she was fit enough to start and gave her injections to deaden the pain.

The women's 100-meter final was held the next day. Once again it was overcast and even colder, at sixty-three degrees Fahrenheit. It was the first time since Stephens's win in St. Louis a year and a half earlier that the world's two best female sprinters were squaring off. According to a United Press International reporter, "It's written all over her [Walsh's] face as she digs her starting holes with a shovel. Next to her is the girl who displaced her as the fastest femme—Helen Stephens, the country girl from Missouri. Helen laughs as she readies herself for the run down the straightaway. She knows she is tops."[35] Dollinger was in lane one, Stephens in lane four, Krauss in lane five, and Walsh on the outside in lane six. Stephens could see Walsh from the middle lane.

At the starter's gun, Stephens got off the line together with Krauss and Dollinger, while Walsh lagged behind, her start slowed by the injury. After thirty meters, Walsh was fourth. According to the Official Record of the Berlin Olympics, "by the 50 meter mark she [Stephens] had left all her competitors behind and sprinted across the finishing line in 11.5 seconds with a running style that many men athletes might well envy."[36] Stephens cruised to the tape in an Olympic record time, Walsh came in second at 11.7, and Krauss was third at 11.9. Stephens's Olympic record stood for twenty-four years, until U.S. sprinter Wilma Rudolph broke it at the 1960 Rome Olympics. Disappointed but resigned to the fact that Stephens was simply faster, Walsh congratulated her with a handshake and even managed a faint smile. A photo of the three medalists on the awards stand during the playing of the U.S. national anthem captures Krauss's right arm raised in the Nazi salute, Stephens in a traditional military salute, and Walsh, looking forlorn, with her arms at her side. If Walsh had run for the United States in 1932, American women would have won three straight 100-meter gold medals.

On the same day as the women's 100-meter final, Jadwiga Wajs placed second in the discus. *Przegląd Sportowy* [Sports Review] hailed "our brave women" with the headline, "Two Starts, Two Silver Medals."[37] "Bravo!" declared *Kurjer Warszawski* upon Walsh earning the silver medal, while pointing out that she had been bothered by a bad leg.[38] Indeed, the performances of the Polish women far outdid those of their male counterparts. Maria Kwaśniewska took bronze in the javelin, giving the Polish women three medals. Although the Polish men outnumbered the women 127 to seventeen at Berlin, they also brought home three medals (one silver and two bronze), but none in track and field. The other big Olympic news in Polish newspapers was the success of the Polish soccer team, which reached the semifinals before losing to Austria. The Polish

Walsh congratulating Stephens on her victory in the 100 meters at the Berlin Olympics.
Kurier Codzienny, Narodowe Archiwum Cyfrowe [National Digital Archive].

press proudly reported that on the medals table, Poland came in fifteenth of the forty-nine participating countries.

The Poles were disappointed that their "flyer" had lost the most prestigious medal in track and field, but it came as a surprise when a Polish journalist from *Kurjer Poranny* [Morning Courier] hinted that Stephens was not really a woman. It smacked of sour grapes for the Poles to call her a cheat. One paper suggested that Helen should be called "Henry." On August 4, 1936, *Kurjer Warszawski* wrote,

> [Stephens] could not have been more comfortable running around in Berlin, even if the Olympics had been held in the time of Frederick the Great: without any doubt she would have been drafted into the grenadier's regiment. Miss Stephens does not betray femininity. She has broad shoulders, fully masculine arm muscles and legs, and runs like men. In this [record] time Stephens would have gotten the top place in the Polish men's championships.

The Associated Press relayed the story to several prominent American newspapers. It was rumored that the IOC had forced Stephens to undergo a visual examination from German doctors, which she passed. In an interview with the *Los Angeles Times*, Stephens's mother was incredulous: "Helen is absolutely a girl. I had better not say what I think of anyone who would charge that she is anything else. No one else in all Helen's life has ever raised such a question. Helen leads a normal girl's social life. She enjoys dancing and attending dances regularly at college."[39] The controversy continued in February 1937, when *Look* magazine ran a photo of Stephens next to an article titled "Is This a Man or a Woman?"

Evidently Hitler saw something he liked in the 5-foot-11, 165-pound sprinter from Missouri. After the 100-meter final, he invited Stephens back to his reception room beneath the stands. The *Volkischer Beobachter* published a big front-page photo of Hitler giving Stephens an autograph. According to Stephens, who sometimes embellished her stories, Hitler made a pass at her and invited her to his Alpine retreat in Berchtesgaden: "He came into the room and gave me this Nazi salute. Well, I just gave him an old-fashioned Missouri handshake, but that didn't seem to faze him none. He even pinched me and invited me back to his place for the weekend, that old rascal." Stephens also claimed that Hitler told her, "You should be running for Germany. You're a true Aryan type, tall, blonde, blue eyes."[40]

Several days later, Stephens won another gold medal in the 4 × 100 relay when the favored German team, including Krauss and Dollinger, dropped the baton on the last pass to Ilse Doerffeldt. The Germans were leading at the time, but Stephens probably would have caught Doerffeldt on the last leg. Newsreels showed Hitler throwing up his hands in despair when the German team fumbled the pass.

Forty years later, Walsh gave an interview to a Connecticut journal claiming that after the 100-meter final, Hitler had made a pass at her as well:

> Hitler wanted to show Poland what a good neighbor he was. He came down and put his arm around me, shook my hand, and introduced me to [Heinrich] Himmler, Goering, and his whole clique. Even though I had finished in front of two German girls who were supposed to win, he made a big fuss for the press about how happy he was to have a Polish girl win a medal.[41]

If these stories are true, there was an epidemic of romantic advances at the Olympics. Even Riefenstahl got into it. She claimed that when the stadium lights went down for the decathlon awards ceremony, gold medalist Glenn Morris "headed straight to me. I held out my hand and congratulated him. Then he grabbed me in his arms, ripped off my blouse, and kissed my breasts, right in the middle of the stadium, in front of a hundred thousand spectators."[42] Of course, this was not the only time that the most famous Nazi film director hedged the truth. After the war she claimed that she had had little to do with the Nazi regime.

Both Stephens and Walsh were probably flattered by the attention they got from the leader of one of Europe's great powers, even if the guy was pasty white, doughy, and homely. From the inception of women's events at the Olympics, women athletes had struggled to gain acceptance. They were often ridiculed for breaking customary gender roles and their lack of femininity. Their critics grew louder two years after the Berlin Olympics, when a story broke about the sex of German high jumper Dora Ratjen. Ratjen won the German high jump championship before the Olympics, but teammate Elfried Kaun won the bronze medal in Berlin with a jump of 1.60 meters, matching Bergmann's personal best. Ratjen jumped 1.58 meters, placing fourth and just missing the medal stand. Ratjen's finish precluded any further inquiry into her somewhat odd behavior and questions about her masculine voice. Amid the discussion about the women athletes at the Berlin Olympics who looked like men, the German press wrote that the deepest voice actually belonged to Helen Stephens:

> [She had] a raw cowboy bass voice that sounded as if it came from a deep ravine. . . . On the first days, when this had not yet generally got around, there was always a bit of a panic in the Friesenhaus when Helen Stephens's masculine voice echoed through the corridors, for every girl of course thought that some male visitor had crept into the building, and that it was strictly forbidden.

Velma Dunn, the American silver medalist in the 10-meter platform dive, noted that Stephens acted "very mannish" and talked "lower than most men."[43]

Bergmann had roomed with Ratjen several times at high-jump competitions. Bergmann found her "strange" for avoiding the shower room with other women, wearing swim trunks in the locker room, and preferring to use a private bath, claiming that she was a little shy. Other athletes had made some of the same observations about Walsh's behavior.

Two years later, at the European Athletic Championships in Vienna, Ratjen won the high jump with a world-record jump of 1.70 meters. Walsh was there too, winning the 100 and 200 meters. As Ratjen got off the train from Vienna in Magdeburg, she was apprehended by the local police. Ratjen was charged with impersonating a woman, and her European championship medal was confiscated. Ibolya Czák of Hungary was moved up to first place.

The case was an embarrassment to the Reich. In 1939, the Magdeburg prosecutor dropped charges against Ratjen because she had lived as a woman her entire life, although she had now changed her gender identity and name to "Heinrich": "Fraud cannot be deemed to have taken place because there was no intention to reap financial reward," the prosecutor argued. "His activities and relations were always feminine."[44] Westerners were inclined to believe that the unscrupulous Nazis were behind a conspiracy to have Ratjen pose as a woman to win the high jump at Berlin, supposedly to make up for banning Bergmann.

Given the brutal character of the Nazi regime, many assumed that Hitler and his henchmen would go to any lengths to win, even by putting Ratjen up to the scam. During the Cold War, the West suspected the same gender-bending shenanigans of the Soviet Union. When Soviet women began to dominate the Olympics in the 1960s, the sex of some of the most successful Soviet women athletes, for example, sisters Tamara and Irena Press, was questioned.

In 1966, *Time* magazine falsely quoted Ratjen blaming the Nazis for concocting the hoax. Ratjen supposedly said that he ran "for the sake of the honor and glory of Germany. For three years I lived the life of a girl. It was most dull." Bergmann also saw it as a Nazi plot to replace her.[45] Germany easily topped the list of medal winners at Berlin anyway, capturing thirty-three gold, twenty-six silver, and thirty bronze medals.

The doctor who delivered Ratjen in 1918 determined that she was a girl, and she was raised that way all of her life. But early in puberty, Ratjen began to question her gender designation: "My parents brought me up as a girl," Dora told authorities after her arrest in 1938. "I therefore wore girl's clothes all my childhood. But from the age of ten or eleven I started to realize I wasn't female, but male; however, I never asked my parents why I had to wear women's clothes even though I was male."[46] There was precedent for Ratjen's case. Czechoslovakian Zdenka Koubka was a world-class middle distance runner in the early 1930s, and shortly after the Berlin Olympics she declared that she was transitioning to be a man. "I always thought I was a girl for the first part of my life," Zdenka told reporters. "And then about a year ago I began to realize that I wasn't a girl. Downy hair began to grow on the side of my face, and my manhood began to assert itself."[47] In 2009, the German weekly magazine *Der Spiegel* reported that there was no evidence that the Nazis had anything to do with a conspiracy to put Ratjen on the women's team.[48]

These controversies provided fodder for Olympic functionaries who had opposed women competing in track and field events from the start. After the Berlin Games, Brundage declared, "I am fed up to the ears with women as track and field competitors . . . [their] charms sink to less than zero. As swimmers and divers, girls are beautiful and adroit, as they are ineffective and unpleasing on the track."[49] Many of those who opposed women participating in track and field thought that swimming and diving were acceptable for females, but Velma Dunn recalled the following after she returned from the Olympics:

> At the end of the first week at USC [University of Southern California], the head of the department called me in, and she said that she hoped that I wasn't going to continue my competition, because it wasn't ladylike. That's the first

time I had ever thought of diving as not being ladylike. . . . I didn't dive for two years.[50]

None of the three ascendant women in American track and field in the 1930s, Walsh, Stephens, and Didrikson, were physical beauties in the classic sense. Their relatively plain and muscular traits did little to counter the existing biases about women athletes. As historian Jennifer H. Lansbury observed, "Their working-class backgrounds and 'mannish' appearances upset the middle-class sensibilities of physical education instructors, pushing women's track and field even further to the margins of white society."[51] Many fellow athletes commented on Walsh's masculine looks and unwillingness to change in the locker room before and after meets; Canadian Olympian Roxanne Atkins Andersen remembered that Walsh had insisted on a private dressing room. Jean Shiley, the high-jump gold medalist at the 1932 Los Angeles Games, called Walsh "strange."[52] Years later, Krauss's teammate Marie Dollinger, who finished fourth in the 100 meters at Berlin, remarked sarcastically, "You know, I was the only woman in the race."[53]

A week after the Olympics, Walsh and Stephens raced again in a meet in the western German town of Wuppertal. Stephens soundly beat Walsh twice in the 100 and 200 meters, leaving no doubt about who was the fastest woman in the world. It was the last time the two rivals would step foot on the same cinder track. A few days later, Walsh returned to Warsaw to set an unofficial world record in the 80 meters.

In late September 1936, Walsh took the *Batory* from Gdynia back to New York. She was unhappy with her life in Poland, which had been a disappointment. Despite her Polish background, she was an American through and through, and was used to a vastly different lifestyle, a higher standard of living, and the familiarity of her hometown of Cleveland and the nurturing of her family and fellow Polish Americans. The fact that Walsh spoke Polish fluently was not a strong enough link to her country of birth. On October 11, she was back home in Cleveland.

Athletes need a foil to amplify their accomplishments and fame. In the 1960s, golfer Arnold Palmer had Jack Nicklaus; in the 1970s, Muhammad Ali had Joe Frazier; and in the 1980s, the Boston Celtics and Larry Bird had the Los Angeles Lakers and Magic Johnson. Stella Walsh is often forgotten because her greatest potential rivals—Didrikson and Stephens—quit track. Walsh never mentioned Stephens as her greatest rival. Maybe Walsh acknowledged that the Babe was a great competitor because Didrikson competed in different track and field events than those she participated in and quit track to go golfing. Walsh always had the kindest words for Kinue Hitomi, calling her the finest woman athlete she ever met.

After the Olympics, Stephens returned to William Woods College in Fulton. She turned professional in 1937, playing basketball for the famous All-American Red Heads. Walsh returned to her old Blepp-Coombs team, but there is no record of their meeting on the basketball court. Stephens eventually formed the semipro Helen Stephens Olympics Co-eds, with backing from Harlem Globetrotters owner Abe Saperstein. The Co-eds barnstormed the country before the war and again from 1946 to 1953. Stephens even traveled with the House of David baseball team, doing sprints and throwing the shot put. She was also an avid golfer, bowler, and swimmer.

In 1975, Stephens was inducted into the National Track and Field Hall of Fame, along with her old rival, Stella Walsh. Like Walsh, Stephens could not walk away from the thrill of competition. A year before she died in 1994, the Olympic champion was still running in senior races.

6

The Greatest
Woman Athlete

Naturally I would like to run for the United States this year, but I realize
that is impossible. Since I am now a citizen here, it probably wouldn't
be considered patriotic to compete for Poland, but I would like one more
opportunity to run in the Olympics.

—*Stella Walsh before the 1948 London Olympics*

In the fall of 1938, Polish sport authorities offered Stella Walsh a job as a
national physical education trainer, but Walsh declined the position, explaining that she did not want to jeopardize her amateur status. Walsh wanted to
leave Poland anyway. Life was hard enough in her depressed Cleveland, but
the standard of living in Poland was markedly lower. Every chance she got
she left Poland to compete in meets in North America and visit her parents
back home. In the mid-1930s, she sailed back and forth across the Atlantic at
least ten times.

Walsh was happy that her studies in Warsaw were over. She had never
adapted to life in the country of her birth. She was a relative unknown on
the streets of Warsaw—a university student like any other. It was no time
to be caught in Eastern Europe anyway. With little opposition from Britain
and France to his unilateral breaches of the Versailles Treaty, Hitler was
becoming increasingly bold. In a November 1937 meeting with his financial advisors and top generals, Hitler laid out his plans (in the so-called

Hossbach Memorandum of the meeting) to revise Germany's eastern borders by force in the early 1940s. Western appeasement encouraged him to move up the timetable.

Walsh went back to live with her parents on Clement Avenue. She did not hold down a regular job during this period but was in the prime of her athletic career. She relied on local clubs to subsidize her travel to track and field meets. Walsh joined the Polish Girls' Olympic Club of Ohio, which won the first Polish American Olympic Games in 1937, in Pittsburgh. Walsh was the club's one-woman show, winning all but one of the ten events she entered.

The *Plain Dealer* followed Walsh's exploits closely, and her name repeatedly popped up in the news, even when it had nothing to do with her career on the track. In 1938, Shaker Heights police set up a sting operation to nab muggers who were active in the area. One cop dressed as a woman and chased down a would-be mugger. Sportswriter James Doyle joked that the robber "must have thought for a few seconds that he'd made the mistake of holding up Stella Walsh."[1] On July 7, 1939, the newspaper reported that Walsh had thrown the fastest ball recorded by the "speedometer" at a Cleveland Indians baseball game.

Few athletes of her time, let alone a Polish woman from Cleveland, were such international stars. In September 1937, Walsh represented the American Falcons in the Falcon World Games in Katowice, Poland. Afterward, she went on a tour of Europe, running in meets in Berlin, Vienna, and Budapest. In the Polish city of Drohobycz in August, Walsh unofficially shattered three world records, in the 80 meters, 100 yards, and broad jump.[2] Back in Cleveland the next summer, she supposedly clipped a whopping .4 seconds off her 100-yard world record, but it was wind-aided (it must have been a big gust). At the second Polish American Olympic Games in Pittsburgh in June 1938, Walsh won nine of ten women's events, losing only to her neighborhood friend Frances Sobchak in the high jump. On July 5, Walsh left again for Europe, to compete in the European Athletic Championships, her biggest meet since the Olympics. Several weeks before the championships, she competed in a meet in Warsaw, where she set an unofficial world record in the broad jump.

The European Championships took place on September 17 and 18, in Austria, which by then was part of the Third Reich. Six months earlier, the German Army had marched into Hitler's homeland. The Anschluss of Austria was

Polish ambassador Jerzy Potocki honors Walsh in Pittsburgh, 1938. *Kurier Codzienny, Narodowe Archiwum Cyfrowe [National Digital Archive].*

Hitler's first aggressive move outside of Germany's borders, and the Western powers did not react. The West was divided about the nature of the German threat, in part because of the success of the Berlin Olympics. The Nazis had shown the world that the remilitarization of the Rhineland in March 1936 did not threaten France and that Hitler had nothing but peaceful intentions. Many visitors came away from Berlin believing that anti-Nazi propaganda was unwarranted. Showcasing Germany through the Olympics provided fodder for those in France and Great Britain who had favorable views of Nazism, credited Hitler with bringing the German economy back to life, and wanted to avoid another European war at any cost. Even the Poles were hopeful. Polish artist Jan Parandowski won a gold medal in the art competition at the 1936 Berlin Olympics and wrote these optimistic words about the meaning of the quadrennial event:

> There is an ideal—we can even call it commandment—to which twentieth-century mankind aspires and which it expects; the commandment of peace. In Antiquity the voice announcing the Olympic Games disarmed fighters, put an end to animosity and discord, and, although this divine truce only lasted a few months, sometimes it lasted whole years.[3]

The Berlin Olympics served apologists for Hitler's repression of Jews and political opponents, and justified acceptance of Hitler's disregard for the Versailles Treaty. Even the release of Leni Riefenstahl's seemingly apolitical documentary *Olympia* in 1938, contributed to the Reich's propaganda campaign. In September, Hitler promised British prime minster Neville Chamberlain at Munich that the Czech Sudetenland was his last territorial objective. The brutal Kristallnacht pogrom against German Jews that November belied Hitler's assurances that the Nazi regime was no threat to Europe. Riefenstahl expected a big welcome in Hollywood that fall, but the movie industry shunned her.

Hitler's interest in Austria and Czechoslovakia was strategic rather than a sincere desire to bring the Germans in the former Austrian Empire into the Third Reich. Consolidating control of Germany's southern flank would pave the way for revision of the most hated provision of the Versailles Treaty, the loss of German territory to Poland. Most interwar German leaders agreed that the border with Poland was untenable. Hitler was no different in wanting to revise Germany's eastern border with Poland, but he knew that a war on

Poland might again bring the World War I alliance against Germany. He was not ready for that yet, so he moved cautiously to prepare for war.

His first objective was to control Austria, either through a puppet government or annexation. As the crisis unfolded in the spring of 1938, Austrian chancellor Kurt Schuschnigg proposed a plebiscite, asking Austrians if they wanted to stay independent or go into the Reich. Worried that Austrians would oppose the Anschluss, Hitler hurriedly ordered the German Army to invade Austria. Cheering crowds along the way to Vienna prompted Hitler to incorporate the country into the Reich. The British and French had no stomach for fighting Germany on behalf of the independence of the Austrians, who were, after all, ethnic Germans.

There is historical controversy about the depth of Austrians' support for the Anschluss. Many Austrians were opposed to the Third Reich, as evidenced by numerous manifestations of Austrian patriotism at sporting events with Germany. In early April, the German national soccer team played Austria in the so-called *Anschluss* match at Vienna's famous Praterstadion (today the Ernst-Happel-Stadion). Austria won the game, 2–0, and fans put on a display of anti-Germanism that shocked attending Nazi officials. Austrians jeered and whistled during the playing of the German national anthem, chided German fans, and taunted the German players. In games between Austrian and German teams during the war, the German secret police reported many incidents of Austrian fans heckling and committing acts of vandalism against German players and other representatives of the Third Reich.

Despite Hitler's saber rattling, there was no significant opposition in Europe to holding the European Championships in Austria. Walsh was still one of the most well-known figures on the women's European track and field circuit, and at age twenty-seven she had already won four "best athlete" awards from the Polish journal *Przeglad Sportowy*, a mark that still stands. The European championships at the Praterstadion promised a rematch between Walsh and Käthe Krauss, the veteran German sprinter who had finished third to Walsh's second in the 100 meters at the Berlin Olympics. Running for Poland, Walsh bested Krauss in both the 100 and 200 meters, and took second in the broad jump. Walsh also anchored Poland's silver medalist 4 × 100 relay team. She was the star of the meet and looked forward to competing for Poland again at the 1940 Olympics in Tokyo. World War II scuttled the Games.

Walsh at the 1938 European Track and Field Championships in Vienna. *Kurier Codzienny, Narodowe Archiwum Cyfrowe [National Digital Archive].*

The European Championships took place in the midst of the Sudetenland crisis, which put Europe on the precipice of war. After the Anschluss of Austria, Hitler set his sights on Czechoslovakia, which was now surrounded on three sides by Germany. Three million Germans lived in the Sudetenland, and Hitler was intent on a war against Czechoslovakia to incorporate the region into Germany. Czechoslovakia was defenseless without this strategic, mountainous area. If Czechoslovakia went, Poland was exposed too.

Chamberlain went to Germany three times in September, in a desperate attempt to keep the peace. In complete disregard of the Czechoslovaks, on September 12 Chamberlain offered Hitler the Sudetenland—if Hitler agreed not to invade the rest of rump Czechoslovakia. Hitler agreed, and on September 22, Chamberlain met Hitler again at the Rhine River resort of Bad Godesberg to finalize the deal. Hitler, disgusted with Chamberlain's diplomacy and bent on a military campaign against Czechoslovakia, rejected it. Chamberlain flew back to Britain and told the nation to prepare for war.

That same night, Walsh was on a train from Austria back to Poland. Czechoslovak president Edvard Beneš had mobilized the army, and the border was swarming with Czechoslovak troops. Interwar Czechoslovak-Polish relations had been strained because Czechoslovakia had grabbed the predominantly Polish town of Cieszyn in 1919, and Poland had an eye on retaking the town if the Germans were awarded the Sudetenland. Walsh thought that the Czechoslovaks suspected her of being a Polish spy:

I was returning to Warsaw, Poland, from the international championships at Vienna, when I was detained for several hours while passing through the Sudetenland. . . . Passports were being examined in routine manner, but when my Polish service passport was seen I was picked up and held for several hours. When I asked what the confusion was, I learned that the border had been closed, and I was told that "if I knew what was good for me I would not even look through the windows." I was not even allowed to leave the train for a cup of coffee. I began to worry that war had been declared and was too frightened to ask questions.

The *Plain Dealer* wrote, "Walsh must have known how the celebrated Mata Hari felt during some of her harrowing escapades."[4]

Walsh was fortunate that war was narrowly averted. Facing an alliance of Czechoslovakia, Britain, France, and possibly the Soviet Union, Hitler finally agreed to the Munich Conference on September 30, and the Sudetenland was ceded to Germany. Chamberlain's critics forget the tense week after Bad Godesberg, when Britain and France stood resolute. If Hitler had not agreed to Mussolini's offer to broker another compromise at Munich, Europe would have been at war. Hitler reluctantly opted to take the deal for peace, but six months later he broke the Munich Agreement by occupying Bohemia and Moravia. Slovakia became a puppet state, and Czechoslovakia was no more. Poland was next on Hitler's agenda.

In late October 1938, Walsh took the *Batory* back to the United States. She was scheduled to go on a track and field tour of Europe in the fall of 1939, but Hitler attacked her homeland on September 1. Three years after the Berlin Olympics, Europe was again at war. On September 17, the Soviet Union invaded Poland, and the country fell within a month. The German and Soviet occupation of Poland was the most brutal of the war, and when the Wehrmacht attacked the Soviet Union in June 1941, the Germans' persecution of the Poles worsened. Five and a half million Poles lost their lives in the conflict, of those 3 million Jews in the Holocaust. One British historian of Poland labeled this period "Golgota," Polish for Golgotha—or Calvary—the place of Christ's crucifixion.[5]

With war raging in Europe, Walsh became a regular on the North American track and field circuit. Three days after Hitler attacked Poland, Walsh leapt 19 feet, four inches at the AAU Championships in Waterbury, Connecticut, to beat her own nine-year-old broad-jump record by almost seven inches. She also took the 200 meters.[6] At the 1940 AAU Championships in Ocean City, New Jersey, Walsh took home the individual all-around award by winning the discus and broad jump, and coming in second in the 100 and 200 meters.[7] The *Washington Post* reported that Stella Walsh, the "queen of America's women dash athletes," had been dethroned in the 100 and 200 by another Ohioan, Jean Lane, a seventeen-year-old student from Wilberforce University in Xenia, the oldest private, historically black university in the country.[8] Walsh had not won the 100 at the AAU Championships since 1930, but her loss in the 200 was a big upset.

Walsh said that she had pulled a muscle before the AAU meet and promised to beat Lane—the "speedy colored girl," as the *Plain Dealer* put it—in future races. Lane won the 100 again in 1941, and Walsh finished second to Lane in the 200. Walsh won the broad jump and discus, however, continuing a remarkable fifteen-year run in the AAU Track and Field Championships. Somehow she regained her explosiveness off the starting line and won the 100-meter title three more times. When she got beat, it was always a headline. Walsh dominated the 200 meters in the 1940s, losing only once from 1939 to 1948 (in 1941, to Lane). She won the broad jump in 1930, then eight straight broad jump titles from 1939 to 1946, again in 1948, and finally in 1951, at the age of forty. She also garnered two championships in the discus (1941 and 1942).

At the Northeast Ohio AAU Meet in Cleveland in June 1942, Walsh proved that she was still a world-class track and field athlete by setting four unrecognized world records, in the 50-, 100-, and 220-yard sprints, and the broad jump. She also took first in the javelin, placed second in the discus, and led her Polish Olympics team to victory in the 440-yard relay. A month later, at the AAU Championships in Ocean City, Walsh won three titles, in the 200 meters, discus, and broad jump.

Most athletes in her day quit playing games in their early twenties, sometimes for physical reasons, but more so because games were ultimately considered child's play. Walsh could not give it up. Sport was her vocation, her love, her soul. In 1941, she played on the Lakewood Bakery Olympics softball team, winning the city championship. Walsh also organized a basketball team called the Polish Olympics and won the Polish American championship in 1942 and 1943. She was the MVP in both tournaments. In 1943, she played for the Waldorf Beer basketball team, winning thirty-one of thirty-two games. As her reputation as a basketball player grew, Walsh was recruited to play for one of the country's best women's teams, the Rochester Filarets, which is said to have won more than 200 straight games from 1940 to 1944. *Life* ran an article on them on April 3, 1944, but by that time Walsh had left the team.

After Japan attacked Pearl Harbor in December 1941, to bring the United States into World War II, many of baseball's greatest stars, for example, Ted Williams, Hank Greenberg, and Joe DiMaggio, left the game to serve in the armed forces. Chicago Cubs owner Phillip Wrigley started the All-American Girls Professional Baseball League (AAGPBL) in 1943 (depicted in the 1992 film *A League of Their Own*). The National Girls Baseball League was founded in 1944, with six teams playing in the Chicago area.

EXTRA! EXTRA! EXTRA!

ALL STAR ★ *ALL STAR* ★ *ALL STAR*

BASKETBALL CARNIVAL
SUN. EVE. FEBRUARY 11th
at Imm. Heart of Mary Gym
6800 Lansing Avenue

SPILLS! THRILLS! ACTION! SPEED!

POLISH FALCON NEST 141 JRS.
vs.
ALLIANCE OF POLES JRS.

UNION OF POLES JRS.
vs.
IMM. HEART ALTAR BOYS

U. S. NAVY
vs.
U. S. COAST GUARD

FEATURE ATTRACTION

STELLA WALSH'S
OLYMPIC GIRLS
U. S. POLISH CHAMPS
vs.
CANTON, OHIO
BULL DOG GIRLS

MAPLE HEIGHTS A. C.
vs.
CARLING'S

First Game 6:00 P. M.

Dynamic Stan Orzech will Referee.

STELLA WALSH

Poster advertising Walsh's Polish Olympics basketball game at Immaculate Heart of Mary, where she went to elementary school. Notice that the "dynamic" Stan Orzech refereed. Orzech owned a bar in the Slavic Village frequented by Walsh. *Courtesy of Grace Butcher.*

Playing mainly in Midwestern cities, the AAGPBL eventually had ten teams and drew 1 million fans between 1943 and 1954. The AAGPBL purposely feminized its players to sell a women's brand of baseball. As the league office put it, they "had only two things to sell the public, baseball and femininity." At the first few spring trainings, players went to a finishing school run by *Chicago Tribune* beauty editor Eleanor Mangle and beauticians from Helena Rubenstein's salon. The players wore skirts and makeup but were carefully portrayed as "nice girls" with a "high moral tone." No "freaks or Amazons" needed apply, but rather girls who evoked the image of a Hollywood pinup girl. Just to make sure that the girls were chaste, chaperones accompanied the teams.[9]

Neither Walsh nor Helen Stephens tried out for the league, but then their mannish features did not fit into the way Wrigley wanted his women to look. One player recalled that the "league stressed femininity. It wasn't as much about beauty as it was about being *not* masculine."[10] Walsh was also older by about a decade than the youthful girls Wrigley wanted on his teams. Her Polish citizenship was another hurdle. The league had an expressly patriotic purpose during the war; Wrigley had the players form a "V" for victory before every game. Walsh was not a player the AAGPBL could promote as a model patriot.

With the war raging in Europe and Asia, it was not clear if the Olympics would ever be held again. Walsh wanted to keep her amateur status, however, and if she played baseball for money, her AAU and Olympic career would be over. Olympic athletes only have a small window of opportunity, and Walsh was at the peak of her physical abilities in the early 1940s; at a Knights of Columbus indoor meet in Cleveland in March 1941, Walsh unofficially broke the world indoor record in the 220-yard dash. The dozen years between the Berlin and London Olympics in 1948 cut short Walsh's Olympic career. She never ran in another Olympics.

As long as she could find funding, Walsh tried to compete in any big track and field meet in the Western Hemisphere. Bristling under U.S. hegemonic policies in Latin America, Argentina tried to tap into the region's resentment by taking the lead in hosting a Pan-American Games. In 1939, as war seemed imminent and the 1940 Olympics were in jeopardy, the Argentine Olympic Committee launched an effort to hold the Pan-Am Games in Buenos Aires.

Both Walsh and Helene Mayer, who had fenced for Germany at the Berlin Olympics, wanted to go. In late 1941, however, both were ruled ineligible to join the U.S. team because they had competed for another country in the Olympics. The *Plain Dealer* wrote that Walsh was the "girl without a country."[11] After Pearl Harbor, the United States decided it could not divert resources from the war effort to send a team to Buenos Aires, and the Pan-American Games were called off. The first Pan-American Games did not take place until 1951, in Buenos Aires.

One of the most embarrassing episodes in Walsh's life took place in the fall of 1942, when she, Harry Jakubiak, and Lois Mattheson were arrested for pilfering six fur coats worth $275 from stores in Logansport, Indiana, about 250 miles southwest of Cleveland. Walsh had met Jakubiak—alias Harry Stron—at a basketball game in Cleveland. Jakubiak allegedly bragged that "he was the smoothest shoplifter in the country." Walsh acknowledged, "I knew he was in some kind of racket, but I didn't know what it was." According to Walsh, she had nothing to do with the thefts: "When we arrived in Logansport in my car, Jakubiak went away with Mrs. Mattheson, and he said he was going to buy her a present. I walked around town window shopping." When Walsh returned to her car, she saw the police surrounding her car, so she hitchhiked to the nearby town of Ober. "I was afraid it might hurt my athletic career if I was seen there [in Logansport]." In Ober, Indiana, she went to the police and reported that her car had been stolen.[12]

Walsh pled innocent to the grand larceny charges, although the coats found in her car were damning evidence. After a few days in jail, Walsh said, "The truth has not much to do with the case. I came to Logansport to do some hunting, and I'm getting all I want. I have killed sixty-six cockroaches in this jail."[13] The *Pittsburgh Press* reported that Walsh had thought she was going to Chicago on a shopping trip. She was released on $3,000 bail, and Mattheson was released without charges. Jakubiak pled guilty and was sentenced to one to ten years. He maintained that the two women were not guilty, but because the stolen goods were found in Walsh's car, she still faced a trial.[14]

In May 1943, Walsh's lawyer requested a postponement. In September, the judge in the case gave Walsh permission to leave the country to play in a softball tournament in Canada, and the trial was again set back to June 1944. On October 11, 1944, the *New York Times* reported that the prosecutor in the case, Kenesaw M. Landis II, the nephew of the famous baseball commissioner, had dropped the charges of grand larceny against Walsh because Mattheson was by that time in the Women's Army Corps, and the Logansport municipal authorities refused to pay her way back to testify in the trial. The incident went virtually unnoticed throughout the rest of the country and did not hurt Walsh's reputation in the long run.

While Walsh was awaiting trial in the fur coat caper, she went back to the track. The larceny charge did not seem to affect her at the 1943 AAU Championships, which were held at Lakewood High School, about seven miles east of Cleveland. Walsh competed in the 100 meters, 200 meters, and broad jump, and won them all.

Stephens was paying close attention to Walsh's career. When she heard that Walsh had tied her Olympic record of 11.6 seconds in the 100 meters at the 1943 AAU Championships, Stephens contemplated a comeback, although as a professional basketball player she was not eligible to run in AAU meets. "[I] just want to show Stella Walsh I can beat her," she said.[15]

Another pioneering woman athlete won the 50 meters and the high jump at the 1943 AAU Championships. At an early age, Alice Coachman was outracing and outjumping boys in her hometown of Albany, Georgia. "The girls were no fun to play with," she scoffed, "because they were always trying to act cute." She came to the attention of the Tuskegee Institute track and field coach, and began competing for that famous club, winning her first national high-jump championship in 1939, at the age of sixteen. In 1948, Coachman qualified for the U.S. Olympic team for the London Games, but she had a potentially debilitating condition. "I didn't really want to go to England," Coachman remembered. "I started crying like a baby. But I couldn't let my country down. . . . I had an ailment that was corrected by the doctor placing a plastic tube in me to turn my ovary around. It was twisted. That was dangerous in high-jumping." The U.S. Olympic team doctor took out the tube the day before the high-jump competition at London, and Coachman won, making her the first African American woman to take home an Olympic gold medal. "I was happy to get my medal awarded to me by King George," Coachman said, "because I had heard so much about the king and queen of England."[16]

In August 1944, Walsh ran a record 24.2 in the 220-yard dash. For the first three years after the war, she won every U.S. National Outdoor 200-meter title. Walsh recognized that as she aged, she was losing some of her explosiveness out of the starting blocks in shorter sprints, so she also began running the 800 meters. Accomplished in both track and field, she also trained for the pentathlon, an event in which sheer speed was secondary to conditioning and athletic skills. At the Northeast Ohio District AAU Championships in June 1945, she set a world mark in the triathlon, which consisted of the high jump, javelin, and 1,000 meters. The *Plain Dealer* also reported that Walsh had run an 11.2 in the 100 meters, supposedly lopping a huge 0.3 seconds off of Stephens's world record.[17] Although this record was never officially recognized, Stephens again repeated her challenge: "I beat her before, and I can do it again."[18] At the 1945 U.S. National Championships in Harrisburg, Pennsylvania, Coachman beat Walsh in the 100 meters, but Walsh won the 200 meters and the broad jump.

Walsh kept up a busy schedule that winter, running indoor track meets and playing basketball for the Polish Olympics. Her team put together a thirty-game winning streak, and in February 1946 they won a fifth straight Northeast Ohio AAU Championship. As usual, Walsh led the team in scoring. At a Polish Olympic Club meet in Cleveland in June 1946, Walsh beat her own record in the 60 meters, which she had set thirteen years earlier in Lwów, and a week later she bested her 50-meter record, set in Katowice in 1933. At the Northeast Ohio AAU Championships, Walsh topped that with an 11.5 time in the 100 meters, tying Stephens's world record. Once again, these records were unofficial.

Germany surrendered on May 8, 1945, and Japan capitulated on August 15, ending World War II. Walsh desperately wanted to compete in the Olympics again, although given the devastation in Europe, it was not clear which city could host it. In August 1945, the IOC decided to hold the first postwar games in 1948. British sporting authorities pushed hard for London, wanting to show the world that Britain was still a world power, recovering from the war and remaining open for business. After the Nazi exploitation of the 1936 Berlin Games, the British argued that their amateur tradition best exemplified the separation of the Olympic movement from political agendas. Cognizant that Britain's economy was foundering, the United States offered to feed the Olympic athletes. In February 1946, the IOC decided on London.

Many members of British prime minister Clement Atlee's Labour Party argued that reconstruction should take precedence over spending on a sporting event. A *New York Times* reporter argued that the psychological lift for Britain was well worth the cost:

> For the British people, weary from two World Wars in thirty years and separated by only twenty-one miles of channel from a Europe split and tense with international strife, the sight of young men and women from the Balkans, from Scandinavia, from Western Europe, and from the Middle East, from the Moslem world, from the British Empire, and from the Western Hemisphere . . . generally competing side by side, will have a tonic effect.[19]

The Soviet Union did not send a team to the 1948 Olympics, but its satellite states in Eastern Europe did, including Poland. Walsh was eligible to run for Poland, but by that time a Communist government was firmly established in Warsaw. Soviet leader Josef Stalin was not about to allow Poland to hold free elections after the war because a democratically elected government would have been antagonistic to Moscow. Poles knew very well that Stalin had divided their country with Hitler when the war began in 1939, and that Stalin had ordered the killing of thousands of Polish Army officers in 1940. The Soviet leader barely trusted the Polish Communists, let alone Polish democrats and bourgeois intellectuals. Stalin had murdered hundreds of exiled Polish Communists before and during the war. After the Red Army began to push the Germans out of Poland in 1944, he immediately installed a Soviet-friendly government made up of Polish Stalinists.

There is an old joke about the chronic divisions within Polish politics that when ten Poles gather together they form eleven political parties; however, after World War II, Polish Americans were united in their hatred of Soviet Russia and outraged that the United States did not prevent the Soviet subjugation of Poland. Roosevelt was unjustifiably blamed for giving free rein to Stalin in Eastern Europe, when, in fact, Roosevelt had no way to prevent Stalin from doing what he wanted there. Poland became the crucible of the Cold War in Eastern Europe.

In the early postwar period, the Western powers held out hope that Stalin would allow free elections in Poland, and Walsh continued to run in Poland and for the Polish national team. Hers was still the most recognizable name on the European track circuit. In 1946, Walsh won her last five titles at the

Polish National Track and Field Championships. In August, she competed for Poland for the final time at the European Championships in Oslo, but at thirty-five she was beginning to show her age. She did not place in the 100 and 200 meters, the high jump, the broad jump, or javelin. Walsh finished fourth in the shot put.

The Polish Communists held phony elections in January 1947, solidifying their hold on power. Given the Polish American community's virulent hatred of Stalin and the Polish regime, there was no way that Walsh could run for the People's Republic of Poland at the London Olympics. Despite her failure at Oslo, she was still one of the best female athletes in the United States. At the AAU Championships in Buffalo in late August 1946, Walsh captured her twenty-ninth and thirtieth national titles, winning the 200 meters and the broad jump. She came in second in the 100 meters. At the AAU Championships in San Antonio in June 1947, she again won the 200 and came in fourth in the broad jump, while complaining of a pulled muscle. Tuskegee Institute won its tenth women's AAU team title in eleven years. The only year they lost during that string was to Walsh's Polish Olympics team in 1943.

In December 1947, at the age of thirty-six, Walsh finally received her U.S. citizenship papers. By that time, the Soviet-backed Polish United Workers Party was firmly in control of the Polish government. Walsh was fixated on competing again in the Olympics. Now that Poland was no longer free, it was a remote possibility. Walsh was well aware of the IOC rule that an athlete could not switch countries to compete in the Olympics. According to the *Plain Dealer*, she was "looking forward to the possibility of competing in the 1948 Olympic Games in London," but the newspaper cited the Olympic rule that would rule her out: "An athlete having once competed for one country cannot compete for another country, except in the case of conquest or the formation of a new state." If she had remained a Polish citizen, she could have continued to live in Cleveland and still run for the Polish Olympic team. She was resigned to the political reality of the Cold War:

> Naturally I would like to run for the United States this year, but I realize that is impossible. Since I am now a citizen here, it probably wouldn't be considered patriotic to compete for Poland, but I would like one more opportunity to run in the Olympics. This absolutely will be my last season of competition, and that would be a great way to finish my career. Maybe fate will decide for me.[20]

Surely Walsh would have made the 1948 U.S. Olympic team. Helen Stephens had retired from running to play basketball, and at the 1948 U.S. Track and Field Championships in Grand Rapids, Michigan, Walsh placed first in the 100 and 200 meters, and the broad jump. Frances Sobczak Kaszubski, Walsh's Polish American pal from Cleveland, emerged as a star in Grand Rapids, winning the discus and shot put. The *Plain Dealer* headline on July 14 read, "Cleveland Housewife Snares Two Track Titles." Walsh was proud and yet envious of her friend, who qualified for the U.S. Olympic team in both events. Kaszubski said that she had been inspired by the great Stella Walsh:

> My mother tried to discourage me. She and dad both wanted me to be lady-like. But I persisted. We lived next-door to Sokół, the Polish Falcons Hall, on Broadway at 72nd, and I finally talked them into letting me become a member. They even let my younger sister join also. Because we were so close, my mother believed no harm could come to us, and she could keep her eye on us.[21]

Kaszubski did not finish in the top ten in either Olympic event at the 1948 London Games, but she won the U.S. championship in the shot put in 1945, 1948, and 1950, and the discus in 1945, and from 1947 to 1951. She went on to become an official with the AAU. Her most controversial decision came at the 1958 U.S. Track and Field Championships, when she called a foul on Lillian Greene for allegedly getting paced by a teammate on the infield in the last lap of the 880 yards. Although the teammate was simply cheering on Greene, she was disqualified. Walsh, running for the Southern Pacific Athletic Club, finished fifth in that race but was selected for the U.S. team to go to Moscow for a duel meet against the Soviets that summer.

Helen Stephens wanted to go to the London Olympics as well, but she had lost her amateur status by playing basketball with the semiprofessional All-American Red Heads. Stephens and Walsh probably would have challenged for the medals' stand in both the 100 and 200 meters. The Netherlands' Fanny Blankers-Koen's winning time in the 100 meters at London was two-tenths of a second slower than Walsh's second-place finish at Berlin twelve years earlier. Walsh told the *Chicago Herald-American*, "I've beaten Koen every time I have run against her—about four times."[22] Walsh did not mention that she had lost every race to Stephens.

Walsh was thirty-seven years old in 1948. Even if she could somehow find a way to compete in the 1952 Olympics, whether for Poland or the United States, she would be out of her prime. Walsh began to run in longer races, which took more training and endurance. The 400 and 800 meters were still not on the Olympic program for women, however. The pentathlon, which Walsh dominated in the United States in the early 1950s, was not an Olympic event either. The 800 meters for women finally returned at the 1960 Rome Olympics, women ran the 400 meters for the first time at the 1964 Tokyo Olympics, and the heptathlon and marathon for women debuted at the 1984 Los Angeles Games.

In 1949, Grace Butcher was a sophomore at Chardon High School, about forty miles east of Cleveland. The sixteen-year-old wanted to run track but found no outlet to do it. Butcher tried to start a girls' track team at Chardon, but the boys' coach told her that she could not do it because there were no other girls' teams to run against: "You know, Grace, we can't really have girls' track here. To have a team here, you'd have to have one at other schools, too. Nobody has girls' track," he said.[23] Butcher's mother Mary then contacted Walsh, who was coaching girls at the Polish Falcon club in Cleveland. Butcher's diary entries recall her excitement to work out with the Olympic champion:

MOM CALLED STELLA WALSH, AND THIS FRIDAY I AM GOING TO CUYAHOGA HEIGHTS TO WORK OUT WITH HER TRACK TEAM! [*sic*]. My break! It's unbelievable. . . . Boy, talk about being nervous—I'm scared. Will I make good tomorrow? If praying my heart out helps any, I should because I've been praying my heart out this past year. . . . Will I be able to think about school tomorrow? I doubt it. Just thinking about going makes my heart beat faster and my stomach thrill.[24]

On the first day of practice, Walsh asked Butcher what event she wanted to do. Butcher said that she wanted to run the mile, but of course there was no mile run for women in those days, so Walsh told her, "You have good, long legs, you can try the hurdles. The 220. Maybe high jump." Butcher was ecstatic about her first workouts at Cuyahoga and thrilled to get a pair of Walsh's track shoes: "I put them under my pillow the way Stella says she used to."[25]

Grace Butcher trained with Walsh in 1949, and is still
running today. *Photo by Darlene Fritz.*

That summer Butcher ran with Walsh on a 4 × 110 relay team. Butcher
recalled,

At my first-ever meet on June 11, 1949, wearing the bright satin uniform of the
Poland Falcons (I guess that was really wasn't kosher, seeing as how I'm not
Polish), I ran on the winning 440-relay team with Stella at anchor, but we were
disqualified to second because one of our runners ran out of her zone. I was
third in the 220 behind Stella and a teammate.

Butcher said that it was a thrill of a lifetime: "To run in the same race as Stella!
To see her take off her warm-up suit struck me as rather like seeing a statue

unveiled. I was almost glad I was so far behind in the race so I could watch her run. She almost never ran like that in training. Her acceleration seemed out of this world."[26] For months, Grace's mother drove her to Cleveland to train with Walsh. Mary and Stella became good friends, often sharing a few drinks after practice.

Disappointed at not being able to run in the London Olympics, Walsh once again said she would call it a career. In 1948, the *Plain Dealer* ran a photo of Walsh sitting in her room at home, surrounded by a clutter of plaques, medals, and trophies. That is all she had to show for her many victories on the field of play. In August 15, 1949, the newspaper announced, "Stella Quits Track, Will Write Memoirs." One of the reasons Walsh thought about retiring was to find work in physical education, which Olympic rules prohibited if she wanted to remain an amateur. "In recalling the highlights of her career," the newspaper wrote, "Miss Walsh regards her victories in the 1930 and 1934 women's Olympics and her sweep of the 60-, 100- and 200-meter dashes and broad jump at the 1932 Olympics at Los Angeles as her greatest triumphs." The newspaper probably misquoted Walsh and conflated her women's Olympic victories with the Los Angeles Games, because she only won the 100 meters in the latter.

Walsh could not stop competing, and she went back on her pledge once again. Sport was in her genes; her grandfather, during a visit from Poland to Cleveland in 1929, dared his granddaughter to take him on in a 100-yard dash. Walsh barely beat the sexagenarian. In the United States, vocation often defines a person's identity, and running was Stella Walsh. She had received great adulation from sports and, like many retired athletes, had trouble transitioning to life without sports. What would be her new mission in life? She had business cards made with a drawing of a sprinter, with the name "Stella Walsh" on the left-hand side and "Stella Walsh Olson Walasiewiczowna" on the right. Beneath the runner is the inscription, "Olympic and U.S. Champion Holder of 65 World and National Records." She once said, "Every year I think of retiring, but I get out on the track with the youngsters and want to run myself."[27] She challenged everyone, young and old, to a race.

A new AAU event rejuvenated Walsh's career. In 1950, she won the national pentathlon championship (shot put, high jump, broad jump, 200 meters, and 80-meter hurdles). The next year, she successfully defended her title at the national championships in Berkeley. Walsh won five con-

Walsh used her married name and Polish name on her business card. *Western Reserve Historical Society.*

secutive pentathlon titles from 1950 to 1954, competing for the Polish Falcons in 1950 and 1951, Dreyer AC in 1952, and the Knickerbocker PC in 1953 and 1954.

For a quarter-century, Walsh was among the most famous Polish American athletes. Another Polish Clevelander, spitballing pitcher Stan Coveleski, led the Cleveland Indians to the 1920 World Series championship, the first of only two Indians World Series wins. St. Louis Cardinals Hall of Fame first baseman Stan Musial won seven batting titles and three MVP titles, played in twenty-four All-Star Games, hit .331 for his career, and led the Cardinals to three World Series championships. Cincinnati Reds slugger Ted Kluszewski was the other Polish American baseball player of note in Walsh's cohort, walloping a major-league high of 171 home runs from 1953 to 1956. Middleweight Tony Zale, whose real name was Anthony Zaleski, was the most famous Polish American fighter. In three epic fights with Rocky Graziano, Zale retained the middleweight title in 1946, lost it in 1947, and regained the title in 1948. Zale lost the championship later that year to Frenchman Marcel Cerdan, who was famous for his love of French songstress Edith Piaf. Cerdan died in 1949, in a plane crash, on his way to New York to see her.

In a 1950 poll of Polish American daily newspapers, Walsh, not Musial or any of the others, was voted the greatest Polish American athlete of the first half of the twentieth century. Musial came in second, and 1947 Notre Dame

Heisman Trophy winner and Chicago Bears quarterback Johnny Lujack finished third.[28]

In 1936, Southern California bakery magnate Paul H. Helms founded a
philanthropic organization that honored athletes from throughout the world.
Helms had supplied the bread for the Olympic Village at Stella Walsh's first
Olympics in Los Angeles in 1932. From then onward, Helms marketed his
product as "Helms Olympic Bread, the Bread of Olympic Champions." In
1949, he inaugurated the $10,000 World Trophy, which recognized the best
amateur athletes from each continent. The Helms Athletic Foundation Hall
on Venice Boulevard became a museum of sports artifacts. "[The Founda-
tion] has been set up in trust and financed so that it can be perpetuated
perhaps forever and can never be altered," promised Helms. "Otherwise, I
could not accept these valuable trophies, which now have a permanent place
in Helms Hall."[29]

In 1951, the Helms Foundation named its greatest woman athlete of the
first half of the twentieth century; surprisingly, it was not Babe Didrikson
Zaharias, Helen Wills, or Helen Stephens, but Stella Walsh. She deserved the
award. For nearly twenty-five years—from the early 1930s to the mid-1950s—
Walsh piled up victory after victory in the U.S. Track and Field Championships. Walsh won thirty-two U.S. Outdoor Championships, by far the most
of any woman in history. In 1955, Walsh and Kaszubski were elected to the
Helms Foundation Women's Track and Field Hall of Fame. In gratitude,
Walsh gave the Helms Foundation her first medals from the 1927 Junior
Olympics in Cleveland and her 1932 Olympic gold medal.[30] In 1952, Walsh
moved to Los Angeles, residing close to where her medals were on display
until the Helms Foundation shut its doors in 1982, two years after her death.

7

The Move to Los Angeles and an Arranged Marriage

I didn't go out with boys till I was twelve! . . . People keep asking me why I never married. I tell them that I've been running all my life—and where men are concerned, I'm just too fast for 'em!

—*Stella Walsh*

In 1952, Walsh left her parents and lifelong home in Cleveland and moved to Los Angeles, the city of her Olympic victory two decades before. During that brief stay in Southern California in 1932, Walsh was smitten with the "land of perpetual spring"—the blue skies, the Pacific Ocean, and the wide-open spaces of the City of Angels. California was a place for Walsh to get a fresh, new start, an escape from her parents' cramped house on Clement Avenue and the congested Polish neighborhood where the rumors and crude jokes about her gender swirled. There she endured many snide, derogatory comments about her masculine looks, muscular body, and lack of feminine curves.

After two difficult decades of economic depression, war, and political rancor concerning New Deal legislation, General Dwight Eisenhower's election as president in 1952 marked a return to normal. First Lady Mamie Eisenhower was emblematic of that conservative era for middle-American women. She often appeared in public in a long skirt, dainty little hat, and white gloves.

Most television fare in the 1950s, for instance, *Father Knows Best* and *Make Room for Daddy*, portrayed women in a subordinate, domestic role.

Los Angeles had that conservative side, but Walsh could more easily blend into an anything-goes Bohemian culture. As one historian of the movie industry put it, "The passionate melodramas surrounding Hollywood's birth challenged the nation's gendered boundaries by celebrating the exploits of these exotic, glamorous workers out West."[1] In 1947, a secretary at RKO Studios in Culver City published the first issue of *Vice Versa*—a groundbreaking magazine for women seeking unconventional relationships. *I Love Lucy* was television's top show in the 1950s, and in her zany way Lucille Ball nudged the norm of a traditional, submissive housewife. Nonetheless, Ball's role as a mother was central to the show. One episode in 1953 featured the birth of her son, "Little Ricky," and it was watched by some 44 million viewers. In the last half of the decade, Elvis "the Pelvis" Presley began to rock this conservative world, foreshadowing the counterculture Woodstock generation of the 1960s.

Walsh left behind a tight-knit Polish community that was an important part of her identity and had nurtured her running career. The Polish population in the sprawling city of Los Angeles was small. In the late nineteenth century, a group of notable Polish intellectuals and artists had settled in and around the southern suburb of Anaheim, among them the famous actress Helena Modjeska and Poland's greatest historical novelist, Henryk Sienkiewicz.

In the 1860s, Modjeska was a sought-after player on the Kraków and Warsaw theater scene. She was regarded as Poland's best actress. The Stary Teatr [Old Theater] in Kraków still bears her name. Modjeska arrived in California in 1876. As a reporter for *Gazeta Polska* [Poland Gazette], Sienkiewicz saw her first performance in San Francisco. Modjeska became the most acclaimed Shakespearean actress in the United States, while Sienkiewicz returned to Poland in 1879, to write his most famous works, including *The Deluge*, a historical novel depicting the Swedish and Russian onslaught on Poland in the mid-seventeenth century. The book's title was apropos for Poland's fate in the twentieth century.

Modjeska built a house about twenty miles southeast of Anaheim, near the Cleveland National Forest, in what is now known as Modjeska Canyon. She called the house "Arden," after the English forest that is the setting of Shakespeare's *As You Like It*. The residence is on the list of National Historic

Landmarks. Her son, engineer Ralph Modjeski, helped build San Francisco's Golden Gate Bridge.

Walsh moved to Glendale, about five miles north of downtown Los Angeles. In 1960, there were only about 600 Angelinos of Polish heritage in the Glendale area and approximately 44,000 in the entire city. Walsh was a U.S. citizen now, so her move to Los Angeles—the quintessential American city of freeways, movies, television, and free-wheeling lifestyles—put a distinctly American stamp on her naturalization.

Furthermore, Southern California had a perfect climate for a woman who had dedicated her life to sport. Walsh could participate in year-round softball, basketball, and track. On one trip home to Cleveland in 1953, she told the *Plain Dealer* that in contrast to California, the northern Ohio climate "stinks in spades."[2] In Los Angeles, Walsh could train all she wanted. She even wanted to play more golf, after having won the Polish National Open Golf Tournament in 1948, shooting an 80. A year before she moved to Los Angeles, the *Plain Dealer* had reported, "Stella Walsh, 40, Eyes Golf Career." The newspaper wrote that Walsh liked playing softball and basketball more than track and field.[3] There was ample opportunity to do it all in California.

Walsh used her connections to the Waldorf Brewery Company to land a job there and then went to work for the Knickerbocker Plastics Company in Burbank, where she played for and coached the company-sponsored baseball and basketball teams. She also became a trainer for the San Fernando Valley Women's Athletic Club. The North Hollywood Knickerbockers basketball team won the California AAU title in 1955, and Walsh was named the tournament's MVP.

The U.S. Olympic tryouts for women were scheduled for Harrisburg, Pennsylvania, in July 1952. Walsh was still good enough to qualify for the Helsinki Games. She dominated the Pacific Coast and the Southern Pacific track meets that summer. Running for the Dreyer Athletic Club of Berkeley at the U.S. National Championships in Los Angeles in late October 1952, Walsh bested her own world pentathlon record, which she had set a year earlier at the National Championships in Houston. On July 2, 1952, the *Los Angeles Times'* Jeanne Hoffman, in her column on women athletes called "Skirting All Sports," noted, "The gal can still run."

At the risk of being ostracized by the Polish American community, however, Walsh would not contemplate running for Communist Poland in the

Olympics. As the *Plain Dealer* put it, "She declined an invitation to represent Poland in the 1952 Helsinki Games, disapproving as she did of the red complexion of the remnant that's left of the land of her birth."[4] The United States and the Soviet Union were in the depths of the Cold War in the early 1950s; the Soviet Union successfully tested an atomic bomb in 1949, and the United States countered with a hydrogen bomb in 1952. In 1950, North Korea attacked South Korea, and President Truman set a precedent by sending in U.S. troops to contain Communist expansion. As the Korean War was raging, Wisconsin senator Joseph McCarthy conducted a witch hunt for Communist sympathizers in the United States. Julius and Ethel Rosenberg were executed in 1953, for spying for the Soviet Union.

At first, the *Plain Dealer* overlooked the IOC rule against running for two different countries in the Olympics and predicted that "Stella Walsh of Glendale, California, is given a good chance to qualify [in the broad jump]. She will also try in dashes and discus."[5] Several days later the newspaper corrected itself, reporting that Walsh was ineligible to compete at the Helsinki Olympics. Walsh pled her case to the IOC as a woman without a country:

> I'm an American citizen now, and Poland is no longer a state. It's recognized as an overrun country. It's a satellite of Russia. . . . The rules governing entrance into the Olympics also specify that exception is made for naturalization through right of conquest. That would certainly take in Poland.[6]

The AAU and the IOC would hear none of it. Walsh was among many émigré athletes from Soviet bloc countries who could not or would not compete for their native national teams. One hope was to form an Olympic team without national designation. Before the Helsinki Olympics, Hungarian émigré Count Anthony Szapary organized the "Union of Free Eastern European Sportsmen." According to the *New York Times*, "During World War II, he had been sent to a concentration camp for activities with the Hungarian Red Cross and his relief work for Polish and Jewish refugees. He was released through the intervention of King Gustav V of Sweden."[7] Szapary created the Hungarian National Sports Federation after the war, but when the Communists seized power in 1947, he defected to the United States.

Szapary's Hungary and Walsh's Poland were the most recalcitrant Soviet satellites. Both countries had deep historical grievances against the Russians.

Russian tsar Nicholas I helped Austria crush a Hungarian national uprising in 1849. Hungary fought against Russia in World War I and again in World War II, this time on the side of Hitler's Wehrmacht in 1941. The Red Army occupied Hungary at the end of the war, ushering in more than forty years of Communist rule. Most Hungarians hated the Soviet-backed government.

The Communist regime tried to gain domestic support by building on a long and successful Hungarian sporting tradition. For such a small country, Hungary had won a disproportionate number of Olympic medals and international soccer matches. Hungarian Olympic teams (separate from the Austrian ones) were among the top medal winners at the 1908 London and 1912 Stockholm Olympics. Budapest sought the 1920 Olympics, but World War I precluded that bid.[8] From 1924 to 1936, Hungary won more medals than any other East European country, garnering the third most gold medals at the 1936 Berlin Olympics (behind Germany and the United States). Hungary fielded one of the best national soccer teams in the world in the 1950s. From 1949 to 1955, the Hungarians played sixty games and won or tied all but three.

Szapary hoped that the IOC would recognize the union and allow Walsh and other East European émigrés to compete in the Olympics. Walsh was not optimistic: "I have heard that [IOC president] Avery Brundage favors a free nation unit, but many [IOC] members feel that if the group is admitted, Russia would lodge a protest. . . . I suspect that our chances are slim, as undoubtedly more are curious to see what Russia has to offer." Walsh was right. The IOC had long tried to keep political issues out of the Olympics and only recognized national Olympic committees, not athletic organizations. Furthermore, the IOC wanted the Soviet Union to go to the Helsinki Games, and Moscow and the other Soviet satellites vehemently opposed Szapary's group.[9]

In the run-up to the Helsinki Olympics in the fall of 1952, Walsh found herself in trouble with the law again when she allegedly tried to shoplift groceries from Mack's Farm Market in Glendale, not far from her apartment on Mayfield Avenue. Walsh had already had several brushes with the law. In 1931, she was booked for hitting a bystander during a discus completion in New Jersey, and in 1942, she was jailed as part of a fur heist in Logansport, Indiana. Neither charge stuck. Three years later, she hit a truck and trailer driven by Howard Bartell in Bay Village, a town on Lake Erie about ten miles west of Cleveland. Walsh and her passenger were slightly injured in the crash. Three months later, Bartell took Walsh to court to pay for the loss of his truck and trailer, charging her with careless driving.[10] There is no record of what became of that case.

The *Logansport Press* in Indiana, recalling Walsh's alleged theft of fur coats there a decade earlier, covered the grocery store story: "A store manager picked her up after he saw her put a half-pound of butter, some peach preserves, and a carton of cottage cheese in her purse and walk out." Walsh offered to pay for the goods, but store owner S. L. McKernan refused, and Walsh was arraigned on September 6. A week later, the manager of the market, Leon Benon, asked for the charges to be dismissed.[11]

The failure of Szapary's organization was a great disappointment to Walsh. In 1954, she again declared her intention to retire. But life without competition seemed impossible. Now in her forties, Walsh surprised herself with her continued success:

> I can't figure it out myself. Each year I say I'm going to retire. Each year I run just as fast. Just this summer I equaled my world record of 6.4 in the 50-meter run, which I established back in 1930. . . . I'm hoping to stay in condition in hopes the AAU will revise its rules and let me compete for the United States in the 1956 Olympics.[12]

The *Los Angeles Times* carried a cartoon of an aging Walsh running behind a wheelchair, with the quip, "OLD? Who's OLD?" Following Walsh is a banner that reads, "Stella Walsh in 1980." Ironically, that was the year she would be murdered.[13]

Walsh also continued to play basketball for the Polish Olympics. She was getting better at it, scoring thirty-four points in one Municipal Basketball League game. Jeanne Hoffman called her "Bevo Stella," a not-so-complimentary comparison to Clarence "Bevo" Francis, the giant center who starred for Rio Grande College in the early 1950s.

In October 1954, the AAU Track and Field Championships were held at Thomas Edison Field in Cleveland. Walsh returned to her hometown to go for a fifth straight pentathlon title. Competing for Knickerbocker Plastics Company, the hometown favorite won the event. That was the last of Walsh's forty-one indoor and outdoor national championships. A year later, in Morristown, New Jersey, Barbara Mueller dethroned the forty-four-year-old defending pentathlon champion.

Denied the chance to run in the Helsinki Olympics, Walsh turned her attention to supporting American female track and field athletes. She even went on television with California governor Earl Warren, Lillian Copeland, and other former Olympic athletes to raise money for the U.S. Olympic team to go to Helsinki. Soviet women won twenty-three medals at Helsinki to only eight for the Americans. According to an article in *Life* magazine, Walsh was so disappointed in this poor performance that she started a women's training center in Van Nuys, California. The magazine also wrote that Walsh, at age forty-five, was still hoping to qualify for the 1956 U.S. Olympic team. In the mid-1950s, she began coaching the women Marines at the El Toro Marine Corps Air Station near Irvine, California. She admitted that improving the performance of the American women athletes was a long-term project: "I'm afraid we must concede complete superiority to the Russian women, especially in the field events. What we must think of now is the 1960 Olympics."[14]

Walsh's continued success on the track and the basketball court kept her name in the sports sections of the Los Angeles press. In December 1953, the Cocoanut Grove hosted the annual *Los Angeles Times* Sports Awards. Walsh was given a special award for "particularly meritorious performances during 1953." According to the newspaper, Walsh "stole the show" with her acceptance speech:

> My Glendale neighbor, [famed New York Yankee manager] Casey Stengel, asked me the other day, "Stella, what's the secret of your ability to stay on top?" I looked at ol' Casey, who hasn't done so bad himself, and told him, "It's this way, Case: I don't smoke. I don't drink. And—I didn't go out with boys till I was twelve!" . . . People keep asking me why I never married. I tell them that I've been running all my life—and where men are concerned, I'm just too fast for 'em! . . . I'm starting to take up golf seriously this spring, and you tell that Didrikson to watch out. I'll catch her in two years![15]

Walsh was even a minor celebrity in Tinseltown, appearing on Groucho Marx's television quiz show *You Bet Your Life*. The show was as much Groucho's vehicle to crack jokes at the expense of the contestants as it was a real quiz show, but Walsh loved the publicity and was proud to recount her remarkable career. The exchange went as follows:

Groucho: Stella Walsh, eh? One of the greatest women athletes of our time. The female Bob Mathias.[16] It's a great honor to have you here, Stell. Stella, where are you from?

Stella: Well, I come from a little village in Poland called Wieś Wierzchownia.[17]

Groucho: And your name is Stella Walsh? That isn't a Polish name.

Stella: My name is really Stanisława Walasiewiczowna.[18]

Groucho: What was your name again?

Stella: Stanisława Walasiewiczowna.

Groucho: That's good with a heavy cream sauce, isn't it? Well, Stella, I know you've been a headliner in the sports pages for a good many years, and this is kind of a delicate question, but how old are you?

Stella: I'm forty-three.

Groucho: Well, you don't look it. What are some of the titles you hold?

Stella: Forty United States championships, twenty-two Polish national titles. Of course the Olympic title, and a number of world titles. . . . I won the greatest woman athlete of the half-century award, in a poll.

Groucho: Who did the voting?

Stella: It was a newspaper poll.

Groucho: One "poll" would naturally vote for another "Pole." How many records do you hold, Stella?

Stella: I hold over one hundred records in various countries.

Groucho: Now that you are too old for competition do you keep in condition?

Stella: Oh, I'm not too old for competition. Last year I won the overall pentathlon title. And of course I expect to defend it this year. And the interesting part about my competitors, most of the contestants weren't even born when I was winning my first championship twenty-five years ago.

Groucho: Stella, I must say I admire your athletic achievements. I can say that because I'm an old sport myself. There's an old joke . . . the guy says to the girl: "Do you like indoor sports? Yes, if they go home early."

Stella: If they go home early it's no sport.

Groucho: Well, I just thought I'd throw that in . . . a joke.

Stella: I thought I'd just throw mine in too.

Groucho: Would you mind picking me up and throwing me out?[19]

Groucho then moved on to the quiz part of the segment. Walsh had moved to California in part to train for the 1952 and 1956 Olympic Games. She was well aware of where the Olympics were held. Groucho asked, "What is the proposed site of the 1956 Olympic Games?" Walsh quickly answered, "Melbourne, Australia." Groucho then tossed another softball question: "The last Olympic Games were held in 1952. In what city were they held?" Walsh blurted out, "In Helsinki, Finland." Now confident, Walsh and her fellow contestant risked half of their money on the last question, which, of course, had little to do with the Olympics. "In fencing," Groucho asked, "What do you call the protective pad on the end of a foil." Neither Walsh nor her partner had a clue that "button" was the right answer.[20]

In the mid-1950s, the IOC again took up cases like Walsh's—athletes who had competed for one country in the Olympics but had changed citizenship. The IOC also considered athletes who had married a foreigner and taken the citizenship of the spouse. Walsh kept abreast of these developments with the hope of trying for one more Olympics, although she would be forty-five years old in 1956. She was still dominating Southern California track meets, and in May 1955, she ran in the Command Performance track meet in East Los Angeles to raise money for the 1956 U.S. Olympic team. Walsh was pessimistic about the U.S. women's chances of beating the Soviets at Melbourne, "but we'll give them a good run for their rubles," she said. On January 31, 1956, *Los Angeles Times* columnist Jeanne Hoffman joked, "Yankee hanky-carriers would stand a still better chance if stellar Stella, 44-year-old 'jumping bean' who refuses to be a jumping has-been, were eligible."[21]

The Olympic Charter of 1955 still prohibited competitors from competing for two different countries, stating, "It is not permissible for a competitor having once worn the colours of a country in the Olympic Games to wear those of another country on a future occasion except where his former country or place of birth has been incorporated in another state."[22] Walsh petitioned the IOC on the basis that the Communist People's Republic of Poland was an illegitimate successor to the interwar Republic: "The government which

I represented [in 1932 and 1936] does not exist," she argued. "The Russians are opposed to it, but I believe it will pass if it comes to a vote."[23] In the fall of 1955, Walsh decided that if she was not allowed to compete for the U.S. Olympic team in Melbourne, she would quit running.

In early 1956, Walsh wrote John Jewett Garland, the U.S. delegate on the IOC, saying, "If I were now to represent Poland in the Olympic Games, I would have to accept the Communist faith, which I do not want to do; and, of course, I will not do."[24] Brundage, who was a strict constructionist of the Olympic Charter, would not budge. Walsh's exhortations fell on deaf ears.[25]

The IOC met shortly before the start of the 1956 Winter Games in Cortina d'Ampezzo, Italy, and proposed adding the wording that a "woman competitor having once worn the colours of her native country in the Olympic Games is granted the right to wear also the colours of her country through marriage."[26] The resolution was adopted, and as Ned Cronin of the *Los Angeles Times* wrote, "Stella could take a crack at the 1956 Olympics if she corners an American husband between now and the tryouts this summer."[27] He doubted that Walsh could find love in such a short time.

Walsh had to find an American spouse quickly, with or without love. One possibility was Harry Olson, an old acquaintance from Cleveland now living in the Los Angeles area. The arranged marriage happened fast. On August 15, 1956, Walsh and Olson drove from Los Angeles to Las Vegas, Nevada, where they were married in a quick ceremony at one of the many wedding chapels in the gambling mecca. There are no known witnesses or photos of the ceremony.

Little is known about Olson, an aviation company draftsman from Northridge, California, about twenty-five miles northwest of Los Angeles. Some reports claimed that he was a former prizefighter. This fact would have suited Walsh fine, because Babe Didrikson had been able to tamp down criticism of her masculine mien by marrying professional wrestler George Zaharias, whose bad-guy act earned him the ring moniker the "Greek Hyena." Didrikson could look positively demure and feminine next to her muscle-bound spouse, and she knew it. A Los Angeles newsman once asked her, "Tell me, Mrs. Zaharias, of all the records you've broken and all the events you've won, what was the single most thrilling experience of your life?" Without a pause Babe replied, "The first night I slept with George."[28]

Walsh's marriage to Olson is a mystery. Walsh told the *Los Angeles Times* on August 16, that she had met the thirty-three-year-old Olson six years earlier in Cleveland and that they had reconnected in Los Angeles: "She said they had been going together for the last year and a half, and had been planning marriage." If it is true that they had discussed marriage, it was connected to Walsh's hope to become eligible to run for the United States at Melbourne.

Walsh used her husband's last name on and off for the rest of her life, either Stella Walsh Olson or Stella Walasiewiczowna Olson. "Olson" at the end of her name helped mute the whispering about Walsh's sexuality, which had only increased as Walsh, now in her forties, continued to dominate the U.S. Track and Field Championships. Although she was married for only a short time, the name Walsh Olson confirmed her status as a married woman for the rest of her life. She kept the name until she died in 1980, although the *Plain Dealer's* obituary did not call her Walsh Olson and "Olson" does not appear on her gravestone.

Walsh was desperate to compete in another Olympics, and this was clearly a marriage of convenience. The *Los Angeles Times* headline on August 16 read, "Stella Walsh Marries; Eligible for the Olympics." She even told the press that "her marriage would assure her eligibility for the Olympic team if she is successful in the [Olympic] trials." The *New York Times* announced, "Stella Walsh, the forty-five-year-old track star, was married last night in Las Vegas to Harry Olson. . . . The bride hopes to compete for the United States in the Olympic Games at Melbourne, Australia, this year."[29]

Four years later, on March 3, 1960, *Plain Dealer* columnist Hal Lebowitz confirmed that "at age 45, in an effort to become eligible for the '56 Olympics, Stella married a U.S. citizen." Lebowitz added that "at last reports she is still happily married." There is no evidence that Walsh and Olson ever lived together or that they ever divorced. Curiously, many of Walsh's biographical references list the date of her marriage as 1947, the same year she received U.S. citizenship. If Walsh had married nine years earlier, it would inoculate her from accusations that she married simply to be eligible for the 1956 U.S. Olympic team.

Immediately after the wedding, Walsh flew to Philadelphia for the AAU Championships, while Olson stayed behind in Los Angeles. She intended to go on to the U.S. Olympic Trials later that summer in Washington, D.C.

Walsh was confident that she would qualify for the Olympics in the 200 meters at the trials at American University. She was still dominating that event at
AAU meets in California. As the *Los Angeles Times* put it on April 27, 1956,
she was the "ageless wonder of the spike-and-girdle set."

Competing for the Southern Pacific Athletic Association, Walsh finished
third in her heat in the 200 meters and was not among the top three in her
100-meter heat. She failed to qualify for the finals in either event. She finished
a distant sixth in the long jump. Walsh had set a world record at 19 feet, 9¾
inches in 1938, which would have beat the trial's winning mark of 19 feet,
9¼ inches, but in her mid-forties Walsh could no longer jump that far. Once
again she said that her track and field career was over.[30] A month later, Babe
Didrikson died of cancer at the young age of forty-five.

Walsh's failure at the 1956 Olympic Trials seemed to be the end of her
dream to compete again in the Olympics. She would be nearly fifty years old
by the time of the 1960 Rome Olympics, too old to contend. In the fall of
1956, she said she would run in a few more local meets and then hang up her
spikes. "I've had my share. After all, this is my thirtieth season. . . . For years
I've wanted to take up golf but never had the time. From now on I'm going
to concentrate on just two things: being a good housewife and a fair golfer."[31]

Walsh could not stay away from the thrill of competition on the track.
Hoffman called her the "Eternal One." Sport was her claim to fame, her life's
work. Unlike music, art, writing, or other more sedentary endeavors, athletes
face an early end to pursuing their passion, and Walsh kept postponing her
retirement. In 1957, she took a train from Los Angeles to Cleveland to run
again at the AAU Championships in Shaker Heights, a suburb only about six
miles from her family home. Hampered by a pulled thigh muscle, she failed
to qualify for the finals in the broad jump, discus, and the 220 yards. After the
meet, Walsh again pledged that she was done with the track and said she was
taking a position with the U.S. Olympic Women's Track and Field Committee, which was headed by her neighbor and former discus champion Frances
Kaszubski. "It has been my life's dream to get to the Olympics as a representative of the United States," Walsh told the *Plain Dealer*. "And this [job] may
be it. Track has been very good to me, and I hope I can pass on some of my
knowledge to the upcoming young prospects."[32]

In 1958, the AAU added the 440 and 880 yards to the women's track
program, and the IOC resurrected the 800 meters for women after a thirty-

two-year hiatus. Walsh had broken through class, ethnic, and gender barriers to compete in sports, and now she tried to push the limits imposed on her by nature. She no longer had the explosiveness to win the sprints or the broad jump, so she concentrated on the middle distances. The 1958 AAU Indoor Championships happened to be in Akron, Ohio, and an exhibition 880-yard run was on the program. Walsh and three teammates from the Southern Pacific Athletic Club went to the meet. Walsh also wanted to qualify for a nineteen-woman team that was scheduled to go to Moscow in July. There was still opposition to the 800 meters on the Olympic program, so Kaszubski addressed the competitors before the race: "Ladies, please don't collapse and embarrass me. Run under control and with a smile on your face."[33]

Grace Butcher, now running for the Cleveland Magyar Athletic Club, was surprised to see the forty-seven-year-old Walsh, her old mentor, warming up for the half-mile. "I can't picture myself beating the incomparable Stella Walsh," Butcher thought, "but I will do my darndest to stick with her." Butcher's diary entry recalled her winning effort: "I found myself setting pace, having started on the pole. So I settled into an easy tempo and held it, waiting for two things: First, when was I going to get tired . . . and second, when was somebody going to challenge me? And there was nobody."[34]

Walsh came in third and was gracious in defeat. "Nice going, Grace," she said. Walsh was still the biggest name in women's track, and the *Plain Dealer* did not even mention Butcher in the headline, which read, "Walsh Finishes Third."[35] The two met again at the outdoor championships in Morristown, New Jersey, in May. Butcher came in second, and Walsh finished fifth. Butcher went on to win the 800 meters in the 1959 AAU Outdoor Championships, but a foot injury hampered her in the 1960 U.S. Olympic Trials and she did not go to the Rome Olympics. Back in California, Walsh won the 440 and 880 yards in two meets before heading to the Soviet Union in 1958, for the first of a series of groundbreaking dual meets.

In the last years of Stalin's life, relations between the Soviet Union and the United States reached their nadir. After he died in 1953, Soviet premier Nikita Khrushchev opened a new era in relations with the West. Recognizing that a nuclear war with the United States was suicidal, he called for "peaceful coexistence." In 1955, Khrushchev met U.S. president Dwight Eisenhower in Geneva, the first summit between Soviet and American leaders in a decade.

Khrushchev's exposé of Stalin's crimes at the Twentieth Party Congress of the Communist Party of the Soviet Union in early 1956 emboldened Poles and Hungarians to challenge their Stalinist regimes. The Polish Communists resolved their political crisis by putting an anti-Stalinist at the head of the PZPR, but Hungary's rebels called for an end to the Communist regime altogether. The Hungarian revolution in the fall of 1956 was a serious threat to Soviet bloc solidarity, and Khrushchev was not about to give up the security belt in Eastern Europe that the Soviet Union had won in World War II. He called in the Red Army to end the revolt. More than two thousand Hungarians lost their lives. An estimated 200,000 Hungarians left the country after the failed revolution, among them stars from the celebrated national soccer team.

The lowlight of the 1956 Melbourne Olympics was the semifinal water polo match between Hungary and the Soviet Union, when a Soviet player hit a Hungarian on the side of the head, opening a deep cut above his right eye, leaving the pool red with blood. Outraged Hungarian fans threatened to attack the Soviet players, and the referees ended the match with Hungary ahead, 4–0. Half of the one hundred athletes on the Hungarian Olympic team defected after the Melbourne Games.

During the 1952 presidential campaign, Eisenhower had promised to liberate Eastern Europe from the shackles of Communist rule. That was a hollow commitment; the West made no move to support the Hungarian rebels in 1956. When the Soviets successfully launched "Sputnik" into outer space in 1957, U.S. leaders panicked because the Soviet Union had achieved technological superiority. Still, cultural exchanges between the superpowers became commonplace. In 1959, Khrushchev visited the United States, going to a farm in Iowa and then to Los Angeles. The famed Ambassador Hotel, which had wined and dined Walsh and the other athletes at the 1932 Olympics, hosted a dinner for the Soviet premier. Khrushchev was disappointed when his scheduled trip to see Mickey Mouse at Disneyland, which had been built four years earlier, had to be cancelled because of security concerns.

In 1958, the Soviet Union and the United States began holding annual dual track and field meets. Walsh was selected for the team that went to Moscow in July. She was delighted at the opportunity to run against the country that had crushed Poland's independence after World War II: "The Russians avoided me all during my prime," Walsh declared. "Nothing would give me greater pleasure than to run them off their feet."[36] The Soviets had not ducked Walsh personally, of course, because the USSR did not participate in the Olympics until the 1952 Helsinki Games, when she was still ineligible to run for the United States.

The Soviet women trounced the Americans, and Walsh did not "run them off their feet," finishing far behind the 800-meter winner. The American men beat the Soviet men by seventeen points, while the American women lost by nineteen. The overwhelming victory of the Soviet women gave the Soviets bragging rights. Two of the American javelin throwers sent a postcard home: "The Russians had us going," they wrote, "but wait until next year."[37] The next years brought no better results, as the Soviet women dominated the Americans again. Naturally the Soviets crowed about the superiority of their Communist system because it produced better athletes. The Soviet bloc countries claimed to have emancipated their women and chastised gender discrimination in the West.

This propaganda and the poor showing of the American women in the Olympics and the dual meets with the Soviet Union accelerated a change in American attitudes toward women doing sport. Opportunities gradually increased for women to play games. In 1972, Congress passed Title IX legislation that mandated the devotion of equal resources to men's and women's sports in public schools and universities.

The emergence in the 1950s of the remarkable Tennessee State athletes keyed the resurgence of the U.S. women on the international track and field scene. Led by coach Edward Stanley Temple, from 1955 to 1969 the Tennessee State Tigerbelles won all but one outdoor AAU Track and Field Championship, a truly incredible run. The lone loss came by one point to the Compton Track Club in 1964. Temple coached the U.S. team that went to Moscow in 1958. He said, "We went over there, but they didn't even know we were there. All they were talking about was [decathlete] Rafer Johnson and [shot putter] Parry O'Brien.... The women were nothing. Russia had the Press sisters. The Press sisters had more whiskers than I did."[38]

Tennessee State women registered the only victories in the 1958 and 1959 dual meets with the Soviets, winning the 100 and 200 meters, and the 4 × 100 relay in both years. Led by Mae Faggs in the early 1950s, and then Wilma Rudolph and Wyomia Tyus in the 1960s, the Tennessee State women dominated Olympic sprinting. At the 1962 National Outdoor Championships, Vivian Brown bested Walsh's last surviving U.S. record in the 220 yards.

Rudolph's story was particularly uplifting. As a child, she was stricken with scarlet fever and pneumonia, leaving her left leg partially paralyzed. Through heroic efforts of doctors and her mother, Rudolph recovered and won three gold medals at the 1960 Rome Olympics.

Walsh tried to make one last Olympic team in 1960, but she failed to qualify in the 100 meters and javelin. She finally resigned herself to coaching American women up to the level of the Soviet-bloc athletes. Walsh studied their practice routines and copied their training methods, including weight lifting. She loved coaching and training youngsters almost as much as competing. One of her friends in Cleveland remembered later that "no matter what she undertook, she done [sic] a good job with the children. We went to many track and field meets, and they always became winners because she was very good at coaching and instructing."[39] Grace Butcher never forgot what Walsh meant to her, as a mentor and for breaking barriers in women's sport and master's competitions. In a 1987 interview Butcher recalled,

> My track career has continued now for over thirty years, just as Stella's did, and I am extremely grateful. But it began that day in May 1949, on the track at Cuyahoga Heights, as I felt my hand taken in her strong grip, those intense eyes studying me. . . . She wore real track shoes and real warm-up pants, and she was the greatest woman athlete I have ever known.[40]

Although Walsh would not contemplate running for Poland after it became a Soviet satellite, she continued to do goodwill tours to run in track meets in Poland. In 1962, she took U.S. discus thrower Melody McCarthy with her on a two-and-a-half-month trip. *Sports Illustrated* reported that Walsh, a "spry San Fernando, California, track trainer who won Olympic medals in both the 1932 and 1936 Games, proved her theory on staying in condition—never get out of it—as she nimbly outran younger competitors in eleven of twelve races in her native Poland."[41] The caliber of the competition is not known. Columnist James Doyle wrote this ditty about the middle-aged Cleveland celebrity:

> Though Stella Walsh is all of 50
> She's still a medal-winning swifty
> Our town's erstwhile Olympic wow
> Is on the whizz in Poland now.[42]

In October 1962, the Central Committee of the PZPR awarded Walsh the Champion of Merit Medal for her accomplishments in sports. It was the highest honor that Poland could give an athlete. A street in Górzno—a town about twenty-five miles from Walsh's birthplace—and a high school stadium in Radom were named after Walasiewicz. In contrast to other Warsaw Pact members, Poland's Communist regime was more tolerant of non-Communist cultural institutions and contacts with the West. The hard-line Communist regimes in the Soviet Union or East Germany would not have bestowed such honors on an anti-Communist expatriate living in the United States.

On her way back to Los Angeles from Poland, Walsh detoured to see her aging parents in Cleveland. She also stopped by the offices of the *Plain Dealer* to see Doyle and other sports reporters. She lamented the state of athletics in the United States, ignoring the feats of the Tennessee State sprinters: "We don't have very many newcomers coming up, and our replacements for today's name stars are just not there. I feel we could make rapid strides if more opportunities would be available to school-age boys and girls." She noted that the Soviets were doing strength training to improve speed.[43]

In the summer of 1963, Walsh ran the 75-yard dash in 8.6 seconds, two-thirds of a second slower than the world record. She decided to run in the AAU Championships in July, but any serious competition was over for her. As much as she loved the weather in Southern California and the opportunities to do sport throughout the year, Walsh missed her friends and family in Cleveland.

By the mid-1960s, life in Los Angeles had lost some of its allure for her anyway; the "land of perpetual spring" had become the "city of eternal smog." A symbol of the dramatic changes in the city was the demise of the once-extensive electric trolley system. The last car ran in 1963. The megalopolis had grown to 2.5 million by 1960 (third largest in the country), suburban sprawl clogged the freeways, and race relations were strained (the Watts riots erupted in 1965). In 1968, Adam Raphael wrote in the *Guardian*, "I reckon LA as the noisiest, the smelliest, the most uncomfortable, and the most uncivilized major city in the United States. In short, a stinking sewer."[44] Marilyn Monroe died of an overdose of drugs and alcohol in 1962; the death of Hollywood's most glittering female star reflected the city's lost luster. After a dozen years away, Walsh went back home to Cleveland.

8

Back to Cleveland and the Murder

With great sorrow and a heavy heart we say farewell to an outstanding athlete, a legend of Polish sport. She left us as a great sportswoman and patriot. Honor her memory.

—*Walsh obituary in* Słowo Powszechne *[Universal Word]*

In the summer of 1964, Stella Walsh moved back to her childhood home in Cleveland. She told *Plain Dealer* sports columnist Dan Coughlin, "I came back to see my parents." Julian and Weronica were in their mid-seventies, and her father was not in good health. Walsh was not altogether happy to be back on Clement Avenue, letting Coughlin know that she was not sure how long she would stay in the tiny house.[1] Eight years later, Julian Walasiewicz died, at the age of eighty-two. His funeral was held at Sacred Heart of Jesus on Kazimier Avenue, about a ten-minute walk from the Walsh house. Stella and Weronica would live on Clement for the rest of their lives.

Cleveland was no longer the bustling city Walsh had left in the early 1950s. At the beginning of the century, Cleveland was the nation's fifth largest city, and at the end of the 1940s, the local media boasted that Cleveland was the "best location in the nation." Two decades later, the city was in precipitous decline. The venerable *Cleveland News* newspaper closed its doors in January 1960, foreshadowing the fate of many of the city's old businesses. From 1958 to 1977, Cleveland lost some 130,000 jobs. The interstate highway system cut right through downtown, dividing many of Cleveland's decrepit neigh-borhoods and prompting white flight to the suburbs. The housing stock of the crumbling industrial town was aging, and urban renewal attempts had mixed results. Downtown Cleveland, like many older eastern cities, struggled to maintain its vibrancy. *Forbes* columnist Kevin Badenhausen called it the "most miserable city in the United States."[2]

From 1950 to 1970, an estimated 144,000 African Americans migrated to Cleveland, and approximately 307,000 whites moved out. Racial tensions were high in the city, especially in 1964, after Reverend Bruce Klunder—pro-testing the building of a segregated school on Lakeview Road—was accidently run over by a bulldozer. In the summer of 1966, the city experienced a serious race riot on Hough Avenue and E. 79th Street on the city's East Side, about four miles north of Walsh's neighborhood. The Ohio National Guard was called in to restore order, but not before four people were killed and more than two hundred fires gutted the community. Another outbreak of violence followed in 1968, despite the election of African American mayor Carl Stokes a year earlier. The unrest had a profound impact on the Slavic Village. As the ethnic character of the neighborhood changed, Poles moved out to Parma and other Cleveland suburbs. Jobs in the steel mills were drying up anyway.

The success of a city's sports teams cannot reverse economic and social decline, but winning teams can provide a temporary morale boost. In the 1940s, Cleveland was called the "City of Champions" or "Title Town." The Cleveland Browns won four All-American Football Conference champion-ships, and the Indians won the World Series in 1948, led by fireballing pitcher Bob Feller and power hitter Larry Doby. Even the minor league hockey team, the Cleveland Barons, garnered titles. The city's pro teams were also in the vanguard of desegregating football and baseball; the Browns signed Marion Motley in 1946, and in 1947, Doby joined the Indians to become the first black player in the American League.

In the 1960s, the misfortunes of Cleveland's pro teams mirrored the city's troubles. The Cleveland Indians won 111 regular-season games in 1954, the fourth-highest total in Major League Baseball history, but the New York Gi-ants swept the Tribe in the World Series, beginning four decades of Indian futility. From 1960 to 1993, their highest finish was third once and fourth six times. The team played to sparse crowds in cavernous Cleveland Municipal Stadium on the shores of Lake Erie, which seated almost 80,000 people. In

1974, a "Ten-Cent Beer Night" promotion resulted in a fan riot and fights with the players on the field. The Indians had to forfeit the game. In the 1980s, some wag dubbed the stadium the "Mistake on the Lake." The city got a new baseball stadium in 1994, and the resurgent Indians made it to the World Series in 1995, losing in six games to the Atlanta Braves. Two years later, the Indians played in the World Series again and were three outs away from Cleveland's first championship in thirty-three years. The Florida Marlins rallied for the win in extra innings.

The National Football League's (NFL) Cleveland Browns also played in Municipal Stadium, but with little more luck. The Browns won the NFL Championship in 1964, but after losing the National Football Conference title game in 1969, the Browns became a patsy, making the playoffs three times in the next ten years and losing every time. The Browns reached the American Football Conference championship game in 1987 and 1989, but Clevelanders had their hearts broken in two narrow losses to the Denver Broncos. Cleveland fans were devastated when Browns owner Art Modell moved the franchise to Baltimore in 1996, taking the name Ravens. Cleveland got an expansion team in 1999, but a team named the Browns has never played in the Super Bowl.

Cleveland got a National Basketball Association (NBA) franchise in 1970, but the Cavaliers were usually lousy too. Cleveland businessman Ted Stepian bought the team in 1980, promising to change the racial character of the team: "I need white people. . . . I think the Cavs have too many blacks. . . . You need a blend of white and black. I think that draws, and I think that's a better team."[3] After a series of money-saving moves that made his team non-competitive, the league adopted a rule to stop any team from trading away all of its best players and draft picks, dubbed the "Stepian rule." In the 2000s, the NBA's greatest star, Akron native LeBron James, could not bring a title to the beleaguered city, losing in the 2007 finals. He left the Cavs in 2010, much to the anger of Cleveland fans. "King James" returned to the team in 2014, losing in another NBA Final to the Golden State Warriors. Finally, in 2016, after a fifty-two-year drought, the Cavaliers beat the Warriors in seven games to bring a championship to Cleveland.

After returning to Cleveland, Walsh coached kids at her old Polish Falcon Nest 141, up the street on Broadway Avenue. She got a job as a supervisor in Cleveland's Division of Recreation and moonlighted as a sports editor for the

Nationality Newspapers Service. She also tended bar at the Sunshine Café, just south of Harvard Avenue on East 71st Street.

Walsh was still in the news because she could not bring herself to hang up the spikes. She trained three hours a day at Cuyahoga Heights High School field, about a mile south of her house. She ran exhibitions anytime she could, basking in the limelight as long as people in Cleveland remembered her. In January 1965, she was recruited to play for the Westerners Basketball Club. At fifty-three, she was three decades older than her teammates. She excelled at volleyball as well, leading her team to the championship in the Polonia Millennium Volleyball Tournament in 1966. She was named one of the top players in the tourney, which commemorated the millennial anniversary of the conversion of Polish ruler Mieszko I to Christianity in 966. Walsh was also the leading scorer on her tournament's basketball team. She even served as an assistant coach for a women's professional football team, the U.S.A. Daredevils, which played any men's team they could. The Daredevils were coached by former Cleveland Browns great Marion Motley.

In 1965, Walsh went to a meet in Columbus, Ohio, to try to qualify in the discus for a spot on a U.S. team that was to go to Kiev and Warsaw. According to the *Sports Illustrated* account of the meet, Mrs. Stella Walsh Olson

> walked happily through the swirl of stopwatch-toting officials and sweat-suited ingénues to the discus circle. She was going to compete against the kids. Although she looked broad-shouldered and powerful enough to put on a juggling act with 16-pound shots, she knew she had no chance to win.[4]

Walsh was envious of the opportunities that young women had in sports during that time. "When I see all these wonderful facilities available to the girls, and the understanding, I wish they had it in our day," she said regretfully. "I guess I was just born thirty years too soon." Walsh did not make the team, but she traveled to Poland anyway for three months to dedicate a new Polish athletic stadium named for her and to put on track and field clinics.[5] At a meet in Warsaw, nineteen-year-old Polish sprinter Irena Kirszenstein stole the show, winning the 100 meters and then anchoring the first-place 4 × 100 relay team. Walsh was on hand to congratulate Kirszenstein on the victory stand.

In her prime, Walsh competed at a time when women were just getting onto the Olympic track and field program. In middle age, she also took advantage of the nascent "masters" sporting competitions that became popular in the 1960s. The first U.S. Masters Track and Field Championships took place in 1968, in San Diego, but the meet was for men only. Three years later, at the age of sixty, Walsh returned to California to compete in the first Masters Championships for women. The meet was held at the Los Angeles Coliseum, the scene of her Olympic victory thirty-nine years earlier. The age limit for women was only thirty-five. Competing against athletes a quarter of a century younger, Walsh did not win any events.

Walsh was still one of the best Polish American woman athletes, however. In the summer of 1977, in Pittsburgh, she won the Polish Falcon District 60-meter championship. In September, Walsh represented her neighborhood Polish Falcon Nest 141 for the last time at the World Polish Olympics in Kraków. Walsh, now sixty-six, won the 60-meter sprint in the masters division. Nest 141 president Bertha Modrzynski accompanied Walsh to Poland and remembered the trip: "Believe me they rolled out the red carpet for us. That's how they honored her as the queen of Poland."[6] This was her last victory in a major competition, but Walsh promised to "continue to exert my very best energies to promote the most positive image of the United States [in Poland]. After all, I am extremely proud to be an American. I want to extend the best image possible 'as a Polish American.'"[7]

After coming back to Cleveland, Walsh became a regular visitor to the newspaper offices of the *Plain Dealer* to chat with Coughlin, and they developed a lasting friendship. Walsh had long shed her shyness. She was now a mature, confident athlete, trainer, and world traveler, renowned in Cleveland and Poland. One newspaper called her the "effervescent platinum blonde."[8] Walsh repeatedly badgered Coughlin—thirty years her junior—to run a 100-yard race. Walsh was still running competitively in meets throughout the Great Lakes area, so she was fit. Coughlin finally relented, and the two met on the Cuyahoga Heights track on July 13, 1967. Walsh gave the rotund, out-of-shape Coughlin a ten-yard head start, just to "make things fair," as she put it. Given the handicap, Coughlin beat her, so Walsh insisted that they race again, this time from the same starting line. Walsh beat Coughlin by six yards. According to Coughlin, after the race they went back to Stan Orzech's Tavern at East 71st Street and Lansing. At the time, Coughlin said that he was too tired to drink, so he had a coke and Walsh had two beers. He admitted later, "She drank me under the table, which gave her a sweep of the doubleheader."[9]

For many years, the Polish American community in Cleveland had whispered about Walsh's sexuality. Stories of her drinking, athletic build, and masculine features contributed to rumors that Walsh was not "all woman." Chuck Schodowski, director of Cleveland's Fox TV, grew up with Walsh in the Slavic Village. He said, "I heard my father and uncles joke, 'she's half-guy' or something like that, but I thought they were kidding and they were half-drunk."[10] Grace Butcher said, "I remember the first time I saw her stripped down to run. I was just astounded at her masculinity. . . . Stella was very mannish looking, but many women are, and we didn't think anything of it."[11] In her early fifties, Walsh started dying her hair blonde, and when she began losing her hair, she donned a cheap, ill-fitting platinum blonde wig. Coughlin, Walsh's drinking buddy, said that as Walsh entered her mid-sixties "she became hideously homely."[12]

Nonetheless, Walsh's name did not come up when doubts arose in the mid-1960s about the gender of some of the female athletes from the Soviet bloc who were dominating international track and field events. Unable to beat the Soviet women on the field, Westerners began to question their sex. The Press sisters, Irina and Tamara, were the first Soviet female Olympic stars; Tamara won the gold medal in the shot put and a silver in the discus at the 1960 Rome Olympics, and Irina won gold in the 80-meter hurdles. Tamara won gold medals in the shot and discus at the 1964 Tokyo Olympics, while Irina took home the gold in the pentathlon. The success of Soviet women athletes on the world stage seemed to confirm Communist propaganda that they were more emancipated than their counterparts in the West.

The Press sisters and other Soviet-bloc athletes were so successful that some people speculated that they were not women at all. The new Soviet sportswoman was also a direct challenge to the bourgeois feminine image cultivated in the West, which valued beauty and grace. Some of the Soviet athletes, as caricatured by Tamara Press, were unadorned and plump. According to historian Geoffrey Smith, "The spectre of the Soviets as he-men and he-women . . . underscored the need for American women to take distance from their Soviet counterparts and become as feminine as the latter were mannish."[13]

The rumors about the "gender-deviant" Press "brothers" spread when they pulled out of 1966 European Athletic Championships in Budapest, where a sex test was to be administered for the first time. *The Times* (London) declared, "The absence, though for firmly stated reasons of injury and family illness, of several *leading Russian women athletes* from the championships has caused a great deal of discussion here on the subject of physiologically 'borderline cases' in women's athletics."[14]

Opportunities for women to do sport in the United States grew rapidly, spurred on by the women's liberation movement and the challenge from the athletes from the Communist countries. Women from the United States dominated the Olympic sprints in the twentieth century, except in the 1970s, when East German runners came to the fore. This was not a question of men posing as women, but doping. We now know that the East Germans ran a sophisticated program to supply their athletes with performance-enhancing drugs.

Poland produced three of the greatest sprinters in history, all women. Beginning at the 1964 Tokyo Olympics, Irena Kirszenstein Szewińska and Ewa Kłobukowska carried on the legacy of the great Stella Walsh. When Nazi Germany attacked Poland in September 1939, Kirszenstein's parents left Poland for Leningrad. Somehow they survived the Germans' nearly 900-day siege of the city, during which 1 million civilians perished. Irena was born in 1946, a year after the war ended. The Kirszenteins returned to Warsaw when Irena was a young child, and she grew into the lithe, sinewy, strong, 5-foot-9 body of a prototypical sprinter. At Tokyo, Kirszenstein won silver medals in the long jump and the 200 meters, and, along with Kłobukowska, helped the Polish team win the 4 × 100 relay. At the 1966 European Championships in Budapest, Kirszenstein won the 200 meters and the long jump, came in second in the 100 meters, and anchored Poland's gold medal–winning 4 × 100 relay team.

After marrying sports photographer Janusz Szewiński in 1967, Kirszenstein Szewińska won gold medals in the 200 meters at the 1968 Mexico City Olympics and the 400 meters at the 1976 Montreal Games, and bronze medals in the 100 at Mexico and the 200 at the Munich Olympics in 1972. She also won four more bronze medals in the European Championships in 1971, 1974, and 1978. In 1974, Kirszenstein Szewińska became the first woman to break fifty seconds in the 400 meters. She established six world records in the sprints and is the only runner in history, male or female, to have held the world record in the 100, 200, and 400 meters simultaneously. Kirszenstein Szewińska ran in her last Olympics in Moscow in 1980, but she failed to make the 400-meter finals. One of the greatest Olympic athletes in history, she was elected to the International Women's Sports Hall of Fame in 1992.

Ewa Kłobukowska came in third in the 100 meters at the Tokyo Games, along with winning gold in the 4 × 100-meter relay. In 1965, she set a world record in the 100. She won the 100-meter gold and a silver medal in the 200 meters at the 1966 European Athletic Championships in Budapest and, with Kirszenstein Szewińska, won the 4 × 100 relay. Kłobukowska, like the other female athletes at the meet, had to submit to a visual examination by three women doctors. She passed the so-called "nude parade."

At the European Cup Championships in Kiev in 1967, Kłobukowska willingly submitted to a chromosome test. After all, she was raised a girl and was attracted to boys. According to a story in *Time* magazine, "Though she had negligible bust development, she seemed, with shoulder-length blonde hair, sufficiently feminine to attract plenty of male dancing partners in Warsaw night spots."[15] Three Russian and three Hungarian doctors determined that Kłobukowska had "one chromosome too many." It is unclear which chromosome, but she probably had some "XYY" or even a single "X."[16]

Kłobukowska was stripped of her medals and banned from international competitions. "It's a dirty and stupid thing to do to me," she grumbled. "I know what I am and how I feel." On the one hand, Polish authorities protested the ruling and took an enlightened attitude toward gender designation: "It is not sufficient to say that there is a dividing line, that this is a girl and this is not. . . . You must allow for those persons who are complicated to be able to take part in sport."[17] On the other hand, the Western press, prejudiced against any Soviet-bloc athlete, chided her with such headlines as "Polish Blonde Eva Kłobukowska Turned into 'Adam'" and "Kłobukowska Misses Test for Misses."[18] She later birthed a son, exposing the myriad problems with sex testing.

When drug testing and chromosome gender verification were instituted for the first time at the 1968 Mexico City Olympics, the Press sisters dropped out, adding to the speculation that there was something amiss with them. The *Chicago Tribune* wrote, "We shall never know the exact number of men who have competed in the Olympics posing as women."[19] If there was any cheating going on, it probably had to do more with steroids than gender. Many women in the Soviet bloc were taking performance-enhancing drugs.

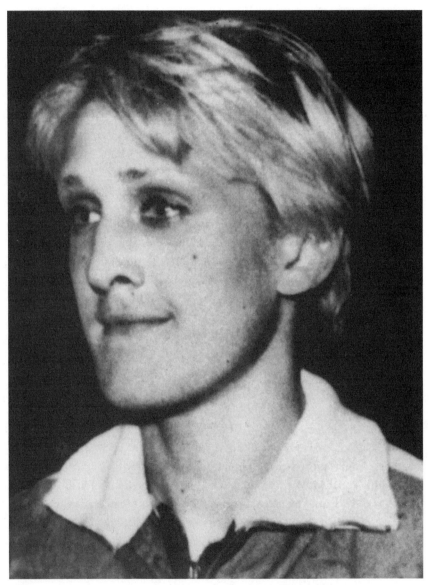

Polish sprinter Ewa Kłobukowska was found to have abnormal chromosomes and was stripped of her European Championship medals in 1967. She later birthed a son, compromising the validity of sex testing. *Smithsonian Institution Archives. Image # SIA2008-4856.*

Chromosome testing was flawed as well, because some women have chromosomal anomalies. The IOC and IAAF ended routine chromosome testing in the 1990s Sydney Games, although both organizations maintained the right to conduct sex tests. The issue surfaced again in 2009, after the IAAF suspended 800-meter world champion Caster Semenya of South Africa for almost a year while trying to determine her sex. Today the IOC sets limits on testosterone for women athletes, which many have charged as unfair. Testosterone does not necessarily improve athletic performance.

In the last decade of her life, Walsh was showered with honors. In February 1970, she was named to the International Women's Sports Hall of Fame, along with Babe Didrikson and Gertrude Ederle. In honor of her induction, Cleveland mayor Carl Stokes designated April 13th "Stella Walsh Day." In the official declaration, Walsh was "acclaimed as the greatest all-around woman athlete of all time and recently inducted into the Hall of Fame for Women . . . the holder of sixty-five world and national American, Canadian, Polish, and Japanese track and field records . . . [and] has triumphed in more than 5,000 events."[20]

Her old Slavic Village friend and national AAU chairwoman Frances Kaszubski was there to hand out the awards. In her acceptance speech, Walsh said she was often asked what it takes to be a champion: "There are many things," she replied. "You have to have good friends and financial backing. You have to adhere to hard training and strict diet. As you know, I don't smoke and drink. And I never went out with boys till I was nine years old."[21] Of course, Walsh was known to put a few beers away, and outrunning boys was more important to her than going to the movies with them.

On June 13, 1974, Walsh was inducted into the National Polish American Sports Hall of Fame, which had been created two years earlier. The track shoes on display at the museum in Troy, Michigan, are signed "Stella Walsh Walasiewicz." The Cleveland City Council issued a resolution honoring Walsh for her induction. Several months later, the council again recognized her at the annual Pułaski Day Dinner Dance and Scholarship Awards Banquet, and lobbied for her to be nominated for the AAU's James E. Sullivan Award: "Council believes that some of her more outstanding achievements qualify her being named as one of the ten most outstanding athletes of the year for the American Sullivan Award."[22] Walsh was nominated but did not win.

Walsh with Polish boxers Zbigniew Kicka and Jerzy Skoczek at the Polish Falcon House, 1975. *Cleveland State University.*

Walsh and her old rival, Helen Stephens, stayed in touch, even exchanging Christmas greetings. On June 14, 1975, Walsh was inducted into the National Track and Field Hall of Fame, which, at the time, was located in Charleston, West Virginia. In an odd twist, Stephens was inducted at the same ceremony. Stephens told her biographer that she had a hotel room next to Walsh, who was staying with a female companion. Stephens, who by that time had made public her homosexuality, claimed that through the shared wall she heard Walsh and her friend having some of their own fun.[23] The story is probably apocryphal.

In June 1978, Walsh entered the Greater Cleveland Sports Hall of Fame in track and field, along with Kaszubski, in part for her work as president of the Lake Erie Association of the AAU. Later that year, Walsh became a member of the newly created Ohio Women's Hall of Fame, which elicited a congratulatory telephone call from U.S. president Jimmy Carter. When Casimir Bielen, president of the Nationality Newspapers Service, nominated Walsh for an "Outstanding Ohioan" award from the Cleveland Public Schools, Polish American Congress president Aloysius A. Mazewski wrote him, saying, "I concur with you that she is the most outstanding woman athlete. She has been a credit to our people."[24] In late November 1980, a week before her murder, Walsh was inducted once again into the Greater Cleveland Sports Hall of Fame, this time for her accomplishments in basketball.

As Walsh piled up award after award in the last few years of her life, recitations of her record elicited repeated exaggerations and falsehoods. In 1979, she was inducted into the Ohio Senior Citizens Hall of Fame. Ohio senator Howard M. Metzenbaum submitted this entry into the Congressional Record, recognizing Walsh:

> We in Ohio are indeed fortunate to have the greatest of woman athlete [*sic*] in history as one of our citizens . . . Stella Walsh. . . . In 1928, as a member of the Polish Olympic team, Stella won a gold medal in the 100-meter dash. She came back to win the silver medal in the same event at the infamous 1932 games in Berlin.[25]

When Metzenbaum was informed that Walsh had won her gold medal in Los Angeles in 1932 and a silver in Berlin in 1936, the senator corrected the mistake on the floor of the Senate the next day.[26]

Walsh's friend from the Slavic Village, Casimir Bielen, issued press releases whenever Walsh was honored. He wrote reference letters for her and hired her on as a sports editor. Bielen played loose with the truth and was the source of the many distortions of her record. He frequently claimed that the "indestructible athlete" was the "winner of five gold and four silver medals in the 1932 and 1936 Olympics."[27] In fact, Walsh won only two Olympic medals, gold in the 100 meters at Los Angeles and silver at Berlin. He included her victories at the Women's World Games in 1930 and 1934 with her two Olympic medals.

On July 6, 1979, the Polish Consulate in New York sent a letter to "Walsh Olson" at Clement Avenue, inviting her to a reception to award her the Srebrna Oznake Zasługi Polskiej Rzeczpospolita Ludowej [Silver Cross of Merit of the Polish People's Republic], one of the most prestigious civilian honors that the government could bestow.[28] Presidents John F. Kennedy and Gerald Ford had previously received the award in Poland. Walsh sent a telegram to the consulate two weeks later, explaining that she had been out of town when the letter arrived. She had tried in vain to get a flight to New York. "Since I missed this important event," she added, "I want to make amends by accepting this high honor of recognition at some future date."[29]

It might have been an embarrassment for Walsh to attend this official function at the diplomatic mission of the Communist People's Republic anyway. She was to receive the award in conjunction with the government's commemoration of "National Day" on July 22, which marked the formation of the Polish Committee of National Liberation in Lublin in 1944. The so-called Lublin Committee was the core of the postwar Communist government. The People's Republic stopped officially recognizing November 11, National Independence Day, which the interwar government had celebrated as the date of the resurrection of Poland in 1918. In May 1980, Polish minister-consul Kazimierz H. Cias bestowed upon Walsh the Silver Cross at a ceremony at Eddy's Chalet West Restaurant in North Ridgeville, about twenty miles east of Cleveland. The Ohio House of Representatives noted the award in its official record.[30]

In 1955, a year before her death, Babe Didrikson wrote an autobiography in which she shored up her claim to be the greatest woman athlete of all time. Didrikson was a national figure, while Walsh was just a local favorite. Walsh contemplated writing her own story. Undoubtedly, she also hoped to make some money on a book deal. She was making a little more than $10,000 a year at her job with the Division of Recreation, the highest salary she had ever earned.

When Walsh was inducted into the International Women's Sports Hall of Fame in 1970, she had sent it some of her memorabilia. Now she wanted some of the items back. In a letter to the Hall of Fame she wrote,

After 50 years of competition, with more than 5,000 awards, plus all the record-breaking victories and championship titles, no matter how short, my autobiography has to be a book!! Anyway, enclosed find two sheets of outstanding highlights. . . . Since, I am writing my Life Story [sic], I would appreciate the return of enclosed material.[31]

A California woman was the unlikely source of some of Walsh's memorabilia. Sick-abed with scarlet fever as a little girl in 1932, Ellen Gibson heard about Stella Walsh when she won her gold medal at the Los Angeles Olympics. "I was quite envious being stuck in the house," Gibson remembered years later, "and knowing that somebody was out there running and breaking records." Gibson's husband dealt in antiques, and in 1978 they bought several of Walsh's things at an estate sale, for two dollars. Gibson phoned the Clement Avenue house to tell Walsh about her find, but Stella's mother Weronica, who spoke little English, hung up on her. On April 13, 1980, Gibson finally tracked down Walsh at her Division of Recreation office. Walsh gratefully accepted the found items, telling Gibson that she was writing her life story. Gibson was surprised to hear that Walsh was still doing road work several times a week: "She didn't seem to be a reflective woman, didn't like to look back," Gibson observed. "She was consumed by this urge to run and to teach kids athletics." Walsh told Gibson that some of the kids she trained were "kind of tough" but that "as long as I can outrun them, they'll respect me."[32] The autobiography was never written. Several months later Walsh was dead.

Cleveland's two greatest Olympic athletes, both winners of the coveted 100-meter gold medal as the fastest man or woman alive, died in 1980. Chain-smoking cigarettes finally caught up with Jesse Owens. On March 31, he lost his battle with lung cancer. He was sixty-six. As Owens neared death, he displayed the grace that had characterized his running style and the way he led his life. "Every night I get down on my knees and thank God for all that's happened to me," he said. "In what other country in the world could a poor black kid like me go to all the places I've been, seen all the things I've seen, and make so many friends." Several days before he died, Owens reflected on his friendship with Luz Long, the German Olympian who had helped him win the broad jump at Berlin in 1936. Nearly forty years earlier, Owens had cried when he heard that Long had died fighting in World War II. The day after Owens passed, the *Plain Dealer* wrote, "Mr. Owens said the Olympic Games were never meant to be contests between nations, or differing political systems. The Games, he said, were meant to be contests between individuals."[33]

Those were also the sentiments of Pierre Coubertin, founder of the modern Olympics, but in reality, the Olympic Games became a fierce competition of nation against nation. Jesse Owens and Stella Walsh ran in the Nazi Olympics in 1936, the first of many Olympics exploited for explicit political gain. During the Cold War, the Olympic Games became a competition to prove whether liberal democracy or Communism produced the best athletes.

Although her days as an Olympic athlete were long gone, in the late 1970s Walsh and her fellow Polish Americans were hopeful that Poland might finally break free of Communist rule. For all but twenty of Walsh's sixty-nine years, her native land had suffered from German or Russian oppression. The worst of it was the genocidal Nazi occupation during World War II. The Red Army's "liberation" of Poland replaced Nazi tyranny with a Communist dictatorship.

In the last few months of Walsh's life, there was real hope for a free Poland. In 1978, the conclave of Roman Catholic cardinals elected a Pole, Cardinal Karol Wojtyła, as the first non-Italian pope in more than four hundred years. Pope John Paul II lifted the spirits of the entire Polish nation and indirectly challenged the Communist dictatorship and its atheist, Marxist ideology. A year later, on his first visit to Poland as pope, John Paul said, "It is impossible without Christ to understand this nation with its past so full of splendour and also of terrible difficulties." He hinted that he had not only a spiritual, but also a temporal calling, and foreshadowed the end of Communist rule a decade later: "I must ask myself . . . why it was in the year 1978 that a son of the Polish nation, a son of Poland, should be called to the Chair of St. Peter. . . . Are we not justified in thinking that Poland in our time has become a land called to give an especially important witness?"[34]

The pope seemed prophetic when a worker's revolt in the Gdańsk shipyard in the summer of 1980, led by electrician Lech Wałesa, brought the Polish government to its knees. That fall the Polish Communist Party recognized "Solidarity," the first free trade union in the Soviet bloc. But hopes for a free Poland were dashed in December 1981, when the Polish government, under pressure from the Kremlin, declared martial law. Solidarity went underground until the late 1980s, when Soviet leader Mikhail Gorbachev renounced the use of force to prop up the Soviet satellite regimes. In the fall of 1989, Solidarity returned to head the first non-Communist government in the Warsaw Pact. The Berlin Wall crumbled in November, and by the end of the year, the Iron Curtain was no more. Stella Walsh would not live to witness these monumental events.

In the midst of Poland's political crisis in 1980, the Polish national women's basketball team left for a tour of the United States. The team was scheduled to play Kent State University on December 10. Ten years earlier, Kent State had gained infamy as the site of the Ohio National Guard's shooting of four student Vietnam War protesters, immortalized in the Crosby, Stills, Nash, and Young song "Ohio" and the lyric "Tin soldiers and Nixon coming . . . four dead in O-hi-o." Dorothy Fuldheim, the pioneering female news anchor of Cleveland television channel WEW, recalled the awful moment: "When I returned from Kent I wept on the air because of the killings of four young innocent Americans and the wounding of others." Some angry Clevelanders who supported the National Guard's action against the students called for Fuldheim's firing.[35]

Cleveland mayor George Voinovich commissioned Walsh, who was still working for the Division of Recreation, to greet the Polish national team and present it with a ceremonial key to the city. Who better to welcome the Polish team to Ohio than the most famous Polish-born woman athlete in the United States?

Shortly before nine o'clock on the frigid winter night of December 4, Walsh drove her beat-up old brown 1973 Oldsmobile Omega to Uncle Bill's discount department store at Broadway Avenue and Aetna Road, about a half mile from her house. Uncle Bill's is long gone, but among the storefronts in the nondescript strip mall today is a sports therapy business. Walsh had several hundred dollars in cash in hand to buy commemorative ribbons for the Polish players. Whenever European teams play a "friendly" against a team from another country it is customary for the players to exchange some small trinkets in a gesture of friendship and goodwill. Usually the players swap a small pennant with the colors and symbol of their respective teams. Walsh was charged with presenting souvenirs to the Polish team on behalf of the Lake Erie District AAU Committee.

This was the Christmas holiday season in the city, but the merry old spirit of Cleveland depicted in the iconic film *A Christmas Story* (1983) was no more. Walsh's Polish neighborhood had changed radically in the seven decades since the Walasiewicz family arrived in the Slavic Village. Facing an energy crisis in the early 1970s and competition from foreign imports, Cleveland and other "Rust Belt" cities along the Great Lakes were losing most of their steel and other heavy industries. Clevelanders fled the city for the suburbs, and the old ethnic communities broke down. Cleveland lost 24 percent of its population from 1970 to 1980, leaving behind a city plagued by violence and despair. It was in the top 20 percent of U.S. cities in rates of poverty, unemployment, dilapidated housing, violent crime, and municipal debt. Homicides rose from fifty-nine in 1962 to 333 in 1972, one of the highest rates in the country. According to the Department of Housing and Urban Development, the murder rate in Cleveland and Detroit was the highest of the Rust Belt cities along the Great Lakes.[36] Voinovich complained, "At neighborhood meetings, sometimes people jump on me for two and a half hours about crime."[37] The median family income in Cleveland fell 11.1 percent between 1970 and 1980.[38] The city defaulted on its bonds in 1979, the first city since the Depression to do so.

In 1969, the heavily polluted Cuyahoga River caught fire, leaving a stark image of the city's sorry state of affairs. Another song commemorated that event, Randy Newman's "Burn On":

> Cleveland, city of light, city of magic
> Cleveland, city of light, you're calling me
> Cleveland, even now I can remember
> 'Cause the Cuyahoga River goes smokin' through my dreams
> Burn on, Big River, burn on.

After buying red and white ribbons (Poland's colors) for the Polish team, Walsh was walking back to her car when two young neighborhood thugs, Ricky Clark and his brother-in-law, Donald Cassidy, sprang out of the dark, brandished a gun, and demanded her purse. This was not the first time that Walsh had been a victim of crime. Since moving back to Cleveland in 1964, her car tires had been slashed, she suffered a broken nose in a mugging, and she had her car stolen.[39] It was not safe for a woman to walk around in the dark alone. According to the police report, powder burns on her hands revealed that Walsh tried to knock the gun away and was shot once in the stomach. Clark and Cassidy panicked and fled the scene, leaving Walsh on the ground next to her car. They left more than $200 on the front seat.[40]

The bullet severed an artery. It took more than half an hour for the ambulance to arrive while Walsh was bleeding to death. The ambulance rushed her the five minutes to St. Alexis Hospital on Broadway, the largest Catholic hospital in the area, and about a mile and a half from the Walasiewicz house. St. Alexis had served the family many times before, but this time it was too late. Shortly before midnight, Stella Walsh died on the operating table. Her body was taken to Komorowski Funeral Home on East 71st Street, a short

The parking lot today of the Slavic Village strip mall where Walsh was murdered. *Author photo.*

walk from Clement Avenue. The Walasiewicz family could not cover the cost of her funeral, so Stella's sister Clara Battiato filed a claim with the state's Victim Compensation Fund for medical and funeral expenses.[41]

The murder was big news in the Cleveland area and in Los Angeles, where Walsh won her gold medal in 1932 and lived for more than a decade. The *Los Angeles Times* wrote, "To track and field fans of the 1930s, Stella Walsh was to women's track and field what Jesse Owens is to men's track, or, to a less vociferous degree, what John [Lennon] of the Beatles was to rock and roll."[42] The national news media barely noticed the shooting. Of the fifteen television news segments on Walter Cronkite's *CBS Evening News* the next night, Walsh's murder was the second to last story. The *New York Times* relegated the story to page twenty.

Coverage of Walsh's death was soon overshadowed by news of another shooting. On December 8, the same day that Walsh's obituary appeared in the *Plain Dealer*, Lennon was gunned down in front of his New York City apartment—like Walsh—by a complete stranger. The next day the Polish national team dedicated their game against Kent State to Stella Walsh. Polish coach Ludwick Mietta commented, "She was very popular in Poland. . . . [The United States] is a dangerous country."[43] Indeed it was. Three months later, President Ronald Reagan barely survived an assassination attempt by yet another handgun-wielding assailant.

The news of Walsh's death was soon forgotten, even by the Polish press, which was consumed at the time by the emergence of the Solidarity free trade union and the political and economic turmoil in the country. Walsh's death was shunted to the back pages and then forgotten when word came of Lennon's murder. In the December 6–7 issue of *Życie Warszawy* [Warsaw Life], there appeared a short article with the headline "Stanisława Walasiewiczowna Is Dead." The newspaper mistakenly reported that she had been shot during an attempted burglary of her apartment. A day later, the paper ran a longer article about her life and a photo of Walsh winning the 100 meters at the 1932 Los Angeles Olympics.

Słowo Powszechne [Universal Word], a Catholic newspaper that generally supported the Polish Communist government, wrote a heartfelt obituary: "With great sorrow and a heavy heart we say farewell to an outstanding athlete, a legend of Polish sport. She left us as a great sportswoman and patriot. Honor her memory." *Sztandar Młodych* [Youth Banner], the organ of the General Council of the Socialist Federation of Polish Youth Associations, did some sloppy research, reporting incorrectly that Walsh had left Poland in 1914, and that her career had ended in 1946. But the paper lauded her efforts on behalf of Poland, saying, "Her connection to the Polish nation manifested itself in stadiums throughout the world."[44]

For several years before her death, Walsh had been working with the POC on developing connections between Polish and American athletes. Unlike their counterparts in the Soviet Union and East Germany, Polish sports authorities generally tried to steer clear of politics. After the murder, the POC issued the following statement:

> In relation to the tragic death of outstanding athletic Olympic record holder Stella Walsh Olson—we are joining with you in sorrow—an irreparable loss—she served Polish sport and was active in Polonia. She was the world's most famous athlete in between the wars—and will remain forever—our pride of Polish sport.[45]

Five days after the murder, more than four hundred people attended Walsh's memorial service at Sacred Heart of Jesus Church, where her father's funeral had been held eight years earlier. The Polish national basketball team, clad in their red and white "Polska" sweat suits, filed into the church and sat across from Walsh's mother Weronica and her two sisters, Clara and Sophia. Two other Cleveland Olympic gold medal sprinters, Harrison Dillard and Paul Drayton, were among Walsh's pallbearers. Father Bartnikowski's eulogy referenced Walsh's life in sports: "There is but one important event—eternal salvation. It is not measured by time clocks or tape measures, only by God Himself."[46] Walsh would not rest in peace, however. A bombshell hit the community when the results of her autopsy were made public.

9

Saving Stella Walsh

When she was a little girl . . . in the heart of the Polish community, everyone was aware that she was a little different from the others. It was accepted. It was something we all knew about. When she was younger, she was teased by the other children.

—*Walsh's friend Casimir Bielen, after her autopsy report*

As Walsh's body was laid to rest in a place called Calvary, her memory was being crucified. Cleveland's Polish American community came out in force for her funeral because controversy was swirling about the results of the autopsy. The day before the funeral, local NBC television station WKYC (channel 3) ran a story on the preliminary autopsy findings, which revealed that Walsh had a small, nonfunctional penis and testicles, a small opening below the scrotum, but no female genitalia or reproductive organs.

Walsh's friends were outraged at charges that Walsh was a fraud and suggestions that "Stella the fella" should forfeit her medals and awards. Walsh's old pal Beverly Perret Conyers said that she was a "victim of every circumstance. A victim of birth, a victim of life, and a victim of death." *Plain Dealer* columnist Hal Lebowitz, who had regularly shared a few beers with her at Stan Orzech's bar, wrote, "The neighborhood men enjoyed talking with her and bought her beers. Her shyness made it difficult for the public to know her. In a sense, she lived in a shadow world, almost a sports oddity. . . . In her death, by a robber's bullet, she again was the victim of the times."[1] When channel 3 cameras showed up at the memorial service, one funeral goer screamed, "Get out of here. You've got a lot of nerve after that garbage last night."[2]

Walsh's condition is known today as intersex or gonadal mosaicism, which occurs in an estimated 0.018 percent of live births.[3] Because she had not undergone any surgery, she was not a transsexual. This issue in women's sports had been headline news several years earlier when Dr. Richard Raskin underwent a sex-change operation to become Renee Richards. Richards caused a stir by going on the pro tennis tour and reaching the quarterfinals of the 1978 U.S. Open. Walsh's case was different.

The uninformed media assumed that if Walsh was not all woman, she must be a man. Some in the press charged her with fraud. One Australian journalist wrote, "Meet the most outrageous transvestite of all time—she won Olympic medals and set world records back in the thirties, and got away with it."[4] A British newspaper claimed, "Her rivals believed that she was a man, and in 1980 an autopsy revealed they were right."[5] Harry Gordon, the Australian Olympic Committee's historian for the 2000 Sydney Olympics, concluded, "An autopsy revealed that she had male sexual organs."[6] One journalist called her life "shadowed by mystery and scarred by shame."[7] Even Walsh's biographical entry in the U.S. Track and Field Hall of Fame leaves doubt about her achievements, saying, "An autopsy revealed that Walsh had male sex organs."[8]

Some in the Polish press also reported that Walsh, one of their most famous track and field athletes, was not a woman. Polish journalist Anna Jakieła wrote, "The immensity of the whole confusion forever darkened the sprinter's achievements, and everyone just remembers now the question of her sex."[9] *Życie Warszawy* [Warsaw Life] wrongly concluded that the autopsy revealed that "Walasiewicz was a man."[10]

If Stella Walsh had died of natural causes, her condition would have gone with her to the grave. Sexual identity is a thoroughly personal, intimate issue, but an autopsy was mandatory in this murder case. The job fell to Cuyahoga County coroner Samuel Gerber, who had gained some notoriety in the sensational trial of Dr. Sam Sheppard in 1954. Sheppard was accused of murdering his wife Marilyn. The doctor was convicted, but twelve years later he was acquitted in a retrial. Gerber's testimony was refuted at the second trial.

Gerber's report on Walsh found that her genetic makeup was both male and female:

The majority of her cells examined had a normal X and Y chromosome, and a minority of her cells contained a single X chromosome and no Y chromosome. Individuals with this form of sex chromosome mixture may present a variety of physical forms ranging from almost normal males to individuals that would be indistinguishable from females with Turner syndrome (a condition in which females have just one X chromosome).[11]

Gerber theorized that Walsh had probably developed more prominent male sex organs as she reached puberty and that she was probably traumatized by it. Two months later, Gerber said, "She suffered from a rare malady known as mosaicism, in which the human body possesses both male and female chromosomes. In her case, Miss Walsh did have male sex organs. That alone does not make her a man. All you can say is that her sex chromosomes were male dominant."[12]

Several weeks after Walsh's murder, Dr. Angus Muir, director of Case Western University's genetics center, commented on Walsh's mosaicism, stating, "You have to take into consideration the whole human being," he observed. "And if biologically you can call someone a male or female by their chromosomes, functionally or psychologically, they may be in fact the other." Muir acknowledged that to discover as a teenager or later in life that one's gender identity differs from one's biological sex, is "very disconcerting. Psychologically, it's devastating."[13]

Mosaicism was still a relatively unknown condition in 1980. At birth a person was either designated male or female. Approximately 1 to 2 percent of the population does not fit into these two biological categories. In 2013, Germany became one of the first countries to acknowledge that some babies are born with traits of both sexes and allow parents to wait before designating the child as male or female and possibly undergoing corrective surgery.

In the early twentieth century, few people, even those in the medical profession, acknowledged that some people were born with genital peculiarities. This might have been the case with Dora Ratjen, the German high jumper at the Berlin Olympics who later identified herself as male. For most of Walsh's life, sexual ambiguity was not a matter of general public discourse. She had no support system to help her navigate a world in which there were only two sexes and two clear gender identities. She lived in a "no-man's—no-woman's—land," but her birth certificate listed her as a female, she was given a female name and raised female, and she thought of herself as a woman throughout her life. That was her gender identity. Biologist Ethel Sloan makes this very point:

> There is more evidence that gender identity differentiation of the brain as male or female occurs postnatally and depends not on hormones, but on the total environment in which a child is reared. Usually, the chromosome constitution, the gonad structure, the morphology of the external ducts, and the appearance of the external genitalia coincide: When they do not, the sex assignment and rearing can apparently override both the genotype and the phenotype.[14]

Stella Walsh lived in a time when few people acknowledged that there should be a category for her condition. Shortly after Walsh's death, Dr. Eduardo Hay of the IOC's Medical Commission wrote,

> Obviously she would not have been allowed to participate nowadays, since she would have undergone and failed the femininity control of the IOC's Medical Commission. What happened almost a century ago cannot be taken into account since there was no desire to break the regulations which were valid at the time, or indeed any awareness of having done so.[15]

Except for her family and a few close friends from Cleveland, no one knew that Walsh was living with a condition that had troubled her throughout her life. Many of Walsh's fellow athletes had noted that she always arrived at track meets or basketball games in full uniform. "Stella never got changed in front of us or took a shower," recalled 1932 U.S. Olympic gold medalist Jean Shiley. "She used to arrive at the track in a tracksuit, with her gear already on underneath."[16]

Walsh's condition was a closely guarded secret in Cleveland's Polish community. Certainly no one was going to "out" the ambiguous sex of their most famous athlete. When Walsh's autopsy was made public, several close friends acknowledged that they knew Walsh had a rare genital abnormality. Beverly Perret Conyers had inadvertently seen Walsh undressing in a local bathhouse, saying, "She asked me if God did this to her. I said, 'No, it was a mistake.' I can't figure it out. She was raised in dresses."[17] Conyers defended her friend to the *New York Times*:

It has never affected anything I felt about Stella all my life. I don't think it changes the image of Stella one bit. When Stella competed, there were no sex tests. . . . You don't turn against your friends just because they may have a birth defect. She was a lady in every sense of the word. . . . The Polish people adore Stella. I don't think anything that comes out of this will destroy their feelings. She was kind to everybody.[18]

Walsh's ex-husband, Harry Olson, made a statement to the *Los Angeles Times* that he was as surprised as anyone at the coroner's findings. "I feel stupid as hell for marrying her. We had sex a few times but with the lights off."[19] That was probably a fabrication. Fearing some sort of legal trouble, Olson was covering up a marriage that had been arranged so that Walsh would be eligible to compete for the United States at the 1956 Melbourne Olympics. He said that they had separated because neither one was usually home:

I wish I could say I had a hot, passionate affair with her, but we never really did. Not really. Maybe I was too naïve to realize anything was wrong. People in Cleveland seem torn between loving her and destroying her. All this vicious energy should have been organized toward finding her murderer. Who is this helping anyway? There's got to be a reason for it. Does it give somebody a morbid sense of satisfaction?[20]

As the controversy concerning the autopsy consumed the Cleveland press, Casimir Bielen became the unofficial spokesman for the city's Polish community. Bielen was Walsh's good friend; on the night she was shot she had stopped by his house on Fleet Street on her way to Uncle Bill's. They worked on planning publicity for the Polish team's appearance at Kent State.

Bielen had also grown up in Cleveland's Slavic Village and attended Cleveland's South High School, fourteen years after Walsh. After graduating from the Cleveland College of Western Reserve University (today Case Western Reserve University), Bielen received a master's degree in education at Kent State. He worked as a secondary-school principal and the executive assistant to the state auditor, and coordinated ethnic affairs in the office of Cleveland mayor Dennis Kucinich. At the time of Walsh's death, he was president of Specialized Ethnic Services at the Nationality Newspapers Service. He was known around the neighborhood as "Mr. Ethnic."

Bielen told the *Washington Post* that he also knew that Walsh had a birth defect: "She was ridiculed. We knew this. . . . It was common knowledge that she had this accident of nature. She wasn't 100 percent pure female." He revealed, "When she was a little girl . . . in the heart of the Polish community, everyone was aware that she was a little different from the others. It was accepted. It was something we all knew about. When she was younger, she was teased by the other children." Bielen added, "We knew she had a mutation or deformity. [She] was a little of each."[21]

Bielen felt that it was a cruel injustice to accuse Walsh of being a fraud. He vowed to rescue her reputation and honor her memory as if he were fighting for the entire Polish community. He defended Walsh as vigorously as Polish Americans had denounced assassin Leon Czolgosz eighty years earlier. Walsh's ethnic identity was foremost in his mind. Bielen was incensed by the WKYC-TV report on the results of Walsh's autopsy. "We were told she was 90 percent female," he said. "What was common knowledge by the family, friends, Polonia, and the world for sixty-nine years and accepted has been turned into an ugly, sensational disclosure smearing the Olympic reputation of Stella Walsh."[22]

Conyers echoed Bielen's call to stop the insinuations that Walsh had posed as a man to win women's competitions: "I had known Stella all my life, since I was ten years old. She was a very dear friend. She was my coach for years. I couldn't sit back and let her be disgraced. . . . Why couldn't they [police and media] have waited until the results of her test before saying anything?"[23] Bielen claimed that Walsh had undergone numerous sex tests during her career, but, in fact, formal sex testing did not exist when Walsh competed in the Olympics or other meets.

Bielen promised, "This will be a battle between the 'Polish Mass Media' and TV 3. Publishers and editors of Polish and other ethnic newspapers are eagerly and willingly looking forward to battle, dressed in their heaviest protective armor." Bielen started the Olympian Stella Walsh Defense Fund with a $5,000 contribution.[24] Clara Battiato, Walsh's sister, said, "I'll do anything to sue that [TV] channel. They made something of nothing." The station's news director, Cliff Alexander, defended the report, declaring, "We knew it was going to be a sensitive story. This was not something we did on a whim."[25]

Cleveland's newspapers were more circumspect in their coverage of the controversy and tended to publish stories that eulogized Walsh. Two days after the murder, the *Cleveland Press* quoted Sophie Solomon, Walsh's fellow employee at the Falcons, as saying,

> She was wonderful with children. Who else could teach them track as she could? She went out of her way to reach the kids. They will feel her loss greatly. . . . Stella liked to dance a few polkas and eat a few Polish pastries. She was a happy person, but athletics and keeping fit were her whole life.[26]

Bielen lauded the print media for not sensationalizing the story. In a letter to the editor of the *Plain Dealer*, he wrote,

> Although I have disagreed with the Press [*sic*] on some issues in the past, the Press deserves to be highly praised for its handling of the untimely death of Stella Walsh. . . . The Press also deserves to be commended for not printing the ugly, sensational rumors being circulated after her death although known by the Press. These rumors, however, were broadcast as fact over some TV stations. An antidefamation lawsuit is pending. In my opinion, the Press has not tarnished the image of this great Olympian. Sound and responsible journalism prevailed.[27]

Bielen likened Walsh's murder to the tragic death several months earlier of Cleveland Indians baseball great Luke Easter, who, like Walsh, had been shot in a parking lot by two young robbers. Easter led the Washington Homestead Grays to the last Negro League championship in 1948, and a year later he joined the Indians. He hit eighty-six homers in three seasons from 1950 to 1952, and is said to have hit the longest home run ever at Municipal Stadium. What Walsh meant to Cleveland's Polish American community, Easter was to African American neighborhoods. According to one reporter, "Schoolboys in Cleveland and Buffalo [where he played minor-league ball] waited in line for a chance to touch his uniform—just like they did for [Joe] DiMaggio and [Willie] Mays." "Easter is one of the many might-have-been greats," wrote biographer Daniel Cattau. "But in reality the poor guy never really had a chance."[28]

Serving as a union steward for TRW Automotive, Easter was cashing union checks at the Cleveland Trust Company in suburban Euclid when he was mugged and killed. Walsh sent a letter to the editor of Cleveland's African American newspaper the *Call & Post* expressing her sorrow at Easter's death. Walsh also wrote this note to the *Plain Dealer*:

> I was saddened by the unfortunate killing of another athlete, Luke Easter; however, on the day of the burial, I was saddened more when I heard several newscasts about his death. One black woman was interviewed live on radio. She said, "The blacks must stop this black-on-black crime in the black community."

Walsh responded to the interview, saying, "The implications to the white community were puzzling, because these remarks implied that crimes committed against whites were less significant. To me all crime should be opposed—black on black, black on white, white on black, and white on white."[29] Walsh's reaction was somewhat tone-deaf, indicative of the tense relations between Polish Americans and African Americans at the time. This was a time of transition for the Slavic Village, where East European ethnic groups were moving out as African Americans moved in.

After Walsh's murder Bielen expected the *Call & Post* to reciprocate Walsh's act of sending a letter of sympathy in response to Easter's tragic death. In a letter to the paper's editor, Bielen pointed out that Cleveland had two Olympic gold medalists in the 100 meters: "Stella Walsh, like Jesse Owens, were citizens of the world [*sic*]. Both cared for all. All newspapers should also care and recognize all achievements or deaths—both black and white."[30]

Meanwhile, Bielen brought charges of slander against WKYC, although Bielen's own lawyers told him that "dead people do not have the rights of privacy." Bielen received an anonymous note warning that the station would play hardball:

> The family of Stella Walsh has been warned to stop their fight against TV stations or the body of Stella Walsh would be dug up by court order to prove that she was a man with male sex organs. And the [station's] lawyers would also get a court order to force [coroner] Gerber to release tests proving that Stella Walsh was a man. Please help them. They [the family] live in fear.

The note was signed "SOS."[31]

Bielen pulled out all the stops to clear Walsh's name. He wrote letters to Ohio senators John Glenn and Howard Metzenbaum, and U.S. House representatives Mary Rose Oakar, Charles A. Vanik, Ronald Mottl, and Louis Stokes, demanding action against WKYC: "In this story they implied, inferred, and stated that Stella Walsh was a male that competed against females. This news broadcast also questioned whether the five Gold and four Silver Olympic Medals [sic] would be forfeited." Stokes wrote back that he thought that a congressional investigation of WKYC "would be more detrimental than useful." He added, "Since congressional investigations and hearings attract publicity, my intervention might only cause the rumors to become more widespread." Metzenbaum also told Bielen that there was nothing he could do.[32]

As the controversy roiled, Bielen continued to inflate Walsh's sporting achievements. He always claimed that Walsh had won nine Olympic medals, although she won seven of those at the unofficial "Women's Olympics," not the IOC's Olympics. Bielen often contended that Walsh had won more than 5,000 track and field events, a figure that is impossible to verify, as is the exact number of world records she set. Measurement was inexact in those days, and most of Walsh's records went unrecognized. For example, in 1948, *Track and Field News* listed the "Best Marks by Women" for that year, including an entry for Walsh's time in the 100 meters: "Stella Walsh—11.5 (rumor)."[33]

Bielen also played the patriotic card, casting Walsh as a loyal American, as well as a true Pole. He told the *New York Times*, "She definitely was anti-Communist, but she loved Poland."[34] Bielen complained that the Polish Communist government was using Walsh's murder to criticize the United States for its excessive and random gun violence. The Communists were right about that, as homicide rates in the United States were far higher than in Europe, including the Soviet bloc.

Two months after the murder, Gerber issued the final autopsy results, which revealed that Walsh had male and abnormal female chromosomes, and only undeveloped, nonfunctioning male sex organs. Gerber courageously tried to put the matter to rest, declaring,

The sex of this infant would be ambiguous at the time of its birth. The baby would then be brought to the attention of experts in the field of genetics, endocrinology [hormones], and corrective surgery. The necessary measures could then be undertaken and the infant raised as either a male or a female. She lived and died a female. . . . Socially, culturally, and legally, Stella Walsh was accepted as a female for 69 years.[35]

The Polish community in Cleveland hung on the words, "Stella Walsh lived and died a female." Bielen called it Stella's "final victory."[36] The local newspaper *Slavic Village Voice* wrote, "Stella Walsh was finally vindicated by the autopsy report of Dr. Samuel Gerber."[37] Nonetheless, WKYC ran another segment titled "Was Stella a Fella?" *Plain Dealer* columnist James Ewinger called it a "tasteless line," adding "touting the story in a cheap, snickering fashion is inexcusable."[38]

A few weeks after Walsh's murder, Beverly Conyers tried to explain the tragic dilemma that had faced her friend throughout her life: "How is a woman or male to tell that he or she has a hormonal imbalance? How is someone to carry on a normal life? Does that mean that you have to be ruined and everything taken away?"[39] Of course, Walsh had more than a "hormonal imbalance," but Conyers was right. Walsh never confessed to anyone that she was unhappy with her assigned sex ("gender dystopia," in psychiatric terms). Probably the best way to determine someone's gender identity is to ask them. On an application for a job with the city of Cleveland in the spring of 1979, on the line that read, "Physical record: List any physical defects," Walsh wrote, "None."[40] She always thought of herself as a woman.

Walsh's family and friends such as Bielen and Conyers were incensed about charges that Walsh had intentionally cheated by hiding her maleness, and that her victories should be vacated and her medals forfeited. There was a precedent for Walsh to be stripped of her titles, however, and it involved another Polish sprinter. In 1967, Ewa Kłobukowska lost her 1964 Olympic and 1966 European medals because tests showed that she had XY chromosomes. The Kłobukowska affair seemed to confirm the suspicions of Western sports authorities that some Soviet-bloc women were, in reality, men. The masculine characteristics of the Soviet Press sisters, East German shot putter Heidi Krieger (who later became Andreas Krieger), and the muscular East German swimmers prompted international sporting associations to force women to undergo various tests to verify their sex. These were, in fact, cases of the abuse of performance-enhancing drugs rather than questions of sex.

The results of Walsh's autopsy added to calls for sex testing. In the long run, however, as more becomes known about people who are intersex or have chromosomal anomalies, international sports authorities have adopted a more enlightened approach to sex and gender designations. The IAAF and IOC were embarrassed when Kłobukowska birthed a son.

The most strident calls for overturning Walsh's victories came from the family and friends of Canadian sprinter Hilde Strike, who finished second to Walsh in the 100 meters at the 1932 Los Angeles Games. When the news of Walsh's autopsy broke, Strike's granddaughter, Cheryl Morris, demanded that her 70-year-old grandmother be awarded the gold medal. According to Morris, when Strike was told about the results of the autopsy, "You could see the smirk on her face. She was thrilled to get the news that she was actually the fastest woman in the world on that day." Another granddaughter, Cheryl Toomey, recalled, "Grandma was getting calls from all over the world . . . and we all thought that they would decide to give her the medal."[41]

Canadian sprinter and hurdler Roxanne Atkins Andersen also lobbied to invalidate Walsh's victories. "Stella had replaced a number of women," Andersen pointed out, "including one of my protégés and a friend of mine, Hilde Strike, in numerous championship meets. In the 1932 Olympic 100m, Hilde lost to Walsh by an eyelash. Hilde started really well, but Walsh cut her down with these powerful strides." Those strides, argued Andersen, were those of a man. "Fair is fair," she said. "If Stella was a man, she had an unfair advantage." Andersen also thought that another Canadian, Mildred Fizzell, should have been given the victory in her close loss to Walsh in the 1934 AAU Championships.[42]

Strike remained magnanimous in defeat. After Walsh's death and the controversial autopsy came to light, she was asked if she should be awarded the gold medal: "No, I don't think so," Strike replied. "When we went out on the track that day, I accepted that field and raced against them. That was what happened that day. Eight of us ran; I came in second."[43] Still, calls for retribution continued. On August 10, 1984, the *Times* (London) mentioned Walsh in an article entitled, "Who Said Cheats Never Prosper?" In a short report in 1989, on Strike's death of a heart attack, *Sports Illustrated* perpetuated the myth that Walsh had had an unfair advantage: "In 1980, it was discovered that the gold medalist in that event, Stella Walsh of Poland, was a hermaphrodite and should have been banned from competing as a woman. Despite speculation that Sisson [Strike's married name] would be awarded the gold, she never was."[44] Roxanne Andersen had a hard time letting the issue go. In late 1991, she said, "I'm in my eightieth year and counting my sins of omission, and I thought, 'I should be fighting for my girl'"—namely Fizzell—whom Andersen had coached in 1934.[45]

At a meeting of the Women's Track and Field Committee of the Athletics Congress (TAC) in 1991, the delegates took up the Walsh case. A spokesperson for the TAC said, "It's a unique thing. This is the first time we've studied it." The committee voted not to strip Walsh of her medals and declared that it would not hear any more petitions to take away any of her victories. The chair of the TAC, Lynn Cannon, observed that gender identity was a complex issue. She said that the charges that Walsh masqueraded as a man were "unfair to Stella Walsh," and Cannon authored a resolution that Walsh had been wrongly accused of being a man, writing, "The women's committee disapproves of all of the unsubstantiated allegations that have been made in regard to Stella Walsh." The motion passed unanimously. Even Andersen now recognized that sex designation was more complicated than she had originally thought and dropped her efforts to take away Walsh's titles: "I feel it is in the interest of track and TAC that I should withdraw that protest," she said.[46]

Cleveland newsman Dan Coughlin, Walsh's old drinking partner, once wrote, "Whatever Stella Walsh was, she was one of a kind."[47] Coughlin's clichéd remark had more gravity than he thought. Walsh was one of a very rare, misunderstood, and ridiculed kind. At the 1996 Atlanta Olympics, eight female athletes failed a sex test. Nonetheless, all of them competed. The IOC stopped sex testing in 1999, but the controversy regarding what constitutes a woman continues. In 2006, Indian middle-distance runner Santhi Soundarajan failed a gender test and was stripped of the silver medal in the 800 meters at the Asian Games. She later attempted suicide. Dr. Myron Genel, an endocrinologist from Yale University and a consultant for the IOC said, "My suspicion is that she has one of these rare disorders of sexual development."[48]

In 2009, Caster Semenya of South Africa won the same event at the World Championships in Berlin. The short, cropped hair and manly looks of the sturdy South African led to speculation that Semenya was not a woman. The IOC has only two categories for competitors in the Olympics, so athletes have to pick one or the other. Semenya won gold in the 800 at the 2016 Rio Olympics.

Eric Vilain, an expert on genetics and sexual development at the University of California, Los Angeles, School of Medicine, concurred that sexuality is a complicated issue: "I'll be damned if I could judge [sexuality]. There would certainly be cases where I could not come up with a definitive answer. . . . If you abide by some social construct hoping it will give you a clear-cut distinction, I think you're in for a lot of trouble."[49] In an August 3, 2008, *New York Times* article about sex testing in women's sport, Jennifer Finney Boylan, a trans woman born as James Boylan, wrote, "It would be nice to live in a world in which maleness and femaleness were firm and unwavering poles." Boylan echoed Gerber's observation: "The best judge of a person's gender is what lies within her, or his, heart. The only dependable test for gender is the truth of a person's life, the lives we live each day." The truth of Stella Walsh's life is that whatever personal anguish she might have felt, she always thought of herself as a woman.

Epilogue

The slow pace of the investigation into Stella Walsh's murder kept the media's focus on the controversy concerning her sex. According to Dan Coughlin, "People lost interest [in the investigation]. The story on her was 'Stella was a fella.' Catching her murderers—that was buried in the back of the metro section."[1]

Homicide cases in which the killer has no relation to the victim are the hardest to crack. For two years, the authorities had no solid leads. One of Walsh's neighbors suggested that a waitress at Lansing Tavern and her "common-law boyfriend should be checked out. [There were] bad feelings between Stella and them for many years."[2] It was a bogus tip.

A break in the case finally came two and a half years after the murder. The Cleveland police got a lead that they should be looking for two local men in their early twenties named Ricky and Donald. During an investigation of Donald Cassidy for the attempted murder of his two-year-old child, homicide detectives learned that his brother-in-law was Ricky Clark. In late May 1983, Clark was arrested and charged with the murder of Stella Walsh. He lived just north of Miles Avenue across from Calvary Cemetery, less than a mile from Walsh's grave. Cassidy surrendered to police two days later.

Before he went to trial in November, Cassidy and two other inmates punched out a small window in the seventh-story commons room at the Cuyahoga County Jail and used a bed sheet to shimmy down to a fourth-floor roof. Cassidy injured his hip in the escape. From a house on East 93rd Street in north Cleveland, the dim-witted Cassidy called for an ambulance, claiming that he had been hit by a car. The police promptly returned him to jail.

Cassidy fired the shot that killed Walsh. He pled guilty to murder and got fifteen years to life and another one to five years for the escape. Clark copped a plea for voluntary manslaughter and was sentenced to six to twenty-five years. They never showed any remorse about the senseless killing. There is no record of how long they were incarcerated. If Cassidy and Clark are back on the street today, they would be about Walsh's age when she died.

The autopsy that revealed Walsh's genital ambiguity was a cruel conclusion to an inspirational story. Walsh made her name in sports, and now that legacy was being questioned. Such noted sports historians as Allen Guttmann and William Murray declared, "Stella Walsh was a man."[3] David Wallechinsky, who compiled a thorough history of the Olympic Games, wrote, "All the while that Walsh had been setting eleven world records, winning two Olympic medals, she was, in fact, a man."[4] They were dead wrong.

The issue of alleged cheating in the Olympics came up again in 1988, when Canadian Ben Johnson, the 100-meter gold medalist at the Seoul Olympics, tested positive for performance-enhancing drugs and was disqualified. NBC sportscaster Ahmad Rashad did a segment on alleged Olympic cheaters, including Walsh, declaring, "She was a man." On September 28, 1988, the *Plain Dealer*, while acknowledging that Rashad was probably just reading from a script, called it an "unfair shot." The newspaper added, "Walsh, a nice person, certainly was not a cheater. If she had been, the Olympic committee would have removed her name from the list of gold medalists. Her name is still there. Rashad and NBC owe her an apology."

Walsh's long career was unparalleled, but she has lost her place in women's sports history to Helen Stephens and Babe Didrikson. The three gravesites bespeak their legacies. Walsh's grave is neglected, as is her memory. The sad, little, weathered grave marker in Calvary Cemetery is barely visible today, in a section of the cemetery that was devastated by a violent rainstorm in the summer of 2009. Most of the trees in the area are gone, leaving it even more desolate.

Stephens and Didrikson have prominent, well-groomed burial sites. Stephens suffered a stroke and died on January 17, 1994. She was buried in Fulton, not far from the family farm. The Olympics figure prominently on the gravestone inscription, which reads, "Winner of two gold medals in the 1936 Summer Olympics in Berlin, Germany . . . the 100-meter dash and the 400-meter relay."

Didrikson is interred at Forest Lawn Memorial Park in Beaumont, Texas, about twenty miles from her birthplace in Port Arthur. Her grave is marked by an impressive four-foot-high granite headstone and a small granite marker on the ground below. As a young athlete, Didrikson was known for her arrogance and boastfulness, and the words on the marker boldly declare, "World's Greatest Woman Athlete." The inscription on the headstone belies Didrikson's fierce competitiveness: "It's not whether you win or lose, it's how you play the game."

Poland, Cleveland, and sports played a central role in Walsh's life. As her athletic career wound down, she returned to live with her parents in the old Slavic Village in Cleveland, where Polish-Catholic schools had nurtured her and Polish sports clubs had helped her gain international prominence. The Polish American community in Cleveland and the Polish Falcons provided a "nest" for Walsh to find comfort and support. Her neighborhood has lost much of its ethnic character, and the memory of Stella Walsh is fading. Many of Walsh's childhood haunts have shuttered. As of 1987, Falcon Nest 141 had only 318 remaining members. The old Falcon building on 71st and Broadway still stands, but it is now the Center of Hope Bible Fellowship.

Four years after Walsh's death, the *Plain Dealer* held a poll to determine the greatest Cleveland athlete of all time. The great Cleveland Browns running back Jim Brown won the poll. Fireballing Cleveland Indian pitcher Bob Feller came in second, while Walsh finished a distant ninth.

In 1982, Cleveland dedicated the Stella Walsh Recreation Center on Broadway Avenue, which is adjacent to her shuttered alma mater, South High. A sports venue was a fitting tribute. Except for on the cinder track, Walsh never found solid ground on which to construct her life. Sports gave her a safe space to run away from any personal problems. She had to keep running, competing in senior events well into her sixties and training right up until her tragic death. After the coroner's report revealed Walsh's mosaicism, the *Plain Dealer* wrote,

> In her own community it was long known that in some ways Walsh's life had been a tragedy. . . . In spite of her sporting triumphs, Walsh's life had an un-

The Stella Walsh Recreation Center on Broadway in the Slavic Village, formerly South High, where Walsh went to school. *Author photo.*

derlying sadness. But she lived it with great dignity and as a woman. Out of her tragic death at the hands of an unknown gunman has probably come a final victory.[5]

On December 9, 1980, Walsh was laid to rest near her father Julian in Calvary Cemetery, less than a mile from her childhood home. Her old neighborhood buddy Casimir Bielen spread some dirt from Poland over her coffin and recalled her birthplace: "Stella had a fierce love of Poland," he said at the gravesite. "She loved the Polish people. We trust that this Polish soil will unite her closer with Poland."[6] A year after her death, Bielen and Walsh's friend Monica Pawlowski wrote a memoriam that alluded to Walsh's personal struggles. The word *suffering* appears four times:

> She suffered on Earth to the End
> In Silence she suffered, in patience she bore
> She suffers no more.
> The World's weary troubles and trials are past
> She who suffered is at rest.
> Gone to heaven with the best
> Peacefully sleeping, resting at last.[7]

Stella Walsh's legacy is not at rest. As one of the greatest woman athletes of her time, her story is an important part of Polish, Cleveland, Polish American, and women's history. Many of her friends revered and loved her. Walsh's protégé, Grace Butcher, still active in her eighties, fondly remembers what Walsh meant to her personally and to other women trying to break into the world of men's sports:

> Even though our time together was minimal, I still think about her sometimes when I'm running. Track was something wonderful that boys did, and I watched with envy. But then Stella gave it to me, and to a lot of other people. . . . I think Stella's legacy was saying you can do this, girls can do this, run fast, throw things, jump. It doesn't matter that you are female, do it and do it well. You don't do it like a girl, you don't do it like a boy, you do it like you are supposed to do it.[8]

Notes

PROLOGUE

1. After the collapse of the Russian Empire and the return of the Polish state at the end of the World War I, by default Walasiewicz became a citizen of Poland.

2. The suffix *-ówna* is the Polish feminine form indicating that she was the daughter of Julian Walasiewicz. Walsh usually left off the diacritic when she signed her name, and it does not appear on her gravestone.

CHAPTER 1

1. "Manifest of Alien Passengers for the United States Immigration Officer at Port of Arrival," *Ancestry.com*, October 28, 2010, http://www.search.ancestry.com/search/category.aspx?cat=40; George Vecsey, *Stan Musial: An American Life* (New York: Ballantine, 2011), 41.

2. Norman Davies, *God's Playground: A History of Poland, Volume II: 1795 to the Present* (New York: Columbia University Press, 1982), 236–37.

3. "Manifest of Alien Passengers for the United States Immigration Officer at Port of Arrival," June 13, 1912; John J. Grabowski and Diane E. Grabowski, *Cleveland: A History in Motion* (Carlsbad, CA: Heritage Media Corporation, 2000), 106.

4. Grabowski and Grabowski, *Cleveland*, 87.

5. Charles W. Coulter, *The Poles of Cleveland*, Cleveland Americanization Committee pamphlet (1919), 10.

6. *Plain Dealer* (Cleveland), September 8, 1901.

7. Howard Dennis, "Emma Goldman and the Cleveland Anarchists," *Modern Culture* 14, no. 3 (November 1901): 182. Italics in the original.

8. Edward T. Roe, *The Life Work of William McKinley* (Whitefish, MT: Kessinger, 2010), 169.

9. Emma Goldman, "The Tragedy at Buffalo," *Free Society*, October 1901, from the microform collection of the *Emma Goldman Papers*, University of California, http://.sunsite.berkeley.edu/Goldman/.

10. University of Buffalo Libraries, "Pan-American Exposition of 1901," http://li brary.buffalo.edu/pan-am/exposition/law/czolgosz.

11. Roe, *The Life Work of William McKinley*, 169.

12. *Literary Digest*, September 21, 1901.

13. *Plain Dealer*, September 9, 1901.

14. Library of Congress, "Immigration: Shadows of War," *LibraryofCongress.gov*, https://www.loc.gov/teachers/classroommaterials/presentationsand activities/ presenta tions/immigration/german8.html.

15. Davies, *God's Playground*, 380.

16. Coulter, *The Poles of Cleveland*, 21.

17. *Dearborn Independent*, April 22, 1922.

18. A. Mitchell Palmer, "The Case against the 'Reds,'" in *Reading the American Past: Volume II*, ed. Michael P. Johnson (New York: Bedford, 2012), 133–34.

19. William J. Baker, *Jesse Owens: An American Life* (New York: Free Press, 1986), 18.

20. Baker, *Jesse Owens*, 17–19.

21. *Chicago Daily Tribune*, October 19, 1962.

22. Eve Curie, *Madame Curie: A Biography* (Boston: Da Capo, 2001), 282–83.

23. Claire E. Nolte, *The Sokol in the Czech Lands to 1914: Training for the Nation* (New York: Palgrave, 2002), 82.

24. Brian McCook, *The Borders of Integration: Polish Migrants in Germany and the United States, 1870–1924* (Athens: Ohio University Press, 2011), 143.

25. Donald E. Pienkos, *One Hundred Years Young: A History of the Polish Falcons of America* (New York: Columbia University Press, 1987), 115, 135.

CHAPTER 2

1. Mariusz Kotowski, *Pola Negri: Hollywood's First Femme Fatale* (Lexington: University Press of Kentucky, 2014), 7.

2. *New York Times*, August 3, 1987.

3. *Los Angeles Times*, August 3, 1987.

4. Kotowski, *Pola Negri*, 3.

5. Kotowski, *Pola Negri*, 64.

6. Heiner Gillmeister, *Tennis: A Cultural History* (New York: New York University Press, 1998), 201.

7. Gillmeister, *Tennis*, 204.

8. *Plain Dealer*, February 16, 1930; *Plain Dealer*, February 17, 1930. The word *parva* means "little."

9. Diane Karpinski, "Frances Kaszubski," *ClevelandSeniors.com*, http://www.cleve landseniors.com/family/kaszubski.htm.

10. Jennifer Hargreaves, "Olympic Women: A Struggle for Recognition," in *Women and Sports in the United States*, eds. Jean O'Reilly and Susan K. Cahn (Boston: Northeastern University Press, 2007), 4; Mary H. Leigh and Therese M. Bonin, "The Pioneering Role of Madame Alice Milliat and the FSFI in Establishing International Track and Field Competition for Women," 73–74, http://library.la84. org/SportsLibrary/JSH/JSH1977/JSH0401/jsh0401f.pdf; Amanda Schweinbenz, "Not Just Early Olympic Fashion Statements: Bathing Suits, Uniforms, and Sportswear," in *Bridging Three Centuries: Fifth International Symposium for Olympic Research—2000*, 136, http://library.la84.org/SportsLibrary/ISOR/ISOR2000r.pdf.

11. Ellen Galford, *The Olympic Century: The Official History of the Modern Olympic Movement, Volume 1: The X Olympiad* (Los Angeles: World Sport Research, 1997), 100.

12. *New York Times*, June 23, 1996.

13. Jeanine Williams, *A Contemporary History of Women's Sport, Part One: Sporting Women, 1850–1960* (London: Routledge, 2014), 138.

14. Louise Mead Tricard, *American Women's Track and Field, 1895–1980* (Jefferson, NC: McFarland, 2008), 188.

15. Joe Gergen, *The First Lady of Olympic Track: The Life and Times of Betty Robinson* (Evanston, IL: Northwestern University Press, 2014), 6.

16. Norman Davies, *God's Playground: A History of Poland, Volume II: 1795 to the Present* (New York: Columbia University Press, 1982), 426.

17. PolskieRadio, "Halina Konopacka—pierwsza złota medlistka olimpijska" [Halina Konopacka—The First Olympic Gold Medalist], February 26, 2013, *PolskieRadio SA*, http://www.polskieradio.pl/39/156/Artykul/789704,Halina-Konopacka-pierwsza-polska-zlota-medalistka-olimpijska.

18. *New York Times*, July 28, 1928; *Plain Dealer*, January 13, 1948.

19. Krzysztof Szujecki, *Życie Sportowe w Drugiej Rzeczpospolitej* [Sporting Life in the Second Republic] (Warsaw: Bellona, 2012), 142.

20. *Plain Dealer*, March 3, 1929.

21. *Evening Independent* (Massillon, Ohio), March 24, 1930.

22. *Wall Street Journal*, February 14, 2014.

23. Ron Hotchkiss, *The Matchless Six: The Story of Canada's First Women's Olympic Team* (Toronto: Tundra Books, 2006), 173.

24. *Plain Dealer*, February 18, 1932.

25. *Plain Dealer*, February 18, 1932.

26. *Florence Times News*, February 20, 1930.

27. *Plain Dealer*, February 16, 1930; *Plain Dealer*, February 17, 1930.

28. Daniel Okrent, "Wayne B. Wheeler: The Man Who Turned off the Taps," *Smithsonian*, May 2010, www.smithsonianmag.com/history/wayne-b-wheeler.

29. *Evening Independent*, March 24, 1930.

30. William J. Galush, *For More Than Bread: Community and Identity in American Polonia, 1880–1940* (Boulder, CO: East European Monographs, 2006), 40.

31. *Plain Dealer*, February 16, 1930; *Plain Dealer*, April 8, 1930.

32. U.S. Department of Labor, Naturalization Service, "United States Declaration of Intention for Stella Walsh," April 7, 1930, *Ancestry.com*, http://www.ancestry.com/cs/us/Immigration-Records.

33. *Plain Dealer*, March 13, 1930.

34. *Plain Dealer*, January 13, 1948.

CHAPTER 3

1. Bill Crawford, *All-American: The Rise and Fall of Jim Thorpe* (Hoboken, NJ: John Wiley and Sons, 2005), 167.

2. *Plain Dealer*, December 3, 1930.

3. *Plain Dealer*, August 16, 1931; *Plain Dealer*, August 20, 1931; Matt Tullis, "Who Was Stella Walsh? The Story of the Intersex Olympian," *SB Nation*, June 27, 2013, http://www.sbnation.com/longform/2013/6/27/4466724/stella-walsh-profile-intersex-olympian.

4. *New York Times*, May 21, 1999.

5. John A. Lucas, "There's a Great Deal More to Elizabeth Robinson's Gold Medal Sprint Victory at the 1928 Olympic Games," *Journal of Olympic History* 13 (January 2005): 17.

6. *New York Times*, May 21, 1999; Louise Mead Tricard, *American Women's Track and Field, 1895–1980* (Jefferson, NC: McFarland, 2008), 139.

7. Joe Gergen, *The First Lady of Olympic Track: The Life and Times of Betty Robinson* (Evanston, IL: Northwestern University Press, 2014), 86.

8. *Chicago Tribune*, May 20, 1999.

9. Tricard, *American Women's Track and Field*, 140; *New York Times*, May 21, 1999.

10. Tricard, *American Women's Track and Field*, 99.

11. J. Thomas Jable, "Eleanor Egg: Paterson's Track and Field Heroine," *New Jersey History* (Fall/Winter 1984): 73–74.

12. Jable, "Eleanor Egg," 76; Tricard, *American Women's Track and Field*, 100–101.

13. Jable, "Eleanor Egg," 78–79.

14. *New York Times*, July 26, 1931.

15. Tricard, *American Women's Track and Field*, 99, 173.

16. Jable, "Eleanor Egg," 79.

17. Jable, "Eleanor Egg," 80–81.

18. Susan E. Cayleff, *Babe: The Life and Legend of Babe Didrikson Zaharias* (Urbana: University of Illinois Press, 1995), 65–66.

19. *Plain Dealer*, July 8, 1932.

20. *Plain Dealer*, July 9, 1932.

21. David Clay Large, *Nazi Games: The Olympics of 1936* (New York: W. W. Norton, 2007), 22.

22. *Plain Dealer*, July 9, 1932.

23. *Washington Post*, July 12, 1932.

24. Polish Olympic Committee, "Poland and Olympism," 176, http://library.la84 .org/OlympicInformationCenter/OlympicReview/1976/ore101/ore101w.pdf.

25. *Washington Post*, July 13, 1932.

26. *Plain Dealer*, July 9, 1932.

27. *New York Times*, July 31, 1932.

28. Krzysztof Szujecki, *Życie Sportowe w Drugiej Rzeczpospolitej* [Sporting Life in the Second Republic] (Warsaw: Bellona, 2012), 142.

29. *Chicago Tribune*, July 14, 1932. A "Chinese rice Christian" was a derogatory term for someone who converted for financial reasons. Pegler later became a harsh critic of President Franklin Roosevelt and the New Deal, which significantly increased federal spending to stimulate the depressed economy.

30. *Plain Dealer*, July 14, 1932.

31. Barbara Keys, "The Olympics, Hollywood-Style: Commerce, Coca-Cola, and the Culture of Celebrity at the 1932 Los Angeles Olympic Games," 43, http://library.la84 .org/SportsLibrary/NASSH_Proceedings/NP2004/np2004aj.pdf.

32. Robert C. Post, *Street Railways and the Growth of Los Angeles* (San Marino, CA: Golden West Books, 1989), 150.

33. Post, *Street Railways and the Growth of Los Angeles*, 150–52.

34. Richard Rayner, *A Bright and Guilty Place* (New York: Doubleday, 2009), 4–5.

35. Willy Meisl, *Die Olympischen Spiele in Los Angeles, 1932* [The Olympic Games in Los Angeles, 1932] (Hamburg: H. F. & Ph. F. Reetsma, 1932), 4–5.

36. Doris Pieroth, *Their Day in the Sun: Women of the 1932 Olympics* (Seattle: University of Washington Press, 1996), 86.

37. Pieroth, *Their Day in the Sun*, 86.

38. Xth Olympic Committee, *The Official Report of the Games of the Xth Olympiad Los Angeles 1932, Part 2*, 235, http://library.la84.org/6oic/OfficialReports/1932/1932spart2 .pdf.

39. Abby Chin-Martin, "The First-Ever Olympic Village was Built in Los Angeles," July 26, 2012, *KCET.org*, www.kcet.org/departures-columns/the-first-ever-olympic-village-was-built-in-los-angeles.

40. Dirk Mathison, "Heartbreak Hotel," *Los Angeles Magazine*, June 1998, 79–81.

41. Mathison, "Heartbreak Hotel," 79.

42. George Hodak, "Interview with Evelyne Hall Adams," 1988, 13, http://library.la84.org/6oic/OralHistory/OHHallAdams.pdf.

43. Pieroth, *Their Day in the Sun*, 89–90.

44. Nakładem Zwiazku Polskich Zwiazków Sportowych, *Polacy Na Igrzyskach X Olimpjady w 1932 r* [Poles at the Tenth Olympiad in 1932], Polskiego Komitetu Olimpijskiego, 39.

45. *Los Angeles Times*, August 12, 1932.

CHAPTER 4

1. Doris Pieroth, "Los Angeles 1932," in *Encyclopedia of the Modern Olympic Movement*, eds. John E. Findling and Kimberly D. Pelle (Westport, CT: Greenwood, 2004), 97.

2. *Kurjer Polski* [Polish Courier], August 7, 1932.

3. *Charleston Daily Mail* (West Virginia), August 2, 1932.

4. *Charleston Daily Mail*, August 2, 1932. Starting blocks had been invented in the late 1920s, but purists in the IAAF prevented their use until 1937. Blocks were first used at the 1948 London Games.

5. Ron Hotchkiss, "Crossing the Line," *Canada's History* 90, no. 6 (2010–2011): 43.

6. Louise Mead Tricard, *American Women's Track and Field, 1895–1980* (Jefferson, NC: McFarland, 2008), 194.

7. *Charleston Daily Mail*, August 2, 1932.

8. *50 Lat na Olympijskim Szlaku* [Fifty Years of Olympic Track] (Warsaw: Wydwawnictwo Sport I Turystyka, 1969), 73; Doris Pieroth, *Their Day in the Sun: Women of the 1932 Olympics* (Seattle: University of Washington Press, 1996), 102–3.

9. Krzysztof Szujecki, *Zycie Sportowe w Drugiej Rzeczpospolitej* [Sporting Life in the Second Republic] (Warsaw: Bellona, 2012), 141.

10. Nakładem Zwiazku Polskich Zwiazków Sportowych, *Polacy Na Igrzyskach X Olimpjady w 1932 r* [Poles at the Tenth Olympiad in 1932], Polskiego Komitetu Olimpijskiego, 84.

11. Martin Winstone, *The Dark Heart of Hitler's Europe* (London: I. B. Tauris, 2015), 64. The AB-Aktion eliminated nearly half of Poland's intelligentsia and political figures. Palmiry is northwest of Warsaw.

12. *50 Lat na Olimpijskim Szlaku*, 421.

13. *Plain Dealer*, July 28, 1932.

14. *Plain Dealer*, August 3, 1932.

15. *Plain Dealer*, August 6, 1932.

16. Pieroth, *Their Day in the Sun*, 90.

17. George Hodak, "Interview with Evelyne Hall Adams," 1988, 17, http://library
.la84.org/6oic/OralHistory/OHHallAdams.pdf.

18. Tricard, *American Women's Track and Field*, 204.

19. Pieroth, *Their Day in the Sun*, 113.

20. Tricard, *American Women's Track and Field*, 209.

21. Pieroth, *Their Day in the Sun*, 29.

22. Susan E. Cayleff, *Babe: The Life and Legend of Babe Didrikson Zaharias* (Urbana: University of Illinois Press, 1995), 92.

23. Robert O. Davies, *Sports in American Life* (Chichester, UK: John Wiley and Sons, 2012), 112.

24. Pieroth, *Their Day in the Sun*, 96.

25. Pieroth, *Their Day in the Sun*, 101.

26. Hotchkiss, "Crossing the Line," 40.

27. Amanda Schweinbenz, "Let the Games Begin," Sixth International Symposium for Olympic Research, 217, http://library.la84.org/SportsLibrary/ISOR/ISOR2002zb .pdf.

28. Allen Guttmann, *Women's Sports: A History* (New York: Columbia University Press, 1991), 176.

29. Randy Roberts and James Olson, *Winning Is the Only Thing: Sports in America since 1945* (Baltimore: Johns Hopkins University Press, 1989), 8.

30. Helen Lenskyj, *Out of Bounds: Women, Sport, and Sexuality* (Toronto: Women's Press, 1986), 88.

31. Lenskyj, *Out of Bounds*, 88.

32. *Milwaukee Journal*, February 18, 1930.

33. *Plain Dealer*, January 13, 1948.

34. Nakładem Zwiazku Polskich Zwiazków Sportowych, *Polacy Na Igrzyskach X Olimpjady*, 79.

35. *Los Angeles Times*, August 12, 1932.

36. Donald Kagan, et al., *The Western Heritage since 1789* (New York: Prentice Hall, 2001), 956.

37. *Plain Dealer*, January 22, 1933.

38. *New York Times*, October 27, 1935.

39. *Plain Dealer*, October 19, 1932; *Plain Dealer*, October 22, 1932.

40. *Los Angeles Times*, January 22, 1933; *Oakland Tribune*, January 23, 1933.

41. *New York Times*, January 22, 1933.

42. *Plain Dealer*, January 22, 1933.

43. *Polacy Zagranica* 5, no. 4 (April 1934): 12–13.

44. *Plain Dealer*, February 15, 1933.

45. *Plain Dealer*, April 13, 1933.

46. *New York Times*, August 15, 1933.

47. Ron Hotchkiss, *The Matchless Six: The Story of Canada's First Women's Olympic Team* (Toronto: Tundra Books, 2006), 127.

48. *Plain Dealer*, February 12, 1935; *Plain Dealer*, December 13, 1935.

49. Winston Churchill, *Winston S. Churchill: His Complete Speeches, 1897–1963*, vol. 7, 1943–1949, ed. Robert R. James (New York: Chelsea House, 1983), 290–91.

50. *Sunday Times*, December 4, 2011.

51. *Plain Dealer*, July 26, 1936.

52. *Plain Dealer*, July 26, 1936.

53. *Plain Dealer*, December 8, 1934.

54. *Plain Dealer*, August 2, 1984.

55. *Plain Dealer*, March 23, 1935; Sharon K. Hanson, *The Life of Helen Stephens, the Fulton Flash* (Carbondale: Southern Illinois University Press, 2004), 26–29.

56. *Plain Dealer*, March 23, 1935; Hanson, *The Life of Helen Stephens*, 26–29; Matt Tullis, "Who Was Stella Walsh? The Story of the Intersex Olympian," *SB Nation*, June 27, 2013, http://www.sbnation.com/longform/2013/6/27/4466724/stella-walsh-profile-intersex-olympian.

57. *Plain Dealer*, March 23, 1935.

58. Hanson, *The Life of Helen Stephens*, 26–29; State Historical Society of Missouri, "Helen Stephens," http://shsmo.org/historicmissourians/name/s/stephens/.

59. *Polish American Review* 1, no. 1 (January 1935): unpaginated.

60. *Plain Dealer*, July 26, 1936.

61. *Plain Dealer*, August 2, 1984.

62. *Daily Capital News* (Jefferson City, Missouri), June 20, 1935.

63. *New York Times*, June 19, 1935.

CHAPTER 5

1. *Polish American Review* 1, no. 7 (August 1935): 7.

2. *Plain Dealer*, December 8, 1935.

3. *Plain Dealer*, October 18, 2015.

4. Robert J. Sinclair, "Baseball's Rising Sun: American Interwar Diplomacy and Japan," *Canadian Journal of the History of Sport* 16, no. 2 (December 1985): 48–49.

5. *Washington Post*, January 13, 1936; *Plain Dealer*, January 13, 1936; *Plain Dealer*, January 16, 1936.

6. *Plain Dealer*, July 26, 1936.

7. *Polish American Review* 2, no. 4 (July 1936): 7.

8. *New York Times*, October 27, 1935.

9. Chris Elzey, "American Jews and the Summer Olympics," in *Jews in American Popular Culture: Volume 3, Sports, Leisure, and Lifestyle*, ed. Paul Buhle (New York: Praeger, 2006), 59.

10. "The Movement to Boycott the Berlin Olympics of 1936," *U.S.HolocaustMuseum. org*, http://www.ushmm.org/wlc/en/article.php?ModuleId=10007087.

11. Allen Guttmann, *The Games Must Go On: Avery Brundage and the Olympic Movement* (New York: Columbia University Press, 1984), 69.

12. *Washington Post*, September 7, 1935.

13. *Washington Post*, January 22, 1980.

14. Paul Soifer, "Lillian Copeland Speaks Out on the Olympics: Los Angeles 1932, Berlin 1936," *Western States Jewish History* 38, no. 1 (Fall 2005): 7.

15. Jeremy Schaap, *Triumph: The Untold Story of Jesse Owens and Hitler's Olympics* (New York: Houghton Mifflin Harcourt, 2007), 98.

16. Walter White, letter to Jesse Owens, December 4, 1935, in *The Unlevel Playing Field: A Documentary History of the African American Experience in Sport*, eds. David K. Wiggins and Patrick B. Miller (Urbana: University of Illinois Press, 2003), 164–65.

17. Norman Davies, *God's Playground: A History of Poland, Volume II: 1795 to the Present* (New York: Columbia University Press, 1982), 260.

18. *Polacy Zagranica* 7, no. 7 (July 1936): 42.

19. *Polacy Zagranica* 7, no. 7 (July 1936): 42.

20. *Polish American Review* 2, no. 5 (July 1936): 7.

21. *Lawrence Journal-World* (Kansas), June 17, 1936.

22. Gretel Bergmann, *Ich war die grosse judische Hoffnung: Erinnerungen einer aussergewöhnlichen Sportlerin* [I Was the Greatest Jewish Hope: Memoirs of an Extraordinary Athlete] (Baden-Wuerttemberg: Haus der Geschichte, 2003), 128.

23. Volker Kluge, "Scandal about 'Dora' and the 'Bergmann Case,'" *Journal of Olympic History* 17, no. 3 (December 2009): 22.

24. David Clay Large, *Nazi Games: The Olympics of 1936* (New York: W. W. Norton, 2007), 86.

25. *Los Angeles Times*, August 14, 1932.

26. *Los Angeles Times*, February 4, 2004.

27. *Washington Post*, January 22, 1980.

28. Organization Committee for the Berlin Olympics, *The XIth Olympics, Berlin 1936, Official Report, Volume I*, 547, http://library.la84.org/6oic/OfficialReports/1936/1936v1sum.pdf.

29. *Washington Post*, January 22, 1980.

30. Arnd Krüger, "Germany: The Propaganda Machine," in *The Nazi Olympics: Sports, Policy, and Appeasement in the 1930s*, eds. Arnd Krüger and William Murray (Urbana: University of Illinois Press, 2003), 27.

31. Joe Gergen, *The First Lady of Olympic Track: The Life and Times of Betty Robinson* (Evanston, IL: Northwestern University Press, 2014), 151

32. David Clay Large, *Berlin* (New York: Basic Books, 2000), 296.

33. William Murray, "France, Coubertin, and the Nazi Olympics: The Response," *Olympika: The International Journal of Olympic Studies* 1 (1992): 47.

34. Murray, "France, Coubertin, and the Nazi Olympics," 47; Arnd Krüger, "What's the Difference between Propaganda for Tourism or for a Political Regime?" in *Post-Olympism? Questioning Sport in the Twenty-First Century*, eds. John Bale and Mette Krogh Christensen (Oxford, UK: Berg, 2004), 37.

35. *Lincoln Evening Journal*, August 5, 1936.

36. Organization Committee for the Berlin Olympics, *The XIth Olympics, Berlin 1936, Official Report*, 639, http://library.la84.org/6oic/OfficialReports/1936/1936v1sum.pdf.

37. *Przegląd Sportowy*, August 6, 1936.

38. *Kurjer Warszawski*, August 4, 1936.

39. *Los Angeles Times*, August 4, 1936.

40. *Sunday Times*, December 4, 2011; *Los Angeles Times*, July 31, 1984; Louise Mead Tricard, *American Women's Track and Field, 1895–1980* (Jefferson, NC: McFarland, 2008), 237.

41. *Polish American Journal*, January 16, 1981.

42. Karin Wieland, *Dietrich and Riefenstahl: Hollywood, Berlin, and a Century in Two Lives* (New York: Liveright, 2011), 301.

43. Guy Walters, *Berlin Games: How the Nazis Stole the American Dream* (New York: William Morrow, 2006), 210.

44. Stefan Berg, "The 1936 Berlin Olympics: How Dora the Man Competed in the Women's High Jump," *Spiegel International Online*, September 9, 2009, http://www.spiegel.de/international/germany/1936-berlin-olympics-how-dora-the-man-competed-in-the-woman-s-high-jump-a-649104.html.

45. "Preserving la Difference," *Time*, September 16, 1966.

46. Berg, "The 1936 Berlin Olympics."

47. *New York World-Telegram*, August 12, 1936.

48. Berg, "The 1936 Berlin Olympics."

49. Jennifer Hargreaves, "Olympic Women: A Struggle for Recognition," in *Women and Sports in the United States*, eds. Jean O'Reilly and Susan K. Cahn (Boston: Northeastern University Press, 2007), 11.

50. *Los Angeles Times*, May 19, 2007.

51. Jennifer H. Lansbury, *A Spectacular Leap: Black Women Athletes in Twentieth-Century America* (Fayetteville: University of Arkansas Press, 2014), 235.

52. *Herald Sun* (Australia), July 12, 2008.

53. Walters, *Berlin Games*, 211.

CHAPTER 6

1. *Plain Dealer*, October 13, 1938.

2. *New York Times*, September 19, 1937.

3. Polish Olympic Committee, "Poland and Olympism," 176, http://library.la84
.org/OlympicInformationCenter/OlympicReview/1976/ore101/ore101w.pdf.

4. *Plain Dealer*, October 27, 1938. Mata Hari was a Dutch woman who was executed
by the French in 1917, for spying for Germany during World War I.

5. Norman Davies, *God's Playground: A History of Poland, Volume II: 1795 to the
Present* (New York: Columbia University Press, 1982), 435.

6. *New York Times*, September 4, 1939.

7. *Plain Dealer*, August 6, 1941.

8. *Washington Post*, July 7, 1940.

9. Susan K. Cahn, *Coming on Strong: Gender and Sexuality in Twentieth-Century
Women's Sport* (Cambridge, MA: Harvard University Press, 1994), 150–51; Susan E.
Cayleff, *Babe: The Life and Legend of Babe Didrikson Zaharias* (Urbana: University of
Illinois Press, 1995), 187.

10. Patricia Vignola, "The Patriotic Pinch Hitter: The AAGPBL and How the
American Woman Earned a Permanent Spot on the Roster," *NINE: A Journal of
Baseball History and Culture* 12, no. 2 (Spring 2004): 105.

11. *Plain Dealer*, December 24, 1939.

12. *Plain Dealer*, November 9, 1942.

13. *Plain Dealer*, November 9, 1942.

14. *Eugene Register-Guard*, November 11, 1942; *Pittsburgh Press*, November 11, 1942;
Plain Dealer, November 11, 1942.

15. *Plain Dealer*, August 24, 1943.

16. Louise Mead Tricard, *American Women's Track and Field, 1895–1980* (Jefferson,
NC: McFarland, 2008), 301–3.

17. *Plain Dealer*, June 18, 1945.

18. *Plain Dealer*, June 25, 1945; *Plain Dealer*, June 30, 1945.

19. Richard Espy, *The Politics of the Olympic Games* (Berkeley: University of California Press, 1981), 24.

20. *Plain Dealer*, January 13, 1948.

21. Diane Karpinski, "Frances Kaszubski," *ClevelandSeniors.com*, http://www
.clevelandseniors.com/family/kaszubski.htm.

22. Sharon K. Hanson, *The Life of Helen Stephens, the Fulton Flash* (Carbondale:
Southern Illinois University Press, 2004), 260.

23. *Plain Dealer*, March 7, 2000.

24. Grace Butcher, "Remembering Stella Walsh," *Ohio Runner* 9, no. 1 (July 1987): 15.

25. *Plain Dealer*, March 7, 2000; Butcher, "Remembering Stella Walsh," 15.

26. *Plain Dealer*, March 7, 2000.

27. *New York Times*, December 6, 1980.

28. *Plain Dealer*, June 23, 1950.

29. Joe Jares, "A Baker's Dream Needs Dough," *SI Vault*, September 7, 1970, http://www.si.com/vault/1970/09/07/611481/a-bakers-dream-needs-dough.

30. *Plain Dealer*, August 5, 1951.

CHAPTER 7

1. Hilary A. Hallett, *Go West, Young Woman! The Rise of Early Hollywood* (Berkeley: University of California Press, 2013), 113.

2. *Plain Dealer*, June 12, 1953.

3. *Plain Dealer*, August 5, 1951.

4. *Plain Dealer*, June 12, 1953.

5. *Plain Dealer*, June 29, 1952.

6. *Los Angeles Times*, July 3, 1952; *Plain Dealer*, July 3, 1952.

7. *New York Times*, March 3, 1998.

8. Nikoletta Onyestyák, "Boycott, Exclusion, or Nonparticipation? Hungary in the Years of the 1920 and 1984 Olympic Games," *International Journal of the History of Sport* 27, no. 11 (August 2010): 1920–41.

9. *Los Angeles Times*, July 2, 1952. In 2016, the IOC broke that precedent and recognized an Olympic Refugee Team, inviting ten athletes to the Rio Olympics.

10. *Plain Dealer*, August 1, 1945.

11. *Sarasota Herald-Tribune*, September 7, 1952; *Los Angeles Times*, September 13, 1952.

12. *Plain Dealer*, July 3, 1952.

13. *Los Angeles Times*, January 22, 1954.

14. *Los Angeles Times*, August 7, 1955.

15. *Los Angeles Times*, January 22, 1954.

16. Mathias won the gold medal in the decathlon at the 1948 and 1952 Olympics.

17. Wieś Wierzchownia can be translated as the "village of Wierzchownia."

18. A "secret word" was chosen before the show, and if the contestants said the word during the interview, they won $100. Stella said the secret word "name" right away, winning $100 for her and her fellow contestant.

19. *You Bet Your Life*, episode 150, https://archive.org/details/You.Bet.Your.Life.

20. *You Bet Your Life*, episode 150, https://archive.org/details/You.Bet.Your.Life.

21. *Los Angeles Times*, June 13, 1956.

22. International Olympic Committee, *The Olympic Games Charter Rules and Regulations*, 1955, 20, https://stillmed.olympic.org/Documents/Olympic%20Charter/ Olympic_Charter_through_time/1955-Olympic_Charter-The_OG-charter_rules _and_regulations_general_information.pdf.

23. *Times Herald* (Pennsylvania), October 15, 1955; *New York Times*, October 15, 1955; *Washington Post*, October 15, 1955.

24. Stella Walsh to John Jewett Garland, April 5, 1956, Avery Brundage Papers, quoted in Toby Rider and Sarah Teetzel, "The Strange Tale of Stella Walsh's Olympic Eligibility," unpublished paper, 2015.

25. Toby Rider, "Eastern Europe's Unwanted: Exiled Athletes and the Olympic Games," *Journal of Sport History* 40, no. 3 (Fall 2013): 444.

26. International Olympic Committee, *Olympic Rules* (Lausanne: International Olympic Committee, 1956), in Rider and Teetzel, "The Strange Tale of Stella Walsh's Olympic Eligibility."

27. *Los Angeles Times*, June 13, 1956.

28. Susan E. Cayleff, *Babe: The Life and Legend of Babe Didrikson Zaharias* (Urbana: University of Illinois Press, 1995), 140.

29. *New York Times*, August 16, 1956.

30. *Plain Dealer*, August 26, 1956.

31. *Los Angeles Times*, October 2, 1956.

32. *Plain Dealer*, August 11, 1957.

33. Amby Burfoot, *First Ladies of Running: 22 Inspiring Profiles of the Rebels, Rule Breakers, and Visionaries Who Changed the Sport Forever* (New York: Rodak Books, 2016), 6.

34. Grace Butcher, "Remembering Stella Walsh," *Ohio Runner* 9, no. 1 (July 1987): 17.

35. *Plain Dealer*, March 7, 2000; *Plain Dealer*, March 23, 2000.

36. *Plain Dealer*, March 10, 1958.

37. Louise Mead Tricard, *American Women's Track and Field, 1895–1980* (Jefferson, NC: McFarland, 2008), 386.

38. Tricard, *American Women's Track and Field*, 423.

39. Jeanette Tuve, "Interview with Bertha Modrzynski," *Cleveland Memory Project*, April 15, 1986, http://flash.ulib.csuohio.edu/cmp/ewc/modrzynski.html.

40. Butcher, "Remembering Stella Walsh," 17.

41. "Faces in the Crowd," *SI Vault*, November 5, 1962, http://www.si.com/vault/ 1962/11/05/670206/.

42. *Plain Dealer*, October 20, 1962.

43. *Plain Dealer*, November 5, 1962.

44. Reyner Banham, *Los Angeles: The Architecture of Four Ecologies* (Middlesex, UK: Penguin, 1971), 16.

CHAPTER 8

1. Dan Coughlin, *Crazy, with the Papers to Prove It* (Cleveland, OH: Gray and Co., 2010), 30; *Plain Dealer*, July 30, 1964.

2. Andrew D. Linden, "Blue-Collar Identity and the 'Culture of Losing': Cleveland and the 'Save Our Browns' Campaign," *Journal of Sport History* 42, no. 3 (Fall 2015): 343–44.

3. Adam J. Criblez, "White Men Playing a Black Man's Game: Basketball's 'Great White Hopes' of the 1970s," *Journal of Sport History* 42, no. 3 (Fall 2015): 378.

4. Joe Jares, "Off to Russia without Love," *SI Vault*, July 12, 1965, http://www.si.com/vault/1965/07/12/606343/off-to-russia-without-love.

5. Memo, Stella Walsh Papers, MS 4999, Container 1, Folder 1; *Plain Dealer*, July 4, 1965.

6. Jeanette Tuve, "Interview with Bertha Modrzynski," *Cleveland Memory Project*, April 15, 1986, http://flash.ulib.csuohio.edu/cmp/ewc/modrzynski.html.

7. Casimir Bielen press release, Stella Walsh Papers, MS 4999, Container 1, Folder 2.

8. *Montreal Gazette*, December 6, 1980.

9. Coughlin, *Crazy, with the Papers to Prove It*, 33; *Plain Dealer*, July 13, 1967; *Plain Dealer*, January 24, 1980; *Elyria Chronicle Telegram* (Ohio), May 18, 2003.

10. Chuck Schodowski, interview in Rob Lucas, director, *Stella Walsh: A Documentary*, 2014.

11. Grace Butcher, interview in Lucas, *Stella Walsh*.

12. Coughlin, *Crazy, with the Papers to Prove It*, 33.

13. Helen Laville, "'Our Country Endangered by Underwear': Fashion, Femininity, and the Seduction Narrative in *Ninotchka* and *Silk Stockings*," *Diplomatic History* 30, no. 4 (September 2006): 643.

14. Stefan Wiederkehr, "'We Shall Never Know the Exact Number of Men Who Have Competed in the Olympics Posing as Women': Sport, Gender Verification, and the Cold War," *International Journal of the History of Sport* 26, no. 4 (March 2009): 562.

15. "Mosaic in X & Y," *Time*, September 29, 1967, 74.

16. Ethel Sloan, *The Biology of Women*, 4th ed. (Albany, NY: Delmar, 2002), 159.

17. Jamie Schultz, *Qualifying Times: Points of Change in U.S. Women's Sport* (Urbana: University of Illinois Press, 2014), 111.

18. Wiederkehr, "'We Shall Never Know," 564.

19. Wiederkehr, "'We Shall Never Know," 556, 560. The IOC now tests testosterone levels, but these can vary significantly.

20. City of Cleveland Proclamation of Stella Walsh Day, April 13, 1970, Stella Walsh Papers, MS 4999, Container 1, Folder 1; *Plain Dealer*, April 14, 1970.

21. City of Cleveland Proclamation of Stella Walsh Day; *Plain Dealer*, April 14, 1970.

22. City Council Resolution, September 13, 1974, Stella Walsh Papers, MS 4999, Container 1, Folder 1.

23. Sharon K. Hanson, *The Life of Helen Stephens, the Fulton Flash* (Carbondale: Southern Illinois University Press, 2004), 203.

24. Aloysius A. Mazewski letter to Casimir Bielen, March 8, 1979, Stella Walsh Papers, MS 4999, Container 1, Folder 2.

25. Howard M. Metzenbaum article for the *U.S. Congressional Record-Senate*, May 6, 1979, Stella Walsh Papers, MS 4999, Container 1, Folder 2.

26. *U.S. Congressional Record-Senate*, May 7, 1979, 10066, Stella Walsh Papers, MS 4999, Container 1, Folder 2.

27. Casimir Bielen press release, Stella Walsh Papers, MS 4999, Container 1, Folder 2.

28. Polish Consulate invitation to Stella Walsh-Olson, July 6, 1979, Stella Walsh Papers, MS 4999, Container 1, Folder 2.

29. Walsh telegram to the Polish Consulate, July 22, 1979, Stella Walsh Papers, MS 4999, Container 1, Folder 2; Casimir Bielen press release, Stella Walsh Papers, MS 4999, Container 1, Folder 2.

30. Casimir Bielen press release, Stella Walsh Papers, MS 4999, Container 1, Folder 2.

31. Walsh letter to Mr. Holtz, Stella Walsh Papers, MS 4999, Container 1, Folder 2.

32. *Plain Dealer*, December 7, 1980.

33. *Plain Dealer*, April 1, 1980.

34. "Homily of His Holiness John Paul II in Warsaw," *Vatican*, June 2, 1979, http://w2.vatican.va/content/john-paul-ii/en/homilies/1979/documents/hf_jp-ii_hom_19790602_polonia-varsavia.html.

35. *Plain Dealer*, November 4, 1989.

36. *Plain Dealer*, June 8, 1981; John F. McDonald, *Urban America: Growth, Crisis, and Rebirth* (Armonk, NY: M. E. Sharpe, 2008), 224, 226.

37. *Plain Dealer*, June 8, 1981.

38. McDonald, *Urban America*, 224, 226.

39. Coughlin, *Crazy, with the Papers to Prove It*, 33.

40. *Plain Dealer*, December 10, 1980.

41. *Plain Dealer*, December 5, 1980.

42. *Los Angeles Times*, December 10, 1980.

43. *Plain Dealer*, December 10, 1980, in Stella Walsh Papers, MS 4999, Container 1, Folder 14.

44. *Sztandar Młodych*, December 6–7, 1980.

45. *Kuryer Zjednoczenia*, December 24, 1980, in Stella Walsh Papers, MS 4999, Container 1, Folder 14.

46. *Plain Dealer*, December 10, 1980.

CHAPTER 9

1. *Plain Dealer*, December 6, 1980.

2. Plain Dealer, December 10, 1980; *Geauga Times Leader* (Chardon, Ohio), December 14, 1980.

3. Robert Ritchie, John Reynard, and Tom Lewis, "Intersex and the Olympic Games," *Journal of the Royal Society of Medicine* 101 (2008): 395.

4. Pat Sheil, "Five-Ring Circus: The Twisted Tale of Stella Walsh," *Australian Broadcasting Corporation*, http://www.abc.net.au/olympics/s177264.htm.

5. *Telegraph* (London), May 31, 2004.

6. Harry Gordon, "Olympic Legends Honoured at Sydney's Games Sites," *Journal of Olympic History* (Summer 1998): 20, n5.

7. Paul Farhi, "The Runner's Secret," *Washington Post*, August 22, 2008, http://www.washingtonpost.com/wp-dyn/content/article/2008/08/21/AR2008082103680.html.

8. "Stella Walsh," *USA Track and Field*, http://www.usatf.org/halloffame/TF/showBio.asp?HOFIDs=177.

9. Anna Jakieła, "Stanisława Walasiewicz—Krótka historia" [Stanisława Walasiewicz: Short History], December 12, 2013, http://treningbiegacza.pl/stanislawa-walasiewicz-krotka-historia.

10. *Życie Warszawy*, July 2, 2004.

11. Matt Tullis, "Who Was Stella Walsh? The Story of the Intersex Olympian," *SB Nation*, June 27, 2013, http://www.sbnation.com/longform/2013/6/27/4466724/stella-walsh-profile-intersex-olympian.

12. *Cleveland Press*, February 12, 1981, in Stella Walsh Papers, MS 4999, Container 1, Folder 15.

13. *Plain Dealer*, February 12, 1981.

14. Ethel Sloan, *The Biology of Women*, 4th ed. (Albany, NY: Delmar, 2002), 159.

15. Eduardo Hay, "The Stella Walsh Case," *Olympic Review* 162 (1981): 221–22.

16. *Herald Sun* (Melbourne), July 12, 2008.

17. *Washington Post*, August 22, 2008.

18. *New York Times*, December 21, 1980.

19. *Los Angeles Times*, December 10, 1980.

20. *Plain Dealer*, February 12, 1981.

21. *Free Lance-Star* (Fredericksburg, Virginia), January 23, 1981; *Plain Dealer*, September 8, 1992.

22. *Plain Dealer*, December 16, 1980, in Stella Walsh Papers, MS 4999, Container 1, Folder 14; Bielen press release, Stella Walsh Papers, MS 4999, Container 1, Folder 7.

23. *New York Times*, December 21, 1980.

24. Bielen press release, Stella Walsh Papers, MS 4999, Container 1, Folder 9.

25. *Plain Dealer*, December 16, 1980.

26. *Cleveland Press*, December 6, 1980, in Stella Walsh Papers, MS 4999, Container 1, Folder 14.

27. Bielen letter to the editor of the *Plain Dealer*, December 15, 1980, Stella Walsh Papers, MS 4999, Container 1, Folder 6.

28. *New York Daily News*, December 9, 2008.

29. *Plain Dealer*, April 13, 1979.

30. Bielen to the editor of the *Call & Post*, December 14, 1980, Stella Walsh Papers, MS 4999, Container 1, Folder 7.

31. Handwritten memo, unsigned, Stella Walsh Papers, MS 4999, Container 1, Folder 2.

32. Bielen letter to Congressman Louis Stokes, December 15, 1980, Stella Walsh Papers, MS 4999, Container 1, Folder 7. Bielen sent the same letter to the others; Louis Stokes letter to Bielen, January 10, 1981, Stella Walsh Papers, MS 4999, Container 1, Folder 7.

33. *Track and Field News* 1, no. 1 (February 1948).

34. *New York Times*, December 6, 1980.

35. *Plain Dealer*, February 12, 1981; *Washington Post*, February 13, 1981.

36. Bielen memo, Stella Walsh Papers, MS 4999, Container 1, Folder 15.

37. *Slavic Village Voice*, June 1983, Stella Walsh Papers, MS 4999, Container 1, Folder 15.

38. *Plain Dealer*, February 14, 1981.

39. *New York Times*, December 21, 1980.

40. Walsh letter to Bob Weissman, Cleveland personnel director, April 7, 1979, Stella Walsh Papers, MS 4999, Container 1, Folder 11.

41. *Toronto Star*, September 12, 2009; *Toronto Star*, March 12, 1989.

42. *Herald Sun* (Melbourne), July 12, 2008; *St. Louis Post-Dispatch*, June 16, 1991; *Plain Dealer*, December 7, 1991.

43. *Toronto Star*, February 28, 2002. Only six women ran in the finals.

44. "A Roundup of the Week," *SI Vault*, March 20, 1989, http://www.si.com/vault/1989/03/20.

45. *Plain Dealer*, December 5, 1991.

46. *Plain Dealer*, December 5, 1991; *Plain Dealer*, December 7, 1991; *Akron Beacon Journal*, December 7, 1991.

47. Dan Coughlin, *Crazy, with the Papers to Prove It* (Cleveland, OH: Gray and Co., 2010), 34.
48. Thomas Mulloy, "Enough Gender Bender Bullying," *Call & Post*, October 21, 2009, http://www.cleveland.com/call-and-post/index.ssf/2009/10/enough_gender _bender_bullying.html.
49. *Washington Post*, August 22, 2008.

EPILOGUE

1. Coughlin interview in Rob Lucas, director, *Stella Walsh: A Documentary*, 2014.
2. Unsigned letter to Bielen, January 8, 1981, Stella Walsh Papers, MS 4999, Container 1, Folder 6.
3. Allen Guttmann, *Women's Sports History* (New York: Columbia University Press, 1991), 111, n57; William Murray, "France, Equality, and the Pursuit of Fraternity," in *The Nazi Olympics: Sport, Politics, and Appeasement in the 1930s*, eds. Arnd Krüger and William Murray (Urbana: University of Illinois Press, 2003), 111, n57.
4. Doris Pieroth, *Their Day in the Sun: Women of the 1932 Olympics* (Seattle: University of Washington Press, 1996), 105.
5. *Plain Dealer*, February 13, 1981.
6. Bielen speech at Walsh gravesite, December 9, 1980, Stella Walsh Papers, MS 4999, Container 1, Folder 8. Walsh's mother lived to be 100, and she is also buried at Calvary.
7. *Garfield Heights Tribune* (Ohio), December 2, 1981, in Stella Walsh Papers, MS 4999, Container 1, Folder 15.
8. Butcher interview in Lucas, *Stella Walsh*.

Bibliography

BOOKS, ARTICLES, AND FILMS

"25 Lat Temu zmarła Halina Konopacka" [Halina Konopacka Died 25 Years Ago], http://www.sport.wp.pl.kat.

50 Lat na Olympijskim Szlaku [Fifty Years of Olympic Track]. Warsaw: Wydwawnictwo Sport I Turystyka, 1969.

Baker, William J. *Jesse Owens: An American Life.* New York: Free Press, 1986.

Banham, Reyner. *Los Angeles: The Architecture of Four Ecologies.* Middlesex, UK: Penguin, 1971.

Basinger, Jeanine. *American Cinema: One Hundred Years.* New York: Rizzoli Publications, 1994.

Benoit, Macon. "The Politicization of Football: The European Game and the Approach to the Second World War." *Soccer and Society* 9, no. 4 (October 2008): 532–50.

Berg, Stefan. "The 1936 Berlin Olympics: How Dora the Man Competed in the Women's High Jump." *Spiegel International Online,* September 9, 2009, http://www.spiegel.de/international/germany/1936-berlin-olympics-how-dora-the-man-competed-in-the-woman-s-high-jump-a-649104.html.

Bergmann, Gretel. *Ich war die grosse judische Hoffnung: Erinnerungen einer aussergewöhnlichen Sportlerin* [I Was the Greatest Jewish Hope: Memoirs of an Extraordinary Athlete]. Baden-Wuerttemberg: Haus der Geschichte, 2003.

Bouzaquet, Jean-Francois. *Fast Ladies: Female Racing Drivers, 1888–1970.* Dorcester, UK: Veloce, 2009.

Burfoot, Amby. *First Ladies of Running: 22 Inspiring Profiles of the Rebels, Rule Breakers, and Visionaries Who Changed the Sport Forever*. New York: Rodak Books, 2016.

Butcher, Grace. "Remembering Stella Walsh." *Ohio Runner* 9, no. 1 (July 1987): 14–17.

Cahn, Susan K. *Coming on Strong: Gender and Sexuality in Twentieth-Century Women's Sport*. Cambridge, MA: Harvard University Press, 1994.

Cayleff, Susan E. *Babe: The Life and Legend of Babe Didrikson Zaharias*. Urbana: University of Illinois Press, 1995.

Chin-Martin, Abby. "The First-Ever Olympic Village Was Built in Los Angeles." *KCET*, July 26, 2012, https://www.kcet.org/history-society/the-first-ever-olympic -village-was-built-in-los-angeles.

Churchill, Winston. *Winston S. Churchill: His Complete Speeches, 1897–1963*, vol. 7, 1943–1949, ed. Robert R. James. New York: Chelsea House, 1983.

Coughlin, Dan. *Crazy, with the Papers to Prove It*. Cleveland, OH: Gray and Co., 2010.

Crawford, Bill. *All-American: The Rise and Fall of Jim Thorpe*. Hoboken, NJ: John Wiley and Sons, 2005.

Criblez. Adam J. "White Men Playing a Black Man's Game: Basketball's 'Great White Hopes' of the 1970s." *Journal of Sport History* 42, no. 3 (Fall 2015): 371–81.

Curie, Eve. *Madame Curie: A Biography*. Boston: Da Capo, 2001.

Davies, Norman. *God's Playground: A History of Poland, Volume II: 1795 to the Present*. New York: Columbia University Press, 1982.

Davies, Robert O. *Sports in American Life*. Chichester, UK: John Wiley and Sons, 2012.

Dennis, Howard. "Emma Goldman and the Cleveland Anarchists." *Modern Culture* 14, no. 3 (November 1901): 180–82.

Dyreson, Mark. "Paris 1924." In *Encyclopedia of the Modern Olympic Movement*, eds. John E. Findling and Kimberly D. Pelle, 79–88. Westport, CT: Greenwood, 2004.

——, and Matthew Llewellyn. "Los Angeles Is *the* Olympic City: Legacies of the 1932 and 1984 Olympic Games." *International Journal of the History of Sport* 25, no. 14 (December 2008): 1991–2018.

Elzey, Chris. "American Jews and the Summer Olympics." In *Jews in American Popular Culture: Volume 3, Sports, Leisure, and Lifestyle*, ed. Paul Buhle, 51–59. New York: Praeger, 2006.

Espy, Richard. *The Politics of the Olympic Games*. Berkeley: University of California Press, 1981.

"Faces in the Crowd." *SI Vault*, November 5, 1962, http://www.si.com/vault/1962/ 11/05/670206/.

Fryc, Adam, and Mirosław Ponczek. "The Communist Rule in Polish Sport History." *International Journal of the History of Sport* 26, no. 4 (March 2009): 501–14.

Galford, Ellen. *The Olympic Century: The Official History of the Modern Olympic Movement, Volume I: The X Olympiad.* Los Angeles: World Sport Research, 1997.

Galush, William J. *For More Than Bread: Community and Identity in American Polonia, 1880–1940.* Boulder, CO: East European Monographs, 2006.

Gergen, Joe. *The First Lady of Olympic Track: The Life and Times of Betty Robinson.* Evanston, IL: Northwestern University Press, 2014.

Gillmeister, Heiner. *Tennis: A Cultural History.* New York: New York University Press, 1998.

Gilmore, Glenda E., and Thomas J. Sugrue. *These United States: A Nation in the Making, 1890 to the Present.* New York: W. W. Norton, 2015.

Goldman, Emma. "The Tragedy at Buffalo." *Free Society*, October 1901. From the microform collection of the *Emma Goldman Papers*, University of California, http://sunsite.berkeley.edu/Goldman.

Gordon, Harry. "Olympic Legends Honoured at Sydney's Games Sites." *Journal of Olympic History* (Summer 1998): 17–20.

Gottlieb, Robert, Mark Vallianatos, Regina M. Freer, and Peter Dreier. *The Next Los Angeles: The Struggle for a Livable City.* Berkeley: University of California Press, 2005.

Grabowski, John J., and Diane E. Grabowski. *Cleveland: A History in Motion.* Carlsbad, CA: Heritage Media Corporation, 2000.

———, Judith Zielinski-Zak, Alice Boberg, and Ralph Wroblewski. *Polish Americans and Their Communities of Cleveland. Cleveland Memory Project*, 1976, http://clevelandmemory.org/ebooks/Polish.

Guttmann, Allen. "Berlin 1936: The Most Controversial Olympics." In *National Identity and Global Sports Events*, eds. Alan Tomlinson and Christopher Young, 65–81. Albany: State University of New York Press, 2006.

———. *The Games Must Go On: Avery Brundage and the Olympic Movement.* New York: Columbia University Press, 1984.

———. *Women's Sports: A History.* New York: Columbia University Press, 1991.

———, and Lee Thompson. *Japanese Sports: A History.* Honolulu: University of Hawaii Press, 2001.

Hall, M. Ann. *The Girl and the Game: A History of Women's Sport in Canada.* Peterborough: Broadview Press, 2002.

Hallett, Hilary A. *Go West, Young Woman! The Rise of Early Hollywood.* Berkeley: University of California Press, 2013.

Hanson, Sharon K. *The Life of Helen Stephens, the Fulton Flash.* Carbondale: Southern Illinois University Press, 2004.

Hargreaves, Jennifer. "Olympic Women: A Struggle for Recognition." In *Women and Sports in the United States*, eds. Jean O'Reilly and Susan K. Cahn, 3–14. Boston: Northeastern University Press, 2007.

Hay, Eduardo. "The Stella Walsh Case." *Olympic Review* 162 (1981): 221–22.

Hodak, George. "Interview with Evelyne Hall Adams," 1988, http://library.la84. org/6oic/OralHistory/OHHallAdams.pdf.

Hotchkiss, Ron. "Crossing the Line." *Canada's History* 90, no. 6 (2010–2011): 40–45.

———. *The Matchless Six: The Story of Canada's First Women's Olympic Team.* Toronto: Tundra Books, 2006.

International Olympic Committee. *The Olympic Games Charter Rules and Regulations*, 1955, https://stillmed.olympic.org/Documents/Olympic%20Charter/ Olympic_Charter_through_time/1955-Olympic_Charter-The_OG-charter_rules_ and_regulations_general_information.pdf.

Jable, J. Thomas. "Eleanor Egg: Paterson's Track and Field Heroine." *New Jersey History* (Fall/Winter 1984): 68–84.

Jakieła, Anna. "Stanisława Walasiewicz—Krótka historia" [Stanisława Walasiewicz: Short History], http://treningbiegacza.pl.stanisława-walasiewicz.

Jares, Joe. "A Baker's Dream Needs Dough." *SI Vault*, September 7, 1970, http://www. si.com/vault/1970/09/07/611481/a-bakers-dream-needs-dough.

———. "Off to Russia, without Love." *SI Vault*, July 12, 1965, http://www.si.com/ vault/1965/07/12/606343/off-to-russia-without-love.

Jensen, Erik N. *Body by Weimar.* Oxford, UK: Oxford University Press, 2010.

Kagan, Donald, et al. *The Western Heritage since 1789.* New York: Prentice Hall, 2001.

Keys, Barbara. "The Olympics, Hollywood-Style: Commerce, Coca-Cola, and the Culture of Celebrity at the 1932 Los Angeles Olympic Games," http://library.la84. org/SportsLibrary/NASSH_Proceedings/NP2004/np2004aj.pdf.

Kluge, Volker. "Scandal about 'Dora' and the 'Bergmann Case.'" *Journal of Olympic History* 17, no. 3 (December 2009): 20–27.

Kotowski, Mariusz. *Pola Negri: Hollywood's First Femme Fatale.* Lexington: University Press of Kentucky, 2014.

Krüger, Arnd. "Germany: The Propaganda Machine." In *The Nazi Olympics: Sports, Policy, and Appeasement in the 1930s*, eds. Arnd Krüger and William Murray, 17–44. Urbana: University of Illinois Press, 2003.

———. "Strength through Joy." In *The International Politics of Sport in the Twentieth Century*, eds. James Riordan and Arnd Krüger, 67–90. London: E & FN Spon, 1999.

———. "What's the Difference between Propaganda for Tourism or for a Political Regime?" In *Post-Olympism? Questioning Sport in the Twenty-First Century*, eds. John Bale and Mette Krogh Christensen, 33–50. Oxford, UK: Berg, 2004.

Lansbury, Jennifer H. *A Spectacular Leap: Black Women Athletes in Twentieth-Century America.* Fayetteville: University of Arkansas Press, 2014.

Large, David Clay. *Berlin.* New York: Basic Books, 2000.

——. *Nazi Games: The Olympics of 1936.* New York: W. W. Norton, 2007.

Laville, Helen. "'Our Country Endangered by Underwear': Fashion, Femininity, and the Seduction Narrative in *Ninotchka* and *Silk Stockings.*" *Diplomatic History* 30, no. 4 (September 2006): 623–44.

Leigh, Mary H., and Therese M. Bonin. "The Pioneering Role of Madame Alice Milliat and the FSFI in Establishing International Track and Field Competition for Women," http://library.la84.org/SportsLibrary/JSH/JSH1977/JSH0401/jsh0401f. pdf.

Lenskyj, Helen. "Femininity First: Sport and Physical Education for Ontario Girls, 1890–1930." In *Sports in Canada: Historical Readings,* ed. Morris Mott, 187–200. Toronto: Copp Clark Pittman, 1989.

——. *Out of Bounds: Women, Sport, and Sexuality.* Toronto: Women's Press, 1986.

Linden, Andrew D. "Blue-Collar Identity and the 'Culture of Losing': Cleveland and the 'Save Our Browns' Campaign." *Journal of Sport History* 42, no. 3 (Fall 2015): 340–60.

Lucas, John A. "There's a Great Deal More to Elizabeth Robinson's Gold Medal Sprint Victory at the 1928 Olympic Games." *Journal of Olympic History* 13 (January 2005): 16–21.

Lucas, Rob. Director. *Stella Walsh: A Documentary,* 2014.

Mathison, Dirk. "Heartbreak Hotel." *Los Angeles Magazine,* June 1998, 77–85.

McCook, Brian. *The Borders of Integration: Polish Migrants in Germany and the United States, 1870–1924.* Athens: Ohio University Press, 2011.

McDonald, John F. *Urban America: Growth, Crisis, and Rebirth.* Armonk, NY: M. E. Sharpe, 2008.

Meisl, Willy. *Die Olympischen Spiele in Los Angeles, 1932* [The Olympic Games in Los Angeles, 1932]. Hamburg: H. F. & Ph. F. Reetsma, 1932.

Murray, William. "France, Coubertin, and the Nazi Olympics: The Response." *Olympika: The International Journal of Olympic Studies* 1 (1992): 46–69.

——. "France, Equality, and the Pursuit of Fraternity." In *The Nazi Olympics: Sport, Politics, and Appeasement in the 1930s,* eds. Arnd Krüger and William Murray, 87–112. Urbana: University of Illinois Press, 2003.

Nakładem Zwiazku Polskich Zwiazków Sportowych. *Polacy Na Igrzyskach X Olimpjady w 1932 r* [Poles at the Tenth Olympiad in 1932]. Polskiego Komitetu Olimpijskiego.

Nolte, Claire E. *The Sokol in the Czech Lands to 1914: Training for the Nation.* New York: Palgrave, 2002.

Ohio History Records Survey Project. *Parishes of the Catholic Church Diocese of Cleveland.* Cleveland, OH: Cadillac Press, 1942.

Okrent, Daniel. "Wayne B. Wheeler: The Man Who Turned off the Taps." *Smithsonian*, May 2010, www.smithsonianmag.com/history/wayne-b-wheeler.

Olson, Leonard T. *Masters Track and Field: A History*. Jefferson, NC: McFarland, 2001.

Onyestyák, Nikoletta. "Boycott, Exclusion, or Nonparticipation? Hungary in the Years of the 1920 and 1984 Olympic Games." *International Journal of the History of Sport* 27, no. 11 (August 2010): 1920–41.

Organization Committee for the Berlin Olympics. *The XIth Olympics, Berlin 1936, Official Report, Volume I*, http://library.la84.org/6oic/OfficialReports/1936/1936v1 sum.pdf.

Palmer, A. Mitchell. "The Case against the 'Reds.'" In *Reading the American Past: Volume II*, ed. Michael P. Johnson, 133–34. New York: Bedford, 2012.

Pienkos, Donald E. *One Hundred Years Young: A History of the Polish Falcons of America*. New York: Columbia University Press, 1987.

Pieroth, Doris. "Los Angeles 1932." In *Encyclopedia of the Modern Olympic Movement*, eds. John E. Findling and Kimberly D. Pelle, 95–103. Westport, CT: Greenwood, 2004.

———. *Their Day in the Sun: Women of the 1932 Olympics*. Seattle: University of Washington Press, 1996.

Polak, Ewa, and Maciej Huzarski. "Participation of Members of Polish Gymnastic Society 'Sokol' in Rzeszów in Polish and International Sokol Slets until 1939." *Kultura Fizyczna* [Physical Culture] 13, no. 1 (2014): 13–28.

Polish Olympic Committee. "Poland and Olympism," http://library.la84.org/ OlympicInformationCenter/OlympicReview/1976/ore101/ore101w.pdf.

PolskieRadio. "Halina Konopacka—pierwsza złota medlistka olimpijska" [Halina Konopacka—The First Olympic Gold Medalist]. February 26, 2013, http://www .polskieradio.pl/39/156/Artykul/789704,Halina-Konopacka-pierwsza-polska-zlota-medalistka-olimpijska.

Post, Robert C. *Street Railways and the Growth of Los Angeles*. San Marino, CA: Golden West Books, 1989.

Pula, James S. *Polish Americans: An Ethnic Community*. New York: Twayne, 1995.

Rayner, Richard. *A Bright and Guilty Place*. New York: Doubleday, 2009.

Rider, Toby. "Eastern Europe's Unwanted: Exiled Athletes and the Olympic Games." *Journal of Sport History* 40, no. 3 (Fall 2013): 435–53.

———, and Sarah Teetzel. "The Strange Tale of Stella Walsh's Olympic Eligibility." Unpublished paper, 2015.

Ritchie, Robert, John Reynard, and Tom Lewis. "Intersex and the Olympic Games." *Journal of the Royal Society of Medicine* 101 (2008): 395–99.

Roberts, Randy, and James Olson. *Winning Is the Only Thing: Sports in America since 1945*. Baltimore: Johns Hopkins University Press, 1989.

Roe, Edward T. *The Life Work of William McKinley*. Whitefish, MT: Kessinger, 2010.

Roszkowski, Wojciech. *Historia Polski, 1914–1990* [History of Poland, 1914–1990]. Warsaw: Państwowe Wydawnictwo Naukowe, 1991.

"A Roundup of the Week." *SI Vault*, March 20, 1989, http://www.si.com/vault/1989/03/20.

Sandberg, Neil. *Ethnic Identity and Assimilation: The Polish American Community: Case Study of Metropolitan Los Angeles*. New York: Praeger, 1974.

Schaap, Jeremy. *Triumph: The Untold Story of Jesse Owens and Hitler's Olympics*. New York: Houghton Mifflin Harcourt, 2007.

Schultz, Jamie. *Qualifying Times: Points of Change in U.S. Women's Sport*. Urbana: University of Illinois Press, 2014.

Schweinbenz, Amanda. "Let the Games Begin." Sixth International Symposium for Olympic Research, http://library.la84.org/SportsLibrary/ISOR/ISOR2002zb.pdf.

———. "Not Just Early Olympic Fashion Statements: Bathing Suits, Uniforms, and Sportswear." In *Bridging Three Centuries: Fifth International Symposium for Olympic Research—2000*, 135–42, http://library.la84.org/SportsLibrary/ISOR/ISOR2000r.pdf.

Sheil, Pat. "Five-Ring Circus: The Twisted Tale of Stella Walsh." *Australian Broadcasting Corporation*, http://www.abc.net.au/olympics/s177264.htm.

Sinclair, Robert J. "Baseball's Rising Sun: American Interwar Diplomacy and Japan." *Canadian Journal of the History of Sport* 16, no. 2 (December 1985): 44–54.

Sloan, Ethel. *The Biology of Women*, 4th ed. Albany, NY: Delmar, 2002.

Soifer, Paul. "Lillian Copeland Speaks Out on the Olympics: Los Angeles 1932, Berlin 1936." *Western States Jewish History* 38, no. 1 (Fall 2005): 3–16.

State Historical Society of Missouri. "Helen Stephens," http://shsmo.org/historicmissourians/name/s/stephens/.

Stewart, Justin. *Wayne Wheeler: Dry Boss*. Whitefish, MT: Kessinger, 2008.

Szujecki, Krzysztof. *Życie Sportowe w Drugiej Rzeczpospolitej* [Sporting Life in the Second Republic]. Warsaw: Bellona, 2012.

Tarapacki, Thomas. *Chasing the American Dream: Polish Americans in Sports*. New York: Hippocrene Books, 1995.

Taylor, Paul. *Jews and the Olympic Games: The Clash between Sports and Politics*. Brighton, UK: Sussex Academic Press, 2004.

Teetzel, Sarah. "Equality, Equity, and Inclusion: Issues in Women and Transgendered Athletes' Participation at the Olympics." *Proceedings: International Symposium for Olympic Research*, 2006, http://library.la84.org/SportsLibrary/ISOR/ISOR2006ae.pdf.

Tricard, Louise Mead. *American Women's Track and Field, 1895–1980.* Jefferson, NC: McFarland, 2008.

Tullis, Matt. "Who Was Stella Walsh? The Story of the Intersex Olympian." *SB Nation,* June 27, 2013, http://www.sbnation.com/longform/2013/6/27/4466724/stella-walsh-profile-intersex-olympian.

Vecsey, George. *Stan Musial: An American Life.* New York: Ballantine, 2011.

Vignola, Patricia. "The Patriotic Pinch Hitter: The AAGPBL and How the American Woman Earned a Permanent Spot on the Roster." *NINE: A Journal of Baseball History and Culture* 12, no. 2 (Spring 2004): 102–13.

Walters, E. Garrison. *The Other Europe.* Syracuse, NY: Syracuse University Press, 1988.

Walters, Guy. *Berlin Games: How the Nazis Stole the American Dream.* New York: William Morrow, 2006.

Warf, Barney, and Brian Holly. "The Rise and Fall and Rise of Cleveland." *Annals of the American Academy of Political and Social Science* 551 (May 1997): 208–21.

Wiederkehr, Stefan. "'We Shall Never Know the Exact Number of Men Who Have Competed in the Olympics Posing as Women': Sport, Gender Verification, and the Cold War." *International Journal of the History of Sport* 26, no. 4 (March 2009): 556–72.

Wieland, Karin. *Dietrich and Riefenstahl: Hollywood, Berlin, and a Century in Two Lives.* New York: Liveright, 2011.

Wiggins, David K., and Patrick B. Miller, eds. *The Unlevel Playing Field: A Documentary History of the African American Experience in Sport.* Urbana: University of Illinois Press, 2003.

Williams, Jeanine. *A Contemporary History of Women's Sport, Part One: Sporting Women, 1850–1960.* London: Routledge, 2014.

Winstone, Martin. *The Dark Heart of Hitler's Europe.* London: I. B. Tauris, 2015.

Wryk, Ryszard. *Sport Olimpijski w Polsce 1919–1939: Biogramy Olimpijczyków* [Olympic Sport in Poland, 1919–1939: Olympic Biographies]. Poznań: Wydawnictwo Poznańskie, 2006.

Xth Olympic Committee. *The Official Report of the Games of the Xth Olympiad Los Angeles 1932, Part 2,* http://library.la84.org/6oic/OfficialReports/1932/1932spart2.pdf.

Zjednoczenie Pabianickie, Organizacja Pożytku Publicznego. "Jadwiga Wajs—Marcinkiewicz," http://zjednoczeniepabianickie.pl/zd.

Zweig, Ferdynand. *Poland between Two Wars: A Critical Study of Social and Economic Changes.* London: Secker & Warburg, 1944.

SELECTED NEWSPAPERS, JOURNALS, AND PERIODICALS
Kurjer Polski [Polish Courier]
Kurjer Warszawski [Warsaw Courier]
Los Angeles Times
New York Times
Plain Dealer (Cleveland)
Polacy Zagranica [Poles Abroad]
Polish American Review
Przegląd Sportowy [Sports Review]
Sztandar Młodych [Youth Banner]
Völkischer Beobachter [Folkish Observer]
Washington Post
Życie Warszawy [Warsaw Life]

DOCUMENTS
Western Reserve Historical Society, Cleveland, Ohio
MS4999 Stella Walsh Papers (Container 1, Folder 11)

Index

About the Author

Sheldon Anderson is a professor in the History Department at Miami University in Oxford, Ohio. He teaches courses on the politics of modern sports, the Cold War, and twentieth-century European diplomacy. He is the author of four books: *The Politics and Culture of Modern Sports* (2015), *Condemned to Repeat It: "Lessons of History" and the Making of U.S. Cold War Containment Policy* (2008), *A Cold War in the Soviet Bloc: Polish–East German Relations, 1945–1962* (2000), and *A Dollar to Poland Is a Dollar to Russia: U.S. Economic Policy toward Poland, 1945–1952* (1993). He is also the coauthor of *International Studies: An Interdisciplinary Approach to Global Issues* (3rd ed., 2014).